Criminal Justice in America

Criminal Justice in America

Advisory Editor

ROBERT M. FOGELSON

OUR
CRIMINAL COURTS

RAYMOND MOLEY

ARNO PRESS
A New York Times Company
New York • 1974

Reprint Edition 1974 by Arno Press Inc.

Reprinted from a copy in
  The Newark Public Library

Criminal Justice in America
ISBN for complete set: 0-405-06135-8
See last pages of this volume for titles.

Manufactured in the United States of America

Library of Congress Cataloging in Publication Data

Moley, Raymond, 1886-
    Our criminal courts.

    (Criminal justice in America)
    Reprint of the ed. published by Minton, Balch, New
York.
    1. Criminal justice, Administration of--United
States. I. Title. II. Series.
KF9223.M635 1974   345'.73'05   74-3835
ISBN 0-405-06181-1

OUR CRIMINAL COURTS

By RAYMOND MOLEY

POLITICS AND CRIMINAL PROSECUTION

OUR CRIMINAL COURTS

OUR
CRIMINAL COURTS

By

RAYMOND MOLEY

MINTON, BALCH & COMPANY
NEW YORK : : : 1930

Printed in the United States of America by
J. J. LITTLE AND IVES COMPANY, NEW YORK

TO

BRUCE SMITH

FOREWORD

Unless, as Matthew Arnold said, "the mere endeavor to see and learn the truth for our own personal satisfaction is indeed a commencement for making it prevail," this essay has in it no purpose to make anything prevail. It seeks no solutions, prescribes no remedies, formulates no program of reform. It is a presentation of what seems to me a pertinent selection from the available range of facts concerning criminal law administration in the American states with such comment and personal opinions as seem appropriate. Presented thus as an essay, or perhaps a series of essays, I avoid the pretense of a treatise or a text. I have sought, however, to make some slight contributions to research by suggesting a number of possibly interesting and useful lines of future investigation.

In this discussion a number of limitations have been recognized. It has been necessary to consider criminal justice only as it is related to serious state offenses. The law enforcement agencies of the Federal government are not considered. Except in one chapter I have excluded any discussion of the causes, effects and treatment of crime. The nature of the book, moreover, has made it possible to avoid the burden of detailed citations, although I have attempted not only to express due acknowledgment of sources but to provide the reader with some not too obtrusive bibliographical guidance. On account of varied sorts of official relationships which I have had with crime surveys and commissions in New York, Illinois, Missouri, Virginia, Pennsylvania, Ohio, Connecticut, Michigan, California, and Indiana it is inevitable that many of my conclusions are derived from situations in those states although I have to a degree sought to confirm these impressions by visits to other states and by an examination of such printed data as are available concerning them.

Throughout this book are illustrations drawn from non-legal writings, particularly fiction and the drama. These are used even to the occasional exclusion of examples drawn from actual cases. This is in harmony with the purpose of the book, which is to present realistically not only what does happen but what may easily and conveniently happen under such a system as ours. They are selected because they are the products of artistic observation which more often than not record the reality with unusual attention to detail. After all, a primary characteristic of an artist is a keen power of observation. In viewing the process of justice he may discern and record what lies directly within the range of vision of the legal eye but which is so associated with custom that its true outlines are never defined. The artist, unconfined by legal rules, has no closely woven professional habits of thought and observation. It was the crowning glory of Dickens that with only such systematic legal knowledge as might be gained from a short term as a clerk and a reporter he should have exerted such a profound influence upon the course of legal statesmanship.

In a book of this kind it is inevitable that indebtedness to others will be much greater than a mere list of acknowledgments can show. Where assistance has been given in preparing the material for a specific section I have indicated the fact at the appropriate place. In addition to these I have profited by the critical judgment of Professors E. R. Keedy, A. M. Kidd, John Dickinson, Lindsay Rogers and Charles S. Baldwin. I am further indebted to Audrey Davies, Agnes Thornton, William Jaffe and Clara Leiser for assembling material and editing the manuscript. The Council for Research in the Social Sciences of Columbia University granted the funds necessary for special studies included in a number of chapters.

RAYMOND MOLEY.

New York
July, 1930

CONTENTS

PART III

THE PUBLIC'S INTERESTS *VS*. THE PUBLIC INTEREST

PERSPECTIVE

In spite of the revered phrase of Aristotle, the administration of criminal justice is a government of men, not laws. Any realistic approach to the subject makes this apparent. Consider, for example, the proportion of initiated criminal cases that reach a final determination of guilt. In those instances for which we have reliable evidence the percentage varies from fifteen to fifty per cent. This means that of those cases in which the state begins a prosecution, a considerable majority result in freeing the defendant. His freedom may come in the preliminary hearing where the magistrate finds no "probable cause." It may come through the "no true bill" of the grand jury. It may come through the *Nolle Prosequi,* moved by the prosecutor. Finally, it may come through action in the trial by judge or jury. Everywhere throughout the process of law administration are officials possessed of discretionary power which they use liberally to terminate prosecutions, which they, for one reason or another, feel that the state should no longer continue.

Not only in those cases in which the defendant is set free but in those in which he is found guilty does this use of discretion hold sway. The jury as an agency in the process of criminal justice has all but vanished. Of thirteen thousand felony prosecutions in Chicago in 1926 which were initiated by arrests, less than five hundred resulted in jury trials. In New York the proportion of jury trials is quite inconsiderable. A large majority of persons whose guilt is established in our criminal courts plead guilty. The proportion varies from state to state and from city to city but it is a fair guess that approximately eighty per cent of those who are found guilty in felony prosecutions plead guilty. The tendency is just as marked in the rural districts as in the cities. It is almost universal. The most reliable data show that the percentage in Chicago was in 1926 as high as 90 per cent. In New York City in 1926 about the same. In Detroit in 1928 it was 70 per cent. In a number of Michigan counties outside of Detroit 90 per cent. In Indianapolis in the same year 60 per cent. In rural districts in Indiana over 90 per cent. In Los Angeles 75 per cent in 1928. In a dozen California counties in the same year 85 per cent. In Connecticut in 1928, 90 per cent. In Iowa in 1928, 93 per cent. The practice is becoming standard. In some places the tendency is as marked as the following statement of an experienced lawyer in a middle western county indicates:

"Of the whole 140 cases, there were only three or four pleas of not guilty. All the rest went off on pleas of guilty, either to the offense charged or to a lesser charge, probably agreed to as the result of bargaining. In at least one case, I happen to know that as a result an attempt to try it without adequate preparation continuances were repeatedly secured, and nothing has yet been done. The sum and substance is that unless the prosecutor can get a plea of guilty, little happens."

This tendency to plead guilty seems to be increasing. The data on which to base an opinion are not easy to get but such as we have show that in New York state over a period of eighty years the percentage of cases found guilty "on confession" has increased from twenty to eighty.

The tremendous importance of the plea of guilty in the administration of criminal justice is not difficult to understand. It is a measure of the extent to which jury trial is supplanted by the process of administrative discretion. The plea of guilty is no mere gesture of conscious guilt on the part of a defendant. Neither is it the symbol of renunciation of evil ways. It is a part of well conventionalized defense strategy. It is the result either of some sort of specific compromise or it rises from the feeling that to relieve prosecutor and judge of the work of a trial will win from them more leniency in the fixing of punishment. It will, in the phrase of the court house, win a "light rap." *

The wide exercise of discretion is not a tendency to be deplored, it is a wholly necessary factor in the process of justice as it is elsewhere in governmental activity. Whenever legislative

---

* I have discussed this subject at length in my "Politics and Criminal Prosecution" (New York, 1929). See particularly the chapters entitled "The Vanishing Jury" and "Justice by Compromise."

power sets out to provide legal restrictions of such a nature as to make law self-operating, troubles arise. The practical operation of the Baumes fourth offender law in New York is an example. The basic purpose of the law was to prevent the judge in fixing sentence from exercising discretion. It makes the imposition of a life sentence mandatory when three previous convictions for a felony are shown. In practice, however, the district attorney, when he feels that a life sentence would work an injustice, frequently permits the defendant with three previous convictions to plead guilty to a crime less serious than a felony. The life sentence is thus avoided through the discretion of the district attorney, with the consent of the judge. Thus a way is found to "save both the law and the criminal," a practice as old as human wisdom.

In the face of the great extent to which criminal law is subject to administrative discretion many well worn assumptions find their validity questioned. One of these is the contention that the way to improve criminal justice is to make procedure less technical and more favorable to the state. The rules, they say, are antiquated, cumbersome, overly favorable to the defendant. The remedy proposed is to sweep away the cobwebs, expedite proceedings and eliminate some of the restrictions upon the prosecution. But set procedural rules are in practice seldom invoked. As we have seen, a large majority of cases are decided before the "game" really begins. Trials are exceptional and the process of compromise is one in which formal rules do not operate to any important extent. The contention that the higher courts are overly technical in appeals is not only somewhat questionable in itself but even when it is true the net effect is not great. Very few cases ever reach appellate court and a study of their disposition does not usually justify the criticism. About the only real significance of such an attitude on the part of an appellate court would be to make defendants slightly more assured in the game of compromising cases before they come to trial.

Much as procedure has been the favorite interest of lawyers the organization of courts has been the theme of the political scientist. Courts should be organized on a business basis, he says. There should be an executive head with large power. There should be integration of effort, specialization of cases. Our ma-

chine is cumbersome, based upon bygone conditions. In those
few instances in which it has been tried, perfection of organization has failed to create marked difference in the net result. Good
prosecutors and strong judges seem to do well in badly organized courts while, as we shall see, inferior persons do badly in
the midst of structural perfection.

Nor does the character of the criminal law itself appear to
be the serious factor that some reformers seem to think. There
are those who say it is too easy, that penalties should be increased.
The answer is that (as under the Baumes law of New York)
the increase of penalties has merely shifted the exercise of discretion from one official to another.* "The socially minded" person who complains of a criminal law "based upon a theory of
vengeance" is equally at odds with the stuff of reality. There is
no "criminal law," there are criminal laws. The inappropriate-
ness to the conditions of the time is no new condition. It is
probable that criminal laws have always been out of harmony
with the conditions of life. Criminal laws have to get themselves
passed. They are the creation of no single theory, and of no
single constructive imagination. They are the result of such complex forces as seem to be almost the creation of pure chance.
Sometimes they are the result of habit, sometimes of tradition,
often of the pressure of special interest. The poultry raisers 'of
one commonwealth succeeded in having the theft of a chicken
made a felony. Appellate courts called upon to harmonize these
laws are scarcely guided by more consistent planning than legislators. If a judge or a legislator should be called upon to state
the theory upon which the law he makes is based, he might
hark back to something he heard a minister of the gospel say
sometime, or to something he has read in the Bible. He is usually
credited with much more planning than he deserves.

Not only in the definition of crimes and in the prescription
of penalties is the body of criminal laws highly confused but in
the interpretation of the well known psychological factors that
the books in criminal law tell about. The "intent," the *mens rea,*
"motives," "responsibility," are terms which to form meaning

* For a discussion of this whole question see my paper read before the National
Conference of Social Work at San Francisco in 1929. Published in the Proceedings.

must be articulated with some fairly defined conception of how the human mind works. Psychology now teaches the importance of mental age, and "responsibility" in the face of this new synthesis, must be conditioned to a new meaning—perhaps no meaning at all. In the face of the devastating sweep of newer conceptions of psychology the basic assumptions of criminality are vastly altered. It is hardly sound to assert, as some of the "socially minded" persist in doing, that "a criminal law based upon vengeance must yield to criminal law based on"—something or other-else. "It" is based upon little that has not changed since "it" was formulated. It was based upon little when it was formulated. It can not be adjusted to a "new" conception because apparently a "new" conception has not yet formulated itself. So we have laws, of all sorts, applied in diverse ways, adjusted by many motives, administered by many persons, moved by infinitely complicated motives and conditions. Little is certain but complexity.

It is not the power of discretion that should be the concern of students of criminal justice but the manner in which it is exercised. In most preliminary hearings carelessness, indifference and confusion hold sway to such an extent that it is unbelievable that an intelligent sifting of cases takes place. The prosecutor who plays the major rôle in the acceptance of pleas and in other vital steps in the process, usually makes his decisions under the most unsatisfactory circumstances. Political influence, incompetence, haste and the pressure of a sensation-hunting public hamper him. Sometimes his method of bargaining with defendants resembles the technique of a poker game rather than that of an act of high justice. He may barter away the plain responsibility of the state in order to avoid the ardors of a long trial. At other times, as is well shown in the prologue of a recent powerful play, *The Criminal Code,* he drives a harsh and cruel advantage. More frequently he tries to accomplish, as best he can, the ends of justice as he sees them. But usually, the limitations implied by his political responsibilities, his lack of training and competence and inadequate facilities seriously impair the quality of his decisions.

It is quite probable that there has always been ample exercise of discretionary power in applying criminal laws. At the present time, however, we have found more concise means to express what is being done. We call the process "individualization." The terms of the law which contemplates only the act and the state of mind of the individual who commits it, are modified in particular cases in accordance with the nature and needs of the defendant. As we have seen, this process of individualization may be guided by all sorts of motives and objectives. When prosecutor and judge are guided by the best of intentions in applying the sort of treatment most likely to benefit the defendant and the state as well, they find the problem to be the extent and character of exact knowledge concerning human conduct. When they seek the advice of specialists they find that there is in the process of development a "science" of human conduct. To an increasing extent this body of knowledge is finding recognition in what is called probation. A few adult criminal courts have borrowed the idea, long since established in juvenile courts, of a probation department, which when wisely used provides a sort of intelligence service to the court in the determination of the human problems which it meets. The extent to which this body of specialized knowledge can guide the exercise of discretion of judges and prosecutors in dealing with individuals will ultimately depend upon the extent to which the diagnosis of human nature can be reduced to scientific accuracy.

The haunting dream of the sociologist and psychologist has always been the possibility of social and individual "control." As William I. Thomas, one of the most significant and enlightened sociologists has expressed it "the ultimate object of scientific study is prediction for with prediction we can control." It is easy to see therefore why the future of criminal justice is so closely related to the future possibilities of a science of human relations. To know of the extent to which an offender can be trusted to adjust himself to society and what kind of treatment will make this adjustment more easy is to provide a guide for the almost limitless exercise of discretion by the agencies of criminal justice. A science of human relations is to criminal justice truly an alternative to chaos.

But the state of knowledge of human relations still indicates vastly more of an art than a science. It is, indeed, an art trying to become a science. The elusive character of the materials, the appalling gaps in psychological and medical knowledge, the persistence of prejudice, self interest, and other subjective factors in those who investigate, the taboos so powerfully maintained by those who are investigated, provide obstacles the conquest of which only supreme optimism can contemplate. Some of these difficulties it should be noted were lying in the way of natural science generations ago, but others are peculiar to social science alone.

All of this is true even of the most hopeful of the new humanities, psychiatry. The modern attempt to apply scientific method to the treatment of individual cases invites an analogy between the diagnosis of human physical ills and the diagnosis of conduct difficulties. Such an analogy is useful if not pressed too far. It is true that a medical diagnosis lists a number of physical facts, which are determinable and to some degree measurable by physical processes, on the basis of certain classified knowledge which is the property of the science of medicine and determines in individual cases what these various physical factors mean in terms of the written and measured experience of the science with innumerable other persons. Thus, the coincidence of four or five symptoms leads a physician to diagnose a disease, which has through experience become identified with these symptoms, and which is presumably the particular disease in which these symptoms coincide. The medical diagnosis does not stop, however, with the classification of ascertained facts and the application of these facts to the experience of the science. It consists in the last analysis of a determination of what these facts mean and what the experience of medical science means in relation to these facts—expressed through the insight and understanding of the person who is making the diagnosis. In other words, the facts themselves do not constitute a complete answer to the question. The diagnosis is complete only when the physician has added to the ascertainable facts of science his own guess as to what is the matter and what ought to be done about it. This guess is much more in the nature of an expression of artistic insight than a scientific analysis. It must in the nature of things be such, because until the science of medicine is complete and every physical symptom can be exactly ascertained and measured and the consequences of every physical symptom determined on the basis of verified experience, it will be necessary for those who apply this science to provide their own interpretations. It is exactly at this point where scientific facts end and artistic guesses begin that the analogy between medicine and what we may call human relations bears the closest watching.*

The truly significant exponents of psychiatry are the most earnest exponents of the limitations of their own knowledge. They pray to be rescued from their more impulsive friends. They warn a public always anxious to achieve short cuts to perfection that psychiatry is a wise counselor but as yet not an infallible judge in dealing with criminals.

The knowledge and technique of the social worker, who as probation officer, is likely to provide the alternative to a lawyer's decision by prosecutor or judge, is a degree more removed from scientific accuracy than that of the psychiatrist. The social worker commonly speaks of the necessity for scientific attitude on the part of those who are diagnosing human ills. His interpretation of this scientific attitude is to rest estimates and predictions not upon the basis of wholly empirical judgments but to accept from certain technicians—such as psychiatrists, psychologists and medical men—their own estimates as a basis for the general recommendation which he must finally determine. The estimate of the social worker, therefore, is several degrees more removed from exactitude than the estimate of the physician, because, of all the scientific guesses which the social worker must use in piecing together his own basic facts for determination, that of the medical man is based upon the most adequate and certain knowledge of the facts. The social worker's guess is a guess based upon the guesses of others. The art with which the decision of the social worker is made will depend to some degree upon his own ex-

---

*It may be that my use of the word, "guess," will be resented. It is used here, of course, in no slighting sense. It is used merely because in the present state of the English language no other word so generally indicates exactly what is done in the situation which I am describing. A guess, according to the Standard Dictionary, is "an opinion formed without any sure ground of inference; a judgment based on the data of probability or contingency; a supposition; a surmise; a conjecture." A great scientist, Tyndall, gives me some justification for the use of the term. He speaks of the "guesses of science" in a highly serious and respectful manner.

perience, to a larger degree upon the intrinsic value of the guesses of those who give him his information, and in the last analysis it will depend upon a subtle, indefinite quality of insight. Nevertheless, the social worker performs the function of articulating the contributions of medical men, psychiatrists, psychologists and others, and of relating these factors to the environment which he himself must know. He does not serve well, however, when he seeks to contrast the "scientific" nature of his knowledge with the "legalism" of the judge. He finds his best usefulness where he is humble, in the sense that the greatest of physicians and psychiatrists are humble, before the obviously tentative and fluid nature of his materials.*

A second problem, perhaps more important than the character of scientific knowledge of human behavior, concerns the persons who exercise discretion in criminal justice. It is clear that the dominant figure in the day by day process of law enforcement is the prosecutor. But it is also clear that there is a slow increase in the powers and responsibilities of the trial judge. Perhaps the most important reason for this is the decline in prestige and power of the criminal jury. The relative position of judge and jury is not a new problem in jurisprudence. Pollock and Maitland after viewing the judge's function in the long perspective of history conclude that the behavior which is expected of a judge in different ages and by different systems of law seems to constitute a dominant problem in law administration.

The unmistakable marks of the revival of the powers of the judge are the recent enactment by states of legal authority by which, on the election of the defendant, a case may be tried by the judge alone, the grant of increased power to the judge in the selection of jurors and the widespread support given to the proposal that judges of state courts be given the right to comment to the jury upon vital questions of evidence. Moreover, under his present powers, he is no mean figure. He can, if he will, control the bail bond problem. His consent is usually necessary for many of the decisive actions of the prosecutor. He may issue bench

---

* Most encouraging efforts have recently been made by Sheldon Glueck, Burgess, and others, to provide the basis for scientific guidance in this perplexing field. See p. 174.

warrants, decide upon probation, control those granted suspended sentences and to a great extent determine paroles. In the actual exercise of all these powers there is a vast spread between what he can legally control and what he actually does control. The extent of his power is largely dependent upon the facilities for gaining information which he has at his disposal. These facilities may, however, be secured for him, if he insists upon them. He can, if he will, become an increasingly potent factor in criminal justice. He is, in an extraordinary degree, at the heart of things. With means for getting information, with broader educational background and with more freedom from political entanglements he can take over much of the power now exercised by the prosecutor and become the master of criminal law enforcement.

A shift of power from prosecutor to judge is not out of keeping with either the traditions of the English law or the plain dictates of the present situation. "As time goes on," say Pollock and Maitland in the greatest of legal classics, "there is always a larger room for discretion in the laws of procedure; but discretion and powers can only be safely entrusted to judges whose impartiality is above suspicion and where every act is exposed to public and pre-criticism." This expression of confidence is not inappropriate to the present status of the judge in American public life. In spite of the handicaps and shortcomings which we shall presently describe he is a hopeful figure. As respect and confidence are given to them in American public life, it is probable that the judge ranks to a considerable degree above other officials.

The political burden, however, that the judge must carry is very heavy. The judicial office and its perquisites are regarded by the machine, particularly in the great cities, as part of the spoils of victory. To achieve the bench a lawyer is expected to perform political service. For this reason judges are to a great extent career men in politics. They rise through a series of public offices rather than from the eminence of a lifetime at private practice. The judicial office usually does not come as the reward of professional diligence but of party service.

Moreover, the direct primary and non-partisan elections, once hailed as the means to political freedom, have enforced limitations upon the judge more serious than party obligations. They have revealed what may be called the politics of non-partisanship. Public favor is a mistress in whose service one may suffer deeper humiliation than is imposed by the stodgy but simple requirements of a political organization. Economic and social groups demand recognition. When these conflict, the way to compromise is often through shoddy hypocrisy. The avenues offered by the press for public notice must be used. The judges in order to achieve news value must do striking and unusual things. This may mean participation in trivial and unworthy but interesting activities. The effect of these demands upon the sensitive lawyer is sometimes to drive him from public life.

The result of a career in politics is the development of a political mind. The judge's mental process is subdued to the color of the materials in which it works. This is not wholly undesirable in the administration of criminal law, however. There are lessons taught by the close contact with human nature so necessary to politics, that illuminate the equally human problems of criminal justice. The disadvantages arise from the political patronage associated with law enforcement. Dealing with this demand constitutes the most difficult question that a conscientious judge must meet. It is difficult to escape the conclusion that the interference of politics constitutes the most serious cause of the imperfections of criminal justice.

But judges are what they are, because we are what we are. Politics has been shrewdly defined as "organized human nature." The judge is the result of the political life under which he rises to power. His mind is a product of the atmosphere in which he lives. Likewise, police, prosecutors and other agencies of law enforcement. In spite of the protestations of reformers, we actually get about as much law enforcement as we wish. If we are lawless, it is because we want to be.

We are vastly interested in our sins. Our attention is devoted to them with an almost fond interest. They constitute one of our major interests. They fill our most precious emotional expressions. Art, music, literature and the stage are full of the portrayals of sin and crime. In fact, if some humorless reformer should suddenly provide us with a sinless world, we should probably as soon as we felt the chill of such a deliverance start the round of sin all over by destroying our well meaning protector.

The exploitation of this great interest in crime constitutes in itself one of the major factors in the breakdown of enforcement. It has probably become much more noticeable in the generation since the art of reading has become so completely democratized. It has made it possible to turn certain causes célèbre into great national carnivals of interest. The yellow press has sought the exploitation of human interest in crime with a vengeance. An interesting crime fills the papers and becomes the table talk of thousands. People take sides under the friendly suggestion of the sensational press with its sob sisters and its feature writers. Vast numbers of people form definite impressions of guilt or innocence merely because of what they have read in the newspapers. Under such a dispensation of prejudice the fundamental conception of a trial by jury becomes a bit grotesque. A jury is a part of the public, and by the time the trial has arrived the public has formed its opinion. The jury is a part of the mob. Trial by the press is an inevitable consequence.

In the face of this tendency a few idealists have held to a method of reform in which the dominating factor is a belief in the curative value of facts. The remedy for the evils of the democracy of reading and of political control is education. We know little of the actual facts regarding crime. Let us find them and so tell them to the public as to encourage self improvement. Let us make programs of reform, support these programs with informing arrays of facts and then let us "sell" them to the public. The facts will prevail. Let us put our faith in them. Thus, their creed.

This faith is the basic factor in much research, even academic research. Where it proceeds from any motive other than sheer curiosity it usually recognizes the sensitiveness of politics and politicians to the influence of opinion. It believes that if academic research can apply its keen edge to the vital concerns of human life it can ultimately change public attitudes, just as research in the mysteries of the causes of disease ultimately made everybody more intelligent with regard to the rules of health. It seeks no easy cure and it recognizes the long spans of time necessary to the attainment of its objective. But it has little to move it but faith, even though that faith is very great.

Faith in the facts in the domain of social problems must overcome mountains that did not confront the progress of science in the physical world. One of the greatest difficulties is the tendency to use facts as a way to power. They can be used to bludgeon the way to an objective conceived wholly without relation to the facts themselves, an objective decided upon before the facts were found. Men want influence, power, recognition—they are seldom interested in truth—mere truth. To discover the facts, moreover, in the field of human relations is to influence the facts themselves. For example, should the process of research determine how the voters in a presidential year were intending to vote weeks before the election and should there be determined over a series of years the exact relation between this early determination and the subsequent election, in other words, should it be possible to predict, the prediction itself would change the current of human intentions sufficiently to destroy this laboriously achieved effect. When the biologist discovers a way successfully to attack a microscopic organism he can affirm as a part of his technique that the organism will forever conduct itself in the same manner under the same physical circumstances. The organism does not come to understand and to react to the calculations of the scientist. It will be difficult for the science of human relations to devise the means to make allowance for the modification of conduct in a human being who learns quite readily what the scientist has found out about him. The other difficulty, frequently expressed, is in the fact that the possession of power and influence is deeply concerned in the results of research in human relations. Those who possess this power and influence are not likely to welcome the development of new scientific knowledge that may impair their vested interests.

To these objections the devoted believer replies that out of the conflict of facts against facts, truth against truth, some things get themselves believed, permanently and incontrovertibly. This, he says, constitutes his reward and his justification.

PART I

PRELIMINARIES TO TRIAL

OUR CRIMINAL COURTS

CHAPTER I

THE APPEARANCE OF JUSTICE

NEITHER in our laws nor in the records that these laws require, nor yet in the statistical reports that mirror these records, do we find those deeper elements of criminal justice which elude precise definition and measurement. Party loyalty, racial bias, personal obligation, intellectual and æsthetic short-comings—one cannot subject the influence of these to nice analysis, but they weigh heavily in the scales of justice, and sometimes they are visible in the stark realities of the daily business of court life. Haste, carelessness, indifference to human values, impatience and impropriety, thus become matters of substance. They mirror themselves in the appearance of things. In a real sense, then, the appearance of justice is justice itself.

I. *Harrison Street*

A vast range of the crime and sin of the world can be seen in the human driftage that passes through the Harrison Street branch of the Chicago Municipal Court. This tribunal, that acts at once as a court for the trial of minor offenses and for the preliminary hearing of major crimes, serves an extraordinary police district. To it are brought all cases arising in an area which stretches from the Chicago River on the north to 22nd Street on the south, and from the Lake on the east to Kinzie Street on the west. This area, which includes the Loop, is one of the great, well-known sections in the history of urban civiliza-tion.

The daily number of cases on call ranges from 150 to 300. During court sessions the room is crowded almost to suffocation. The clamor is nerve-straining. On one side of the room is a run-way fenced off by wire, intended to separate the prisoners coming from their cells from the people in the room. It is an inadequate barrier. It does little to restrict communication between prisoners and visitors, and things can easily be passed through to prisoners. The section before the bench is jammed with policemen, lawyers, bondsmen, reporters, detectives, visitors, some morbidly curious, others genuinely interested—men, women and children, young and old, rich and poor, vicious and innocent. During the entire session the bailiffs go through unavailing motions to secure better order. Constantly they rap for order and plead with the mob to move back from the bench and open the way to the bull pen.

Benches are provided for those who have legitimate business in court, but usually no one is sitting on them. For self-protection, and in order to see and hear better, people prefer to stand. The smoke is always thick. The noise is almost deafening. People are whispering, laughing, talking and spitting. There are the loud shouts of the bailiff, the remarks of the bystanders and the pounding of the gavel. Many cases are probably dismissed for want of prosecution because the complaining witness fails to hear the case called. Signs in the anteroom and in the courtroom warn against loitering, and state that persons found guilty of violating this order will be prosecuted, but there is no visible evidence that the rule is taken seriously.

In the course of a year approximately twenty-five hundred felony cases pass through this court, along with panhandlers, vagrants, dope victims and dope peddlers, exhibitionists and sensitive and refined persons who have violated traffic laws or committed other minor offenses. The professional yeggman who is a grave menace to society is given as cursory treatment as the comparatively harmless vagrant picked up when the first snow falls. It is a court vested with the responsibility of discriminating between the important and the unimportant. In actual practice it exercises very little discrimination, or none at all. No one seems to be concerned with the serious responsibility of distinguishing between those criminals who ought to be vigorously prosecuted and removed from contact with society and those whose conviction or acquittal means practically nothing. Everyone seems to be trying to "get it over with." Faced by an excited, milling crowd of defendants, lawyers, police officers, and curious, gaping, nondescript visitors, and hemmed in from the rear by inattentive and disorderly clerks and assistant prosecutors, eagerly besought by small-time lawyers, political middlemen, professional bondsmen, impatient newspaper reporters, and all of the other gentry who seek some passing dispensation from him, the judge seems harrowed beyond endurance. Apparently his chief concern is to get through with it all so that he can attend a political meeting, play a quiet game with friends at a downtown club, or engage in some of the other activities that occupy most of the waking hours of some of the judges in modern American cities. The prosecutor, whose duty it is to see that the state's case is properly presented, that witnesses tell what they know, and that defendants who deserve to be held *are* held, is the most casual person in the room. The assistant state's attorney jots down the name of each defendant and the disposition, and does no more. Occasionally he barks out an impatient question, usually indicating irritation with the police officer. The latter, tired, perhaps, after a night of walking his beat, cynical because he knows that nobody cares whether his case is dismissed or not, is as anxious as the judge to hurry through the formality of a public hearing.[1]

II. *The House that Justice Built* [2]

"This is the house that justice built. This is the castle of fair play. This is the place where wise men shall sit and contemplate our human jealousies, our petty quarrels, our wrongdoings. This, by the grace of God, is a magistrate's court.

"Set squarely down in a backwater street, it is not, for some disappointing reason, impressive. But the spangled parade of a city's life passes here, gaudy and gay, drab and mean. The push of ambition, the drums of crime, the blare of pretension, and keen quiet of tragedy—all these are integral parts. . . .

---

[1] This passage is, in part, a quotation from my report on the Municipal Court in Chicago, *Illinois Crime Survey* (Chicago, 1929), 405.

[2] This is a first-hand description of a busy Magistrate's Court in New York City. It was written by Milton MacKaye of the staff of the *New York Evening Post* and published in that paper on January 10, 1930, as one of a series entitled "The Magistrate Racket."

"This, then, is a magistrate's court set down on the backwater street. Approach its scummy portals, and an inevitable and inexplicable feeling of miscreancy overcomes one. There is something about its very environment that is repellent.

"The System has made this environment. All around the premises little windowed offices, crowded uncleanly offices. This one says, 'Attorney-at-Law'; the next one says, 'Bail, Bonds, Night or Day.' Rows of them, one after another, all alike.

"On one side of the street, on the opposite side of the street. 'Bail, Bonds,' 'Attorney-at-Law,' 'Bail, Bonds,' 'Notary Public.' These are business men of the court environs. They make their livings from woe. Trouble brings them trade. They sit and smoke in their windows and wait. Their good is a bad day.

"Well, into the court. The hallway is crowded. Rat-faced men in derbies, fat, greasy men in derbies. A few scared, nervous men with mufflers about their throats, indecisive, perhaps waiting for someone, perhaps wondering where to go with their problem. A few young girls, most of them accompanied by two or three men companions. One beautiful girl, quite alone. A dozen old women, and a pimply scattering of side-burned adolescent boys.

"Up the stairs. Loitering along them some important-looking red-faced satraps. They talk with authority from the sides of their mouths, chew on cigars and punctuate their pontification by spitting in the direction of a passerby's shoes. Occasionally they salute a policeman, or hail some newly arrived compatriot.

"Taking a deep breath is difficult. Tobacco smoke is everywhere and fresh air is an unknown quantity. There has been some effort at cleanliness, but the smell of the disinfectant only serves to accentuate distaste into nausea. No wonder a famous judge, broken in health, called these places pest holes. Combined with the odor of unwashed mankind, there is the peculiar taint of old buildings, the effluvium from forty years of life and death.

"Upstairs all is confusion. The court, a little behind time, is about to open. People are crowding into the courtroom, corridors are filled. Policemen push their way here, there and everywhere; a few are listening to hopeful defendants who ask them to tone down their testimony, pal.

"Down the corridor some of the men met on the stairs are

grouped around a closed door. There are the magistrate's chambers. The attendant brushes by them, then stops to shake hands.

" 'The Judge in, Joe?' asks one. 'Just dropped over to say hello.'

"He beckons down the hall to one of the side-burned boys. They confer together in low, secret tones. Then he nods and sticks out his lips reassuringly. Without a knock he walks into the Judge's chambers.

" 'Pat Blank,' boasts the boy to his companion, 'Leader of my district. He knows his eggs.'

"Pat walks out a few minutes later, and another red-faced man walks in. There is the sound of loud laughter. Finally the door opens and magistrate and politicians appear. They are met by other men, all handshakers.

" 'Don't forget that chowder party! Well, see you at the club tonight. Harry and Nate have a bone to pick with you.'

"In the courtroom, the attendant bangs his gavel. Hats are already off. There is silence a moment, but the gum still moves rhythmically in sixty pairs of jaws. The magistrate moves to the bench. He sits down, a short man framed against the American flag behind him. The gavel bounces again, and the wheels of justice begin to grind.

"After that first silence all is confusion again. Policemen, attendants, lawyers, bondsmen click in and out of the gates in the partition railing. The blue-coated bailiff on the bridge below the bench shouts out a number of names. A prisoner, brought in from the detention pen, and seated inside the railing, is pulled forward by a policeman.

"The magistrate is deep in conversation with a friend sitting beside him. The prisoner waits. The bailiff bawls out another indistinguishable name, then another. Two women, both between thirty and forty, pick up their coats and walk self-consciously inside the railing. They are motioned to stand by until the first case is disposed of.

" 'What's this case?' asks the Judge, and glances hastily over the complaint. 'Assault and battery. Where's the complaining witness?'

" 'Not here, Judge.'

"The magistrate looks up.

" 'What do you know about this, officer?'

"The officer doesn't know anything about it. He was called to the premises at 345 Umpty-Umph Street and made the arrest on the request of the complainant, who had a black eye. No, no more details. No, the defendant hadn't been drinking.

" 'Discharged. Next case.'

"And so justice grinds on. The confusion increases. The courtroom is jammed and hot.

"A robbery charge now. The black-haired, languid-eyed Assistant District Attorney stands beside the complainant. No, he hasn't investigated the case. He wants $1,500 bail.

"The defendant's lawyer, little faced and big eared, doesn't know the case either. But he wants $1,000 bail. The two young men are charged with stealing clothing from this woman's store. Of course they plead not guilty. The young man with the waxed mustache and blonde hair—he looks Scandinavian—was released from Sing Sing two months ago. No record of his scared, silent companion. Consent to an adjournment? Yes; $1,000 bail.

"Tumbling along, one after another, the cases. This one dismissed, many adjourned, very many adjourned. Some other magistrate will hear them. Today is a rush day. The oath is given time after time: 'Do yousolswear tell truthotruthnoth but truth?' It's hard to believe it's an oath. Perhaps it isn't; only an old legal custom.

"The bondsmen all around, sleek men, most of them. One silver-haired young man with a big mouth steps forward to handle a felonious assault defendant. The details are complete, but, presto, the prize is snatched away. The defendant's brother, late at the hearing, puts up cash. It's hard to beat a bondsman.

"The air grows hotter, becomes stifling. There is an impulse toward flight, a desire to see someone besides the magistrate (a really handsome man) who has a pleasing face, a face to be trusted. So many snide people here, so many snide lawyers and political hangers-on.

"This is a robbery case. The defendant, a boy of seventeen, has his head bound in crimson bandages. That troubles the magistrate until he hears the story, for it is obviously the result of police manhandling. Then the story: Robbery of a speakeasy.

The bartender killed by bandits. This boy's companions held on a homicide charge. No bail. Take him away.

"A chorus girl appears against a company manager. A beautiful, sulky, frightened girl next. She is a maid, charged with stealing a mistress' dress.

"Now a moment when no case is ready. It is time for the issuing of summons, the time for anyone who wishes to speak to the Judge to step forward. The bailiff shouts.

"An old man stumbles forward. He has a face like Bat Nelson's. It is pinched almost beyond human identification, but there is still the shadow of Kilkenny there. Streaks of dried blood fringe his eyes, and the old man's coat is filthy. He is sober, but he hasn't been for long. Hopeless old man.

" 'I want to be committed for a while, your Honor. I'm sick and I'm hungry and I want to lay up,' he says in brogue.

" 'How old are you?'

" 'Sixty-five, and I can't keep a job.'

" 'When were you hurt there—?' pointing to the eyes.

" 'Two weeks ago.'

"The commitment to the Home for the Aged is made out.

"Another suppliant approaches. He is small and shy and young. His collar is dirty and his voice is so low-pitched and bewildered that he is hard to understand. He wants a warrant for his wife.

" 'She left me in Paterson and came here and I quit my job and came after her. She's under age. She's with another man.'

" 'How old is she?'

" 'Fourteen.'

" 'How long were you married?'

" 'Three months. Her mother lives in Paterson and her father in Philadelphia. They're divorced. I went to the Children's Society, but they couldn't do anything for me, because she's married.'

"There's no law to help the husband. What he needs is a social worker.

"This is a magistrate's court. The spangled parade of life passes here, gaudy and gay, drab and mean. The push of ambition, the drums of crime, the blare of pretension, the keen quiet of tragedy, all these are integral parts."

III. *Harlequinade* [3]

"In spite of the fact that the judge went to Springfield to participate in the councils of his party there, his court was a scene of uncommon activity. Various eyewitnesses gave it as their unbiased opinion that at nine o'clock in the morning some two hundred litigants, defendants, shyster lawyers, professional bondsmen, clerks, bailiffs, attorneys-at-law, witnesses, loiterers, newsboys and others were contributing to an oral hurricane which approximated the Board of Trade with wheat cornered on the floor and 'America First' being rendered by a steam calliope in the gallery.

"The court is in the Harrison Street police building, which houses the first precinct police, the detective bureau, the bureau of identification and several other items of machinery for the application of justice. And all these wheels and cogs and levers and cams and gears were there yesterday. All except the judge. He was in Springfield with twelve other judges.

"About a month ago there was published a list of two hundred and fifteen gambling resorts in Chicago. The police department sprang to action and raided four of them, thus protecting the ends of justice. These four cases were on call. . . . The sounds, as one approached the stairs were those of a multitude of conversations all combining and rushing upward in a wild crescendo toward a climax which could only be the roof.

"Here was the court of justice. Some wore their hats aslant over their right eyes and smoked cigarettes prodigiously. Some wore their hats aslant over their left eyes and smoked cigars prodigiously. All smoked and spat. Some spat into the cuspidors, others at them. Some sat in chairs, some put their feet in them. Altogether some two hundred and fifty citizens were joined in a clamor as dizzy as the ancient First Ward ball.

"On the bench sat the assistant state's attorney, sitting without even a pretense of legal authority. All around him the chattering of many voices, clouds of smoke and carloads of coughing and

---

[3] This passage appeared in the *Chicago Tribune*, April 21, 1928. It was written by Robert M. Lee.

sneezing and spitting and God-damns. A man approached the bench and spoke as follows:

" 'What's going on here?'

" 'This here?' queried the assistant state's attorney. Why this here's a court. I'm the judge.'

"The conversation broke off in a swirl of insistent demands from those gathered about the bench.

" 'I want my case postponed,' cried one as he thrust back his hat belligerently and stood puffing a cigar.

" 'No, you don't . . . not 'til I get mine,' declared a similarly intrusive personage, elbowing the first.

" 'Hey, how do you get that way?' growled a third, bursting through the group and projecting his chin dangerously toward the bench.

"A wailing note arose out of the tumult, 'Well, if this ain't a lunatic asylum I'll go to hell.' It was swallowed up in a blur of banalities.

" 'Continuance!'

" 'Continue my case!'

"Mr. —— chuckled amiably on the bench. 'All right,' he said, 'All right. All right. All right. All . . .'

"A clerk bustled up to the bench. 'Just a minute, Joe,' he said, 'I'll mark this one continued.' He drew the judge's docket toward him and wrote. It was the judge's docket and the judge was in Springfield. Continued. Continued. Continued.

" 'Say,' said the citizen, who had been temporarily muffled in the turmoil, 'what's this?'

" 'This?' said Mr. —— gravely. 'This is a court. Who are you, anyway?'

" 'I'm a citizen,' he repeated, 'and I think it's a monstrous joke, your sitting there continuing cases. You're no judge. None of these cases'll be any good. All these policemen have walked their beats day or night and now lose sleep to come down here, still on duty, to watch this silly performance. You ought to be ashamed of yourself.'

"Thus ridding himself of his spleen the citizen retreated. A woman seated at the right of the assistant state's attorney on the bench whispered, 'He's trying to fix a case.'

" 'I wish I knew what case it was,' said ———. 'I'd fix it.'

"A clerk spoke up. 'Fifty-one cases postponed. That's a day's work.'

"Smoke. Clatter of chairs. Scuffling of feet. Riot of talk. And louder. The citizen returned to the attack.

" 'Say,' said he, 'I'm a reporter. And I'm trying to find out what kind of a circus this is.'

" 'O, you're a reporter,' said ———. 'Well, well! Well, I'm the judge. Send over to your paper for a photographer and take a picture of me.'

"A gale of laughter recognized this sally. The reporter turned and laid hold of a nearby sleeve. 'Come on,' he said, pulling the photographer, 'take the judge's picture.

"The photographer began to unlimber his machinery. The assistant state's attorney turned to the captain of the Harrison Street forces. 'He can't take a picture,' said he, his jaw falling.

" 'Why?' demanded the reporter.

" 'Judge's orders.' Then to the police captain. 'Stop that photographer.'

"The captain smiled dreamily. 'I ain't thinking about nothin'.'

"The photographer raised his camera. There was a sound of a chair knocked over and the rush of feet. The assistant state's attorney fled from the judicial bench as if it had been pestilential. The slam of a door was evidence that he was safe in the judge's chambers.

" 'Come on out,' the photographer said. He perched himself on the judicial railing and coiled up for a long siege. The conversation drifted into cackles of laughter. A few more gamblers crept into the judge's chambers for continuances and the rest clumped down the stairs. Court was adjourned."

.   .   .   .

It may be protested that these realistic examples of minor court decorum are extreme, drawn from cities in which the most seriously unsatisfactory conditions prevail; that they describe conditions not universally, not even generally, true; that they are caricatures. But they are unusual only in the sense that they describe what happens in very large cities and in the busiest courts of these cities. They are faithful descriptions of conditions in two cities with an aggregate population of ten millions.

Careful first-hand observation of minor courts in a dozen large cities revealed similar conditions. Reliable reports from many others show the same conditions. The conclusion that must be reached is, therefore, that the conditions described in this chapter are common to the magistrates' courts in jurisdictions governing a majority of the urban population of the United States.[4] The reader who doubts that such conditions can prevail in his own city should verify his opinions by ocular evidence.

[4] A pleasant contrast was afforded by courts which I saw in Detroit, Los Angeles, and Milwaukee.

CHAPTER II

THE GRIMY COURT OF THE MAGISTRATE

THE two unmistakably important tendencies in present day criminal justice are the vast discretion exercised by the prosecutor and by the committing magistrate and the incredible proportion of felony cases which are terminated through the discretion of these officers. In rural districts the magistrate is largely overshadowed by the prosecutor but in the cities the prosecutor largely through his own indifference permits the magistrate to cut liberally into the cases initiated by the police. In most cities the proportion of felony cases terminated by action of the magistrate is over a third, in New York and Chicago it is over one half, while in Philadelphia the percentage is seventy-eight. This large exercise of discretion is carried out in most cities under the most unfortunate circumstances. The foregoing examples have shown how little semblance of a judicial inquiry is observed. The theory and the law of the preliminary hearing, admirably adapted to protect all interested parties, are quite forgotten in practice.

I. *The Preliminary Examination in English History*

When, in 1664, one Francis Tryon found that his house had been burglarized, he reported his trouble and his suspicions to Aleyn, magistrate (alderman). Aleyn initiated a vigorous and fruitful, although not wholly scrupulous, investigation. He interrogated servants, followed up clews, questioned a man named Turner and officially charged him with the crime. He held an official hearing on the charge and, because Turner denied the charge, "but not as a person of his spirit," he decided to investigate further. With another magistrate, he shadowed Turner, and finally caught him, in possession of certain money which

Aleyn suspected had been stolen. Then he arranged that the prosecuting witness should falsely promise not to prosecute, and tricked the defendant into a full confession. He was thus able officially to commit the defendant to Newgate to await trial. In this case, Aleyn, the magistrate, served as a detective and arresting officer, conducted the preliminary examination, committed the prisoner for trial, and presumably appeared at the trial as a principal witness. In his examination of the accused there was no attorney for the defense, not necessarily a confronting of witnesses, and no particular rules of procedure.[1]

This generalized activity of magistrates was characteristic of the system that prevailed in England prior to the nineteenth century. In the preliminary inquiry into felonies, the method was inquisitorial rather than judicial. The distinction will appear in a comparison between the system of which the foregoing is characteristic and that which now exists both in England and in the United States.

No legal duty to conduct preliminary examinations was imposed upon the justices of the peace when the office was created in 1324; but it is probable that rather early they developed the custom of making some kind of inquiry before they committed suspected persons for trial.[2] In 1554 and 1555 statutes were enacted which legally established the preliminary examination.[3] These statutes were apparently designed to arm justices with new and enlarged powers to bring malefactors to trial. They emphasize the administrative law-enforcing character of the justice. They provided that persons arrested for felony should not be let to bail except by two justices who should, when the prisoner came before them, "take the examination of the said prisoner and information of them that bring him in" and put into writing such material evidence. They also provided that

---

[1] Stephen, *History of the Criminal Law of England* (London, 1883), I, 223. The account of this case is from 6 State Trials, 619, 630. Other examples are cited by Stephen I, 223-225, particularly a case in 1681, in which a magistrate named Gilbert, by an elaborate course of detection, built up a case against one Busby, whom he had charged and committed for the crime of being a Popish priest. Gilbert served as detective, committing magistrate and sole prosecuting witness.

[2] The coroner's inquest has always been a form of preliminary examination. For a discussion of its origins and present powers, see my *Politics and Criminal Prosecution* (New York, 1929), 110 to 126.

[3] I and 2, Philip and Mary, Ch. 13, and 2 and 3, Philip and Mary, Ch. 10.

there should be an examination of such persons even when bail was refused and also that essential witnesses could be held by the justices. Under these laws the justices acted inquisitorially, not judicially. The prisoner was closely questioned. Witnesses for the prosecution were not examined in his presence. Their evidence was for the information of the court only; it did not have to be and, in fact, was not communicated to the accused.[4] The magistrate served as public prosecutor.

The system thus established resembled the Continental system in practically every respect, except that in England torture never became a recognized factor in establishing a case. On the Continent, the normal criminal procedure of the Roman law, which was accusatory and not unduly favorable to the accusers, broke down in the twelfth century under the influence of the inquisition developed by the Dominicans, to the point where not only in preparing for the trial, but in the trial itself, "every safeguard of innocence was abolished or disregarded; torture was freely used. Everything was done that possibly could have been done to secure a conviction. This procedure, inquisitory and secret, gradually forced its way into the temporal courts; we may also say that the common law of Western Europe adopted it." [5] But while torture was not generally adopted in England, "the escape," say Pollock and Maitland, "was narrow." It was averted because there did not develop in England the rigorous law of evidence which the canonists evolved for the Continent. "Our criminal procedure took permanent shape at an early time and had hardly any place for a law of evidence. It emancipated itself from the old formulated oaths, and it trusted for a while to the rough verdict of the countryside, without caring to investigate the logical processes, if logical they were, of which the verdict was the outcome." [6]

The fact that torture never came to be used did not, however, prevent magistrates from practicing treachery and corrup-

---

[4] See Stephen, I, 218-219; and Holdsworth, *History of English Law*, I, 296-297.

[5] Pollock and Maitland, *History of English Law* (Second Edition, Boston, 1899), II, 657. See also Esmein, *History of Continental Criminal Procedure* (Boston, 1913), 78-144.

[6] Pollock and Maitland, *op. cit.*, 660-661. It should be noted that while torture was not permitted under the common law, it was used by the king's prerogative. See Jardine, *Use of Torture* (London, 1837), also Holdsworth, *History of English Law*, V, 185-187.

tion. Until the nineteenth century, English magistrates were paid by fees. In discussing "trading justices," Stephen quotes from the testimony of a Bow Street runner before a Parliamentary committee in 1816:

"At that time before the Police Bill took place at all, it was a trading business; and there was Justice This and Justice That. Justice Welch in Litchfield Street was a great man in those days, and old Justice Hyde, and Justice Girdler, and Justice Blackborough, a trading justice at Clerkenwell Green, and an old ironmonger. The plan used to be to issue out warrants and take up all the poor devils in the street, and then there was the bailing of them, 2s.4d., which the magistrates had; and taking up 100 girls, that would make, at 2s.4d., 11, 13s.4d. They sent none to gaol, the bailing them was so much better." [7]

A vivid picture, not only of magistrates' practices, but of the entire criminal problem of the eighteenth century, can be found in the writings of the great novelist, Henry Fielding. After a youthful period of unprofitable play-writing, Fielding had studied law and served with distinction as Justice of the Peace for Westminster and Middlesex.[8]

His judgment of the quality of justice administered by the magistrates of his day is characterized thus in his reflections written in the last years of his life:

". . . my private affairs at the beginning of the winter had but a gloomy aspect: for I had not plundered the public or the poor of those sums which men, who are always ready to plunder both as much as they can, have been pleased to suspect me of taking: on the contrary, by composing, instead of inflaming, the quarrels of porters and beggars (which I blush when I say hath not been universally practiced), and by refusing to take a shilling from a man who most undoubtedly would not have had another left, I had reduced an income of about five hundred pounds a year of the dirtiest money upon earth to little more than three hundred pounds, a considerable proportion of which remained with my clerk; and indeed, if the whole had done so, as it ought, he would be but ill paid for sitting almost sixteen hours in the twenty-four in the most

---

[7] Stephen, op. cit., I, 231.

[8] He served from 1748 to 1753, and was succeeded by his half-brother, John Fielding, "the blind justice," who served for many years and, according to Dickens' account in *Barnaby Rudge*, was a man of courage and ability. During Henry Fielding's service at Bow Street, he was very active in the creation of the early professional police organization which developed into the great metropolitan police of the next century. His son, William, served as a justice for over fifty years.

unwholesome, as well as nauseous air in the universe, and which hath in his case corrupted a good constitution without contaminating his morals.

"A predecessor of mine used to boast that he made one thousand pounds a year in his office; but how he did this (if indeed he did it) is to me a secret. His clerk, now mine, told me I had more business than he had ever known there; I am sure I had as much as any man could do. The truth is, the fees are so very low, when any are due, and so much is done for nothing, that, if a single justice of the peace had business enough to employ twenty clerks, neither he nor they would get much by their labour. The public will not, therefore, I hope, think I betray a secret when I inform them that I received from the Government a yearly pension out of the Public service money; which, I believe, indeed, would have been larger had my great patron been convinced of an error, which I have heard him utter more than once, and he could not indeed say that the acting as a principal justice of the peace in Westminster was on all accounts very desirable, but that all the world knew it was a very lucrative office. Now, to have shewn him plainly that a man must be a rogue to make a very little this way, and that he could not make much by being as great a rogue as he could be, would have required more confidence than, I believe, he had in me, and more of his conversation than he chose to allow me; I, therefore, resigned the office and the farther execution of my plan to my brother, who had long been my assistant." [9]

The generations immediately following the time of Fielding were characterized by two series of reforms, both of which had a profound effect upon the preliminary examination as an institution. The first was the reform in the magistracy itself; the other the development of an efficient police system. When Fielding served, he was relieved, by a special grant from the government, of the necessity of depending upon fees. So was his successor. Subsequently a statute [10] established several stipendiary magistrates with a prohibition against retaining fees. Since that time the stipendiary system has been repeatedly extended throughout the kingdom. Ultimately the holding of preliminary examinations has come to be exercised in the large cities by trained, professional, salaried persons. This made it possible to transform the preliminary inquiry into a judicial hearing.

[9] Henry Fielding's Works (New York, 1911), XI, 200-201. See also Webb, *English Local Government, The Parish and the County* (London, 1906), 327, 335, 337, for an interesting account of the extent to which the justices of the eighteenth century extended their mercenary practices.
[10] 32 George III, Chapter 53.

The establishment of professional police through the various enactments which culminated in the Metropolitan Police Act of Peel in 1829, differentiated the functions of magistrate and of policeman. It should be borne in mind that tradition had provided that police be subjected to the direction of magistrates and in the late eighteenth century these magistrates in London had become "stipendiary" magistrates. In 1839 the control of police was, however, taken from the magistrates and turned over to commissioners and thus, in the picturesque phrase of Maitland, "the judicial and executive duties comprised in the old conservation of the peace fell apart, and we are left with learned magistrates and gallant commissioners." [11]

The legislation which marked the transformation of the preliminary hearing was enacted in 1836 and in 1848. The Prisoner's Counsel Act of 1836 [12] permitted all persons under trial to inspect all depositions taken against them. The statute of 1848 substantially ushered in a new dispensation.[13] It provided that the witnesses for the prosecution be examined in the presence of the accused, that the accused be allowed to make any statement he pleased or call any witnesses he pleased, that he be free from the obligation to make any statement and that the magistrate inform him of this right.

The distinctions, then, between the early English inquisitorial examination and the present judicial one created by the legislation of 1848 seem to be:

(1) Under the early law the magistrate was a public prosecutor who was frequently responsible for the arrest and who definitely used the examination for the purpose of establishing his case. Under the new law, the magistrate sits as judge, usually with no interest in the case prior to the examination.

(2) Under the old law, the accused was examined without any important limitations. Under the new, there is no compulsory examination of the accused, although he is invited to make a statement.

(3) Under the old law, the testimony was secret and for the

[11] Maitland, *Justice and Police* (London, 1885), 100.
[12] 6 and 7 William IV, Chapter 114.
[13] 11, 12 Victoria, Chapter 42.

information of the court alone. Under the new, the testimony is open, accusatory, and confrontative.[14]

(4) Under the old law, the accused had no right to counsel. Under the new, there is right to cross-examination and right to counsel.

(5) Under the old law, the accused could not get the evidence or copies thereof. Under the new, he is entitled as a right to copies of the testimony given in open court and also to inspect all depositions taken against him.[15]

To sum up, the important characteristics of the English and American preliminary hearings include compulsory processes for the securing of witnesses both for and against the accused, the giving of evidence and the provision for cross-examination, the right of the defendant to waive the hearing entirely and the duty of the magistrate to inform him of this right. The preliminary hearing has, in short, become a further extension of the Anglo-American system of decentralizing the administration of criminal justice largely in the interest of protecting the rights of the accused.

II. *The American Preliminary Hearing in Law*

Whether, prior to the disappearance of the inquisitorial features from the English system, the American magistrates exercised like power is not entirely clear. It is probable that at all times, even now, there have been magistrates who have, in fact, been police, prosecutors and magistrates in one, but the early development of the county prosecutor as an aggressive agent of law enforcement, and the power and prestige of the sheriff in all frontier communities, probably prevented the justice of the peace and the city magistrates from assuming much importance as investigators of crimes and suspected criminals. It is clear that for a long time the accepted status of the magistrate in preliminary examinations has been judicial.

[14] The Act of 1848 specifically provides that the place where the examination is to be held shall not be an open court. It is, however, quite possible for the magistrate to exclude the public; but according to Maitland "any use of this power of exclusion is uncommon." *Justice and Police*, 129.

[15] Under the Prisoners' Counsel Act of 1836, 6, 7, William IV, Chapter 114.

The power to conduct a preliminary hearing in rural districts rests usually with justices of the peace and, in cities, with the court that has criminal jurisdiction of an inferior nature. With the exception of a few of the larger cities, the minor court which hears preliminary examinations also conducts the trial of minor offenses.

The legal provisions surrounding the preliminary hearing in the United States describe an institution which is intended to achieve several very important objectives, some which are of value to those charged with crime, some to the state and some to both:

For the defendant:

The nature of the crime is defined and the allegations concerning its connection with the defendant are set forth.

The defendant when he can easily prove his innocence is enabled to dispose of the charge quickly and without much publicity.

He is partially protected against ignorance and vicious inquisitions by police and prosecuting agencies.

For both state and defendant:

Opportunity to determine bail is provided.

Expensive and lengthy trials are avoided when there is insufficient justification for holding them.

For the state:

The state is enabled to hold the defendant when "probable cause" is shown, with sufficient time to prepare the prosecution.

The state is able to get into some sort of permanent form the testimony of witnesses who may disappear or forget or be tampered with.

Witnesses may be bound over for the grand jury or for the trial.[16]

[16] The purposes of the preliminary examination are well summarized in the following terms:

"The object or purpose of the preliminary investigation is to prevent hasty, malicious, improvident and oppressive prosecutions, to protect the person charged from open and

The legal provisions by which the various states attempt to achieve their objectives vary in detail from state to state but the main pattern is a fairly standardized institution. To set forth their details is not in line with the purposes of this book but it may clarify the discussion to outline the legal provisions in some specific system and to offer a few comments upon each point.[17] Rather than to select a single state for such a description, we have selected the system recommended by the American Law Institute in its Code of Criminal Procedure. On various points a few comparative comments are made.[18] To a very important degree this Code represents the judicial (as distinguished from the inquisitorial) form of the preliminary examination. After assembling the legal provisions governing the preliminary examination in the states, the makers of the code seriously considered whether they should recommend the abandonment of the American system entirely in favor of the Continental system. The decision was in favor of the American system. The provisions of the Code are therefore the embodiment of an enlightened attempt to set up a judicial preliminary hearing with all interests fully protected.

The issue in a preliminary examination is, in the Code of the American Law Institute, described in these terms:

Sec. 54. After hearing the evidence and the statement of the accused, in case he has made one, or his testimony, in case he has testified, if it appears either that a public offense has not been committed or that, if committed, there is not probable cause to believe the accused guilty thereof, the magistrate shall order the accused to be discharged.

public accusations of crime, to avoid both for the defendant and the public the expense of a public trial, and to save the defendant from the humiliation and anxiety involved in a public prosecution, and to discover whether or not there are substantial grounds upon which a prosecution may be based." Rosenberry, J. in Thies v. State, 178 Wis. 98, 103, 189 N. W. 539, 541 (1922).

[17] The detailed constitutional and statutory provisions covering the preliminary examination in the various states are conveniently arranged for reference in Tentative Draft Number 1, of the Code of Criminal Procedure of the American Law Institute, published by the American Law Institute, Philadelphia, 1928, pp. 27-28 and 183-251.

[18] An admirable summary and commentary upon these provisions is an article by Justin Miller entitled The Preliminary Hearing in XV *Am. Bar Assoc. Jour.,* 414. My account of the legal aspects of the preliminary examination to some extent follows this article.

A number of states use expressions other than "probable cause" to describe the same concept. Some of these are "sufficient grounds," "probably guilty" and "prima facie case." Just what degree of proof is necessary to cover these terms is not certain. In practice each magistrate interprets the meaning in accordance with his own notions usually guided by rough "practical" considerations as to the desirability of continuing with the prosecution.

The Code requires that "no information may be filed against any person, except a fugitive from justice, for any offense which may be punished by death or imprisonment in the penitentiary, until such person shall have had or waived a preliminary examination." The Code is silent concerning the necessity of a preliminary examination prior to an indictment, thus indicating a wise acquiescence in the established freedom of a grand jury to initiate prosecutions without a preliminary hearing. With only a few exceptions this provision is in line with the substantial requirements in the states. Some sort of hearing is always necessary after arrest to determine bail.

The rights of the defendant are protected by numerous provisions of the Code. The magistrate upon arraignment must inform the defendant of the nature of the charge against him, of his right to counsel and of his right to waive the examination. His right to have and to communicate with counsel is defined. Prompt hearing of the case and limitations upon adjournments protect the defendant against oppressive delay, which is not unknown in this country. His rights with regard to bail are defined. He is entitled to require the state to summon witnesses. All witnesses must be heard in his presence and are subject to cross-examination. In case a secret examination of witnesses is desired by the state, the grand jury is available. The accused may make an unsworn statement in his own behalf after the state has completed its case in order to clear himself of the charge, and his failure to make such a statement shall not be used against him at the trial, but if he makes such a statement it may be used against him at the trial.

The purposes of these provisions for statements by the accused are thus explained by Dean Miller:

"first, by making such statements the accused may be able to convince the magistrate of his innocence, he is at least entitled to such an opportunity; second, the accused is very apt to tell a direct, truthful story at this early stage of the proceedings, which will prevent his concocting a perjured defense, with or without the assistance of a shyster lawyer, prior to the trial; third, it is hoped by some persons that 'if the person charged with a felony is given a prompt and public opportunity before a magistrate to make his statement, the police will have no excuse for conducting secret, unregulated and oppressive examinations.' " [19]

The advantages provided by the Code for the state chiefly center upon the provisions for taking testimony and preserving it for the trial. As has been pointed out, the statements of the accused, sworn or unsworn, may be under certain conditions admitted at the trial. The testimony of witnesses and of the defendant shall be reduced to writing. This is to protect the state in case of the impeachment or disappearance of witnesses prior or during trial. Testimony of witnesses may be admitted as evidence at the trial "if, for any reason the testimony of the witnesses cannot be obtained at the trial and the court is satisfied that the inability to procure such testimony is not the fault of the party offering it." Provision is also made that the magistrate may order the accused to be held to answer for "any public offense" for which the magistrate believes there is probable cause to believe him guilty. This makes it possible to hold a defendant upon a charge other than that originally made, without loss of time and without the danger involved in releasing him pending new proceedings. The state is unable to hold material witnesses under certain protective provisions which guard against the unjust holding of witnesses that now takes place occasionally. Finally it should be noted that even when the defendant waives a hearing the state may require the examination of witnesses and the recording of their statements.

It is important to note the value of these provisions for the recording and the preservation of testimony under the conditions that exist in modern criminal-law administration. In the trial of gangsters, or persons with powerful political connections in great cities, it is almost impossible to protect the state's wit-

[19] Ibid., 416.

nesses. Bribery and intimidation are very common, and are almost impossible to prevent. The earlier material witnesses should be put into some kind of record.

The use of the preliminary examination as a means of hearing witnesses prior to the trial can be very helpful in prosecution. It is, of course, obvious that a prosecutor or a police department acting without power may have difficulty in getting evidence from witnesses. They are not allowed to subpœna them or to place them under oath. Moreover, the conditions under which they conduct such preliminary questionings do not always tend to preserve the interests either of the state or of the defense. Occasionally, however, a magistrate will provide the compulsion and protection of his power for what actually amounts to interviewing of witnesses for the purpose of preparing the case. It is not uncommon to see the examining magistrate sit at his desk after having sworn in a witness and permit the prosecuting officer to place in the permanent record a great deal of testimony of witnesses. This is done without any particular interest on the part of the magistrate in the proceedings, but it is within his hearing and under the authority of his power. This usually takes place in cases where it is a foregone conclusion that the defendant will be bound over and the examination of witnesses is merely to establish a record.

III. *The Preliminary Hearing in Practice*

As the legal status of the preliminary examination is described, there seems to emerge an institution almost perfectly devised to promote the orderly administration of the law. Both state and defendant seem to be protected in every essential respect. But the anticipation evoked by the legal structure is not fulfilled in practice. The American preliminary hearing, while a most important factor in actual law administration, is carried out under the most unfortunate conditions and circumstances.

The faulty administration of preliminary hearings would not be so serious if so many cases were not finally disposed of at that stage of procedure. But it constitutes a sifting process of very great importance. In some of the large cities a majority of felony cases do not get beyond the preliminary hearing; in all of them, a large proportion die there. The following table shows the proportion of felony cases terminated in this stage of procedure in a number of the large cities for which dependable figures are available:

Proportion of Cases Dismissed or Discharged in Preliminary Hearing

City	Year	Percentage Cases Terminated	Authority
New York	1926	58.7	N. Y. Crime Commission Report 1928
Chicago	1926	48.8	Ill. Cr. Survey
Philadelphia	1926	78	Penna. Cr. Commission
St. Louis	1926	34.7	Mo. Cr. Survey, Supp. 1929
Cleveland	1926	38.6	Cleveland Assn. Cr. Justice
Milwaukee	1926	17.3	Ill. Cr. Survey

It is probable that this large proportion of cases eliminated in preliminary hearing is no recent development. In Chicago there has been no increase in twenty years, in Cleveland none in ten years, and none in New York for a like period. Thus it is clear that in the large cities a great many of the decisions, which in the last analysis determine the course of justice, are made in preliminary hearings by judges of inferior courts. Moreover, these decisions are in most cases final. Without assuming that there is any considerable number of cases in which magistrates deliberately release prisoners whom they have reason to suppose guilty, if the conditions under which the decisions are made are such as to prevent sound and informed judgment, the preliminary hearing may result in the release of important defendants who are not only guilty, but whose continued presence in society results in a multiplication of serious crimes. Therefore, while the preliminary hearing is ordinarily neglected and despised by commentators, it is in every respect a most important link in the process of administering justice. It might be concluded with a good deal of justification that so far as the effective enforcement of criminal law is concerned the preliminary hearing is more important than the trial itself.

A somewhat detailed analysis of the disposition of cases in

a single court may be helpful in illustrating how the preliminary hearing operates in practice. The following describes the preliminary examination in the Chicago Municipal Court in 1926: [20]

In the City of Chicago 10,829 cases entered the preliminary hearing in 1926. These cases were disposed of in the manner indicated in the following table:

	Number	Per Cent
Total number cases entering preliminary hearing.......	10,829	100.00
Never apprehended	391	3.61
Error, no complaint	116	1.07
Complaint denied	35	.32
Bond forfeited, not apprehended....................	68	.63
Certified to other courts..........................	50	.46
Dismissed, want of prosecution.....................	2,501	23.10
Nolle prosequi	766	7.08
Discharged	2,117	19.55
Reduced to misdemeanor, not punished..............	12	.11
Reduced to misdemeanor, punished..................	3	.03
No order	22	.20
Pending	7	.06
No record	36	.33
Total elimination	6,124	56.55
Remainder—Bound over to grand jury..............	4,705	43.45

"In discussing the fate of cases in the preliminary hearing on the basis of the above table, it is not necessary to consider at any length a number of the dispositions indicated. For example, the reduction of charges to 'misdemeanor,' 'no record,' 'pending,' certified to other courts and 'no order' involves a comparatively small number of cases and therefore we need not spend much time on them. Charges 'reduced to misdemeanor' mean that an original felony charge, in the opinion of the municipal judge or the state's attorney, is properly a misdemeanor and is disposed of as such on its merits. This is apparently a way of correcting an obvious error in the charge and does not occur frequently; consequently, we may dismiss it without comment.

"The seven cases indicated as 'pending' were not disposed of at the time the investigation was made.

"Seventy-two cases were 'certified to other courts,' which means that after the complaint was filed, the court discovered that because of the age of the defendant or some other circumstances, the case properly belonged elsewhere, either in the Juvenile Court or in some other jurisdiction. This

[20] Quoted in the *Illinois Crime Survey* and published in that report, 296-298. An analysis of the dispositions in preliminary examination in the entire city of New York will be found in *A Statistical Analysis of the Criminal Cases in the Courts of the State of New York* by C. W. Gehlke and Raymond Moley, included in the 1927 Report of the Crime Commission of New York State, 95-174.

does not happen frequently, because the police usually refrain from bringing a charge against anyone wanted by other authorities, and the case, therefore, would not come within the scope of our study.

" 'No record' means that the files were incomplete and in our investigation we were unable to determine the disposition of the case.

" 'No order' means that for some reason the state does not wish to prosecute to a final conclusion but is unwilling to strike the case from the docket entirely.

" 'Never apprehended' means that a complaint was made, a warrant was issued, but the police or other arresting officer was unable to take the accused into custody. This need not detain us long, because in a consideration of the responsibility of the prosecuting officer for the various items in this study it can scarcely be charged that he is to blame for such a result.

"It will be noted that one hundred sixteen cases are lost because of 'error, no complaint.' In the state-wide study which this survey has attempted, we found that this disposition appears only in Cook County and in the City of Chicago. It is, according to the authorities, a way of indicating the dismissal of a case where the complainant applies for a warrant and after a hearing, it is determined that his complaint is groundless. It would seem, therefore, to be about the same sort of disposition as a straight charge with a subsequent dismissal. If it really were an error, the case should be continued until the proper charge is filed, and then the original case dismissed. There would seem to be grave doubts as to the wisdom of dismissing the case outright and an alert prosecutor would certainly object to such a disposition.

" 'Complaint denied' is also found only in Cook County and the City of Chicago. It means that the complainant has had a hearing and it is decided that his complaint is groundless. The same comment that we made above in connection with 'error, no complaint' applies here. It seems that there is an unnecessary multiplication of dispositions here, when simple dismissal would suffice.

" 'Bond forfeited, not apprehended' means that the defendant who has been in custody of the court has been released upon bond, and, when he has failed to appear for trial, the bond has been forfeited.

"Thus 5,384, or half of the cases which enter the preliminary hearing, are terminated there by three kinds of disposition: 'discharged,' 'nolle prosequi,' and 'dismissed, want of prosecution.'

"The case is 'discharged' when, after the presentation of evidence by the state and occasionally by the defense, the court decides there is not 'probable cause' and that the defendant should not be held for action by the grand jury. Technically, this differs in a marked way from 'dismissed, want of prosecution,' because presumably in the latter case evidence has not been presented at all and there is no action for the court to take except to dismiss the case. In practice, however, it may mean many things. It is sometimes due to the absence of witnesses or the failure of witnesses to offer testimony. In practice it also means that in many instances the municipal judge uses this method of ridding the court of a case, when in reality he has heard evidence and has decided that it was inadequate."

The value of the preliminary examination as a means for getting down the testimony of witnesses in a dependable record, and early in the prosecution, is negligible. In a great many of the magistrates' courts no stenographic record is made at all. The impeachment of a witness who tells a story at the trial different from that told at the preliminary hearing is difficult not only as a matter of law but in practice. The fact that in closely contested cases neither side shows its case in any completeness is another element which prevents the hearing from building up a record.

Finally, the very physical conditions that surround the preliminary examination in nearly all the great cities destroy its value in all of these respects. It is public; but it provides none of the conditions which a public hearing is supposed to guarantee. The proceedings take place in a courtroom usually crowded with all sorts and conditions of people. Noise and disorder prevail. Cases are heard with such great speed that no opportunity is permitted for an orderly presentation of evidence. A casual, careless and unintelligible presentation of evidence precedes a hasty guess of judgment. It is so important that this aspect be appreciated by a person who seeks to understand American criminal justice that we gave the preceding chapter entirely to first-hand· descriptions of magistrates' courts in all their grimy and sordid reality.

The most serious side is that the confusion that is present at the preliminary hearing does little to protect the public interest against back-stair wire-pulling and fixing. The magistrate can usually be consulted by all sorts of persons, many of whom have no proper interest in the case. He is almost unprotected so far as political influences are concerned and the political factors involved are very great. Machine politics is always heavily entrenched in the inferior courts. If there is to be any "fixing" of criminal cases, the wise and effective politician does his work here. He is protected by confusion and haste, and he deals with but one person. If his case slips through the preliminary hearing, his task is multiplied manyfold. He must deal with more persons in a more rarefied atmosphere. There is the danger of attracting newspaper attention. The prosecutor may be recalcitrant, or the grand jury or the trial judge may unexpectedly take special interest in the case. Consequently, the forces which so often effectively prevent the adequate prosecution of professional criminals concentrate their strength upon the preliminary hearing. The weakest spot in the system is the one at which greatest pressure is directed.

In the winter of 1929-30 the New York magistrates' courts were subjected to very serious criticism. A grand jury investigation was held. A report was submitted, March 19, 1930, which so completely describes conditions surrounding the preliminary hearing in one of the great urban jurisdictions, that it deserves extended quotation:

"The testimony before us is not legally sufficient to warrant the finding of any indictment. It leads us, however, to make the following statement:

FIRST—It has been brought to our attention that some magistrates have been indiscreet and lax to a degree which might lead to improper inferences in one or more of the following particulars:

By maintaining too close connection with political organizations and by being unduly active in politics.

By a lack of dignity in the conduct of their courts.

By a lack of consideration of persons having business in the court and permitting the same on the part of court employees.

By being dilatory in opening and premature in closing court.

By granting postponements in such number as to put an undue burden on complainants and witnesses, tending to thwart the administration of justice.

By seeing in chambers too many people who may be presumed to have business which should be heard in open court, giving rise to the suspicion that the magistrate is being subjected to improper influences.

By holding for the grand jury cases which, by the exercise of proper courage or intelligence, or both, could have been disposed of by the magistrate.

By the inadequate supervision of the issuance of bail bonds.

SECOND—The magistrates' courts in the county of New York are, almost without exception, inconveniently subdivided and arranged. The subdivision and arrangement facilitate and in some instances may perhaps lead to abuses. In and about these courts persons are suffered to loiter who have no legitimate business therein or thereabout. The presence of most of these encourages improper practices by court clerks, assistant clerks and attendants, which includes the acceptance by some of gratuities for the performance of acts in violation of the law, such as drawing complaints in a lower degree than the facts warrant, unjustly advancing or delaying cases and allowing persons improperly to have access to defendants.

THIRD—The testimony suggests a pernicious business connection between professional bondsmen and attorneys leading to extortionate charges and in some instances to an illegal division by the attorney of his professional fee with the professional bondsman, through whose activity the attorney has secured the client. Bail agents in some instances are shown to have charged more than the legal fee for obtaining bail bonds.

The clerical staffs of most minor courts in the great cities are not only deep in politics but are unbelievably stupid and inefficient, and favoritism for, and insidious relationships with professional bondsmen and disreputable lawyers are common. One of the most disgraceful features of the minor courts of most of the cities is the quality of the clerical staff. The number of clerks is always much larger than is necessary; political prudence rules; and the order of the day is about half the work that is expected in private enterprises of the same kind. Great, beefy ward workers sprawl over clerical duties that a bank would have performed by eighteen-year-old girls. Records are kept as they were twenty-five years ago. Important papers are frequently lost. Such reports as are sometimes given to the public are unintelligible and uninterpreted jumbles of figures, with liberal picturizations of judges and chief administrative officers.

Perhaps the preliminary hearing in felony cases is usually done badly in the United States because it has never been considered a genuinely important factor in the processes of criminal justice. Nearly everyone in the system believes the preliminary hearing to be practically unnecessary. The police, feeling that a large number of well-prepared cases is unjustly dismissed and that the others are carried through more by chance than plan in the preliminary hearing, are bitterly antagonistic toward the magistrate and seek every means to bring their cases directly before the grand jury or prosecuting officer. The defendant who feels quite certain of his ability to escape the clutches of the law because of the strength of his case will ignore the preliminary hearing to the extent of waiving the right of presenting his evidence there. The prosecution views the preliminary hearing as a mere perfunctory detail. I heard a prosecuting officer remark in one of the branches of the Municipal Court of Chicago, "What does it matter? This is only the preliminary hearing." This general attitude of indifference has undoubtedly resulted in pushing the preliminary hearing into a position of neglect, not only in the actual practice of the law, but in the estimate of those who have written about it.

The grounds for this low estimate are many. In the first place, as a means for the weighing of evidence the value of the preliminary hearing is very slight. Neither the defense nor the prosecution is likely to present important evidence at this stage of the case. Both feel that strategy demands little intimation in public of what the defense or the prosecution is likely to be. The prosecution presents as much as it thinks necessary to induce the magistrate to hold the defendant. The defendant, if he feels that he is likely to be held, will withhold practically all his defense. Hearsay evidence is considered, leading questions are permitted, and insufficient opportunity is given for a cross-examination. Thus, the preliminary examination provides no satisfactory means for a really judicial determination of the merits of a case.

Not only as a judicial hearing but as an inquiry, the preliminary examination is inadequate. Little is done to develop facts and circumstances concerning either the defendant or the crime charged. A preliminary determination of the personality of the one accused of crime is quite infrequently attempted. Even if there were a disposition to make a more careful determination of the kind of person under arrest, there are no facilities for doing it, except in isolated instances such as are provided by the psychiatric services embodied in the court organization of the Municipal Court of Chicago and the Recorder's Court in Detroit. An intelligent and diligent examination of witnesses in order to build up the prosecution is almost never made. The judge himself has never heard of the case before. Utterly unprepared and uninformed, he can do little but follow the story of the police officer and interpolate a few improvised questions. The police officers are usually interested in telling only their own stories. Such questioning as they attempt is done in private, immediately after the arrest and before the hearing. They are, moreover, poorly equipped to bring out in the hearing the essential facts necessary for evidence. The prosecutor, upon whom the American system places so much responsibility in preparing cases for trial, is unbelievably negligent in preliminary examinations. In some cities, notably St. Louis and Cleveland, the prosecutor who is responsible for preliminary hearings is not a member of the office which is responsible for the subsequent trial of the case. There is a complete break in responsibility between hearings and trial—with serious loss of efficiency.[21] When, as in Chicago and New York, the same office is responsible for both, the preliminary hearing is regarded as a sort of unimportant and perfunctory gesture. The following description of prosecution in the Chicago Municipal Court is illustrative.[22]

"In each of the criminal branches of the Municipal Court, there is at least one assistant state's attorney and one assistant city prosecutor. In the branches where the volume of work is heavy there are two assistant state's attorneys. The assistant state's attorneys are assigned to the Municipal Court because the state's attorney has jurisdiction in all matters where the State of Illinois is the plaintiff, including felonies and misdemeanors, and should be represented in the trial at all stages. The city prosecutor has jurisdiction over all city cases, including violations of the city code.

"The work of the assistant state's attorneys who are assigned to the Municipal Court is perfunctory and careless in the extreme. The salaries of these men are from $200 to $300 a month. They are, therefore, the least experienced members of the staff. They are usually assigned to those branches of the court which are located in their own political strongholds. The duty which each assistant seems to feel acquits his responsibility is to fill out a form report which contains the name of each defendant in a felony case, the number of the case, the charge and the disposition. When a defendant is bound over to the grand jury, the assistant is required to

[21] For the consequences of this, see my outline of the Cleveland Crime Survey, 27-29.
[22] Quoted from my report on the Municipal Court in the Illinois Crime Survey, 406-407.

fill out a somewhat more detailed sheet. As is indicated in the report on prosecution to which we have already referred, 'an examination of these sheets indicates that some of the assistant state's attorneys scarcely rise above the literacy grade, and added to this are so meager in the information which they record, that the report is scarcely usable at all.' The assistant is usually lounging against the bench engaged in casual conversation with every passerby, careless, unimposing, undignified and indolent. He permits the judge to put most of the questions. He contributes very little to the process of determining whether a crime has been committed.

"The assistant state's attorney gives practically no time to the preparation of cases. The first time he comes in contact with a case is usually when it is called by the clerk. The assistant at this time usually picks up the complaint and attempts to extract testimony from witnesses whom he has not seen before. This, of course, places him at a decided disadvantage and seriously impairs the interests of the state, while the defendant is, in all important cases, represented by a counsel presumably prepared both as to the law and facts. It is thus obvious that the state is poorly served in the preliminary hearing and undoubtedly many cases which might result in the successful prosecution of important criminals are lost at this stage because of faulty work by the representative of the state's attorney's office."

Preliminary examinations in non-urban jurisdictions are usually conducted by a justice of the peace or a village official. Such officials are usually citizens without any special training in law or in administration. It would be unfair to stress this fact too much, however, because the decisions which must be made in a preliminary hearing are not inappropriate to the generalized practical intelligence usually possessed by such officials. Moreover, they are guided, as will presently be shown, by a prosecuting attorney. It would be the height of folly to characterize by any simple phrase the personal qualifications of such a vast and diversified army as that of the rural and village magistrates of the United States. They include many ignorant and crude Dogberrys, it is true. A tradition that is extant here and there to the effect that the rural squire is an intelligent but shiftless man of affairs has some confirmatory examples. Moreover, since the advent of prohibition, mercenary justices are much in evidence here and there who, by methods which are barely within the law, use the fee system to provide an undeserved but rich income. And yet there are great numbers of rural magistrates who are honest, well-intentioned men, not well educated, but possessed of wide worldly wisdom and an intellectual capacity well above the average of their fellow citizens. It is not improbable that this class is in the majority. This estimate is based upon those whom I have known, several hundred in number, and scattered throughout a half dozen states.

The preliminary examinations conducted by these rural magistrates are not marked, as are those of the cities, by haste and confusion. They are, however, conducted quite informally and without much effort to penetrate beyond the superficial. Not much of a permanent record is made. The written memoranda of a case are usually confined to the notations made upon returned warrants, which are sometimes lost and frequently unintelligible. Occasionally a crude docket is kept. Moreover, the value of the judgment made in a preliminary hearing is usually impaired by the fact that the justice and the constable get no fees if a bind-over does not result.

The most distinct difference between the operation of the preliminary examination in rural and in urban communities is due to the part played by the prosecutor. In rural counties, the prosecutor is practically the head of the law-enforcing machinery and when a serious crime is committed, and someone is charged with it, the prosecutor is usually the motive power in the prosecution from the beginning. He constitutes the police, prosecutor, and, partly because of his influence, the preliminary judge as well. He controls the grand jury and, in practically every instance, if he feels that a certain person should be brought to trial, that person is brought to trial, and if he decides to discontinue the prosecution, the prosecution is discontinued.[23] The justice of the peace, usually a layman wholly subservient to the legal knowledge and political importance of the prosecutor, is generally brought into a case only when the latter wants the approval of an action which he has already determined. In rural districts, consequently, not many cases are dismissed in preliminary hearings. Such data as are available show that the percentage of felony cases dismissed in the preliminary examina-

[23] On this point see my *Politics and Criminal Prosecution*, 48-55.

tion ranges from ten to thirty, while the percentage in cities is two or three times as great.[24]

The extent to which the prosecutor dominates the preliminary hearing has prompted the suggestion that the law plainly recognize this and permit the prosecutor himself to conduct the preliminary hearing. This would, of course, be a partial return to the early English practice, and with prosecution enforcement as aggressive as it has become in the United States, the proceeding would, to some degree, become inquisitorial. It is doubtful, however, whether such a change would make it possible to provide the proper kind of control over the preliminaries to trial by a responsible person. As will be pointed out presently, the thing that is necessary in connection with all of the preliminaries to trial is a magistrate of much more significance than the present one, and with authority to control the whole process of conducting the hearing, accepting bail and, to some degree, controlling the preliminary activities of the prosecutor.[25]

The incompetence of non-professional magistrates points to the necessity for a trained, professional magistracy with jurisdiction perhaps limited to criminal cases. Obviously such a magistrate should travel throughout a county or judicial district. Good roads and more adequate transportation facilities would enable a single magistrate of this kind to take over the criminal cases now heard by many justices of the peace. Such an office has recently been created in some of the Canadian provinces, and in New York State a constitutional amendment providing for such an official was approved in 1929. The creation of such an office would provide a certain degree of training for future judges and be a great improvement over the justice of the peace.

IV. *The French "Instruction"*

In the quest for constructive measures to improve the American preliminary hearing, reference has repeatedly been made to

---

[24] The Illinois Crime Survey, 39, shows that the more urban the county, the greater the percentage of dismissals. The same was shown in the Reports of the New York State Crime Commission.

[25] This suggestion is made in the *Missouri Crime Survey* by A. V. Lashly in his report on prosecution. See discussion of it there on p. 100.

the advantages possessed by the Continental system of inquiry which precedes trial. In France this period is called *de l'instruction*, which means, in general terms, the period of investigation, the gathering of evidence and the formulation of the evidence for the use of the state in the trial. The whole proceeding is strongly colored by the fundamental Continental inquisitorial procedure, although the difference between the English system and the Continental is not so marked as many writers have led us to believe. Since the French system is so largely duplicated in all the Continental countries, it will be most convenient to describe that system and to comment upon what it has to suggest to American reformers.

In the first place, it should be noted that the general meaning of the term "police" in France is such as to include practically all the judicial proceedings which precede trial.[26]

The principal officers of the judicial police are, in each *arrondissement*, the *procureur de la republique* and the *juge d'instruction*.[27] The *juge d'instruction* is the important figure in the judicial investigation of crime. He is "a titular or assistant judge of a court of first instance, appointed by decree to make preliminary examinations for a period of three years." This appointment is indefinitely renewable.[28] In criminal cases it is the duty of the *juge d'instruction* to discover all the evidence pointing to the existence of the crime and, in addition, to discover the author of the crime.[29]

The method of investigation depends upon the character of the crime committed and the circumstances under which it is discovered. In the discussion which follows, references are made to what the French call "crimes," the punishment for which is *"peine afflictive ou infamante."* Certain crimes are called

[26] The meaning of police as it was defined in *Le Code du 3 brumaire* IV is that the police "is instituted to maintain public order. . . . It is divided into administrative police and judicial police. The purpose of administrative police is to maintain public order in each locality. It is principally intended to prevent crime. Judicial police investigate crimes which administrative police have been unable to prevent, by assembling the evidence and the names of the accused for the tribunal charged by law with the trial."

[27] The *prefets* of the departments and the *prefet de police* of Paris have the powers of judicial police without their title.

[28] Garraud, *Précis de Droit Criminel*, 14th Ed. (Paris, 1926), 791.

[29] Ibid., 830.

"*délits flagrants.*" These are cases in which the accused is caught in the act, or while being publicly pursued, or while in possession of incriminating articles, soon after the commission of the crime. In such cases, the examination is conducted by the prosecutor (*procureur*) or by the *juge d'instruction* acting in his stead. At such a hearing, the accused is not permitted to have counsel, nor is he warned that he need not answer.[30]

In the case of all other "crimes" the examination is controlled and conducted by the *juge d'instruction*. In the normal procedure, the *juge d'instruction* issues proper warrants on complaints. Witnesses are heard separately, under oath and out of the presence of the accused, by the *juge d'instruction* and his clerk.

After the arrest, the accused is brought before the *procureur,* who requests the *juge d'instruction* to conduct the examination. The *juge d'instruction* informs the accused of the charges and receives his statement. First, however, he warns him that he need not make any. The accused is then told that he has a right to counsel. Notwithstanding these requirements, the *juge d'instruction* may proceed to an immediate interrogation and confrontation, if such a procedure seems urgent, because a witness is in danger of dying, or if there is a possibility that the evidence may disappear, or again, if the *juge d'instruction* has gone to the scene in a case of "*délit flagrant.*" In the last named situation, presumably the rules given below for examinations in "*délit flagrant*" cases would apply. After the first hearing, the accused may communicate freely with his counsel, and he must never be interrogated or subjected to confrontations, except in his counsel's presence, unless he expressly renounces that right. Counsel may not speak until authorized to do so by the magistrate. Refusals to speak are, however, entered in the minutes. Counsel are called by notice given at least twenty-four hours in advance, and the evidence, etc., must be put in at the disposition of counsel the night before each interrogation.

When the examination is completed, the *juge d'instruction* transmits the information to the *procureur,* who must make his "requisitions" (requests for elaboration) within three days.

[30] Law of May 20, 1863.

The *juge d'instruction* may release the accused if the evidence shows no offense, or no charge against him; but if the *juge d'instruction* is of the opinion that the accused is guilty of an offense, he sends the case to the proper court. If it is a "crime," he orders that the evidence and a written report be transmitted without delay by the *procureur* to the *procureur général* of the *"cour d'appel."* Appeals may be made (by the *procureur,* and by the accused on points of jurisdiction and the terms of provisional release) from the findings of the *juge d'instruction* to the *"chambre de mises en accusation"* of the *"cour d'appel."* [31]

Obviously, the French system in respect to preliminaries before trial has a number of advantages. The highly centralized organization of the French administrative and judicial system provides a degree of efficient coöperation among the various officers concerned which is not possible in the United States. Here the prosecutor, police, preliminary judges and grand jury are all organically unrelated. Each is responsible to a different master and in many cases they are in direct rivalry or hostility. The result is either a disastrous breakdown of prosecuting efficiency or the subordination of three of these agencies to the other. In the latter case, control is often exercised by the prosecutor.

Another advantage of the French system is that, to a certain degree, control over the investigation and preparation of cases for trial is taken out of the hands of the police and vested in a professional and responsible judge. The extent to which this has been done has, however, been exaggerated, because, obviously enough, the police retain a large measure of power.

Still another advantage of the French system is that the examination of the accused is carried on by a skilled, legally minded inquisitor. The bungling and often brutal work of police lieutenants in this country stands out in sharp contrast to the professional competence of the average *juge d'instruction.*

Moreover, the case is better prepared when it goes to trial. The evidence is assembled and written down by an expert. When

[31] This description is based upon *Code d'Instruction Criminelle.* Art. 1er to Art. 136; Art. 217 to Art. 231; Decr. 20 Mai 1903; Loi du 8 dec. 1897; Circ. 10 dec. 1897; Loi du 28 avril 1919; Loi du 22 mars 1921. These are collected in Petite collection Dallez. Code d'instruction criminelle et code pénal. 26th ed. (Paris, 1928). I am indebted to Mr. Thomas Dabagh for a memorandum on which this summary is based.

the *procureur* takes charge in the trial he is not, as are most prosecutors in the United States, compelled to improvise his entire procedure after he gets into the case, frequently with disastrous results to his case. With lawyer-like order and precision, the case has been prepared in the record which comes from the *juge d'instruction.*

It would be folly, however, to accept the idealized conception of the French "instruction" without a number of qualifications. Willoughby, for example, has pointed out many surface advantages of this system which need a great deal of qualification. He says, for instance, that "under this system the accused, if innocent, is at once given full opportunity to establish his innocence and to avoid the odium of an indictment and subsequent trial. Under the accusatorial system the idea is stronger that if the accused is innocent his innocence is to be established at the trial. There can be no question that many cases go to trial in the United States which, under the inquisitorial system, would be settled by the discharge of the accused as the result of the searching examination of the *juge d'instruction.*" [32]

This statement needs a number of qualifications. In the first place, it is doubtful whether any such theory exists in the United States. In the second place, it is still more questionable whether, if a rigorous examination were held before trial, there would be more, rather than fewer, cases dismissed. It should be remembered that in the great cities of the United States fully fifty per cent of all cases are eliminated in preliminary hearing and something more than ten per cent of the remainder are eliminated in the grand jury. The opinion may be ventured that if these cases were closely examined a great many of them would be held for trial.

Another assumption that Willoughby makes is also open to doubt. He takes for granted that the accused is given an opportunity to escape odium. That such odium is not entirely removed by the fact that the examination is private is very clear. Moreover, the statements of persons familiar with French police and their methods make it quite clear that brutality and high-handed methods by police are not all eliminated by the system

[32] *Principles of Judicial Administration* (Washington, 1929), 207.

of examinations. Competent observers who have practiced both in England and in France testify that there is much more use of the third degree in France than in England.

Finally, the *juge d'instruction,* while frequently a trained and experienced officer, is subject to the same desire for promotion and recognition that animates American prosecutors, and he will often use most unjust methods to further his interests. A classic example of this is to be found in Brieux's *La Robe Rouge.* The thesis of Brieux is that "it is not that the judges are venal," but that many magistrates are ready to subordinate the interests of justice to their desire to promote their own careers by making a showing of vigorous prosecution. In this drama, he describes several magistrates in a rural section, who find that they have been too lenient, as compared with magistrates in other districts, and resolve to show better results. The immediate victim of this change of policy is the peasant Etchepare. A prosecution is initiated on the most shadowy evidence and, when it is well under way, Mouzon, the *juge d'instruction,* resorts to browbeating and trickery. He confronts the peasant with statements which he falsely alleges were made by Etchepare's wife, he unearths damaging, though irrelevant, incidents out of the past life of the defendant, and finally he reveals to him certain compromising items concerning his wife. When the case comes before the court, the prosecutor recognizes the injustice of the charge and secures an acquittal; but the injustice is fatal to Etchepare's happiness.[33]

Whether the dramatist pictures a common misuse of the power vested in the *juge d'instruction* cannot be determined by any information readily available. That the system makes much oppression quite possible cannot be denied. There seems to be some such fear in the minds of those Americans who have considered the adoption of the system here. For example, the American Law Institute has definitely rejected the inclusion of the Continental system in its recommendations for the following express reasons:

"1. The tendency in European countries, in which this system was employed, has been to abolish it entirely or to eliminate the drastic features.

[33] See appendix II, a translation of this by Miss Celeste Jedel.

In England and Scotland it has been abolished. In France it has been extensively modified, so that in the ordinary case the accused is permitted to have counsel and is cautioned that he need not answer, while in Italy, although not permitted to have counsel and not cautioned, he is not penalized if he does not answer.

"2. The system requires for its successful operation trained officials. In Continental Europe, where the practice prevails, the examining judges are not only lawyers, but have received special training in the arts of examination and cross-examination and in the weighing of evidence. In this country the magistrates are not equipped for such work, in many instances being laymen.

"3. A large percentage of the lawyers, with whom this matter was discussed, expressed views antagonistic to it, for example, (a) that it would violate fundamental principles of personal liberty, (b) that it is opposed to our tradition of fair play, and (c) that it would result in unjust conviction of innocent persons.

"4. In view of reason 3, there would be so much opposition to such a practice by members of legislatures that it would hinder the enactment of the entire code if the inquisitorial systems were incorporated into it.

"5. While the chief reason advanced by those who favor the system is that it will do away with the 'third degree,' there is no assurance that such results would follow.

"6. This system, if enacted, would violate the constitutions of all but two of the states. It would accordingly be necessary to secure amendment of the 'self-incrimination' clause in the constitutions of most of the states, and in eight states complete new constitutions would be required. After careful consideration it was thought that there would be but slight chance of securing such constitutional changes.

"7. Finally, even if the necessary constitutional changes were made and the system adopted by the legislatures, it was thought that it could not be successfully operated, not only for the reason that there are no properly equipped officials, but because the great body of public opinion would be against it." [84]

[84] *Code of Criminal Procedure*, American Law Institute, 1928, 26-27.

CHAPTER III

BAIL OR GAOL

NOT long ago, in a large American city, a young man was arrested for attempting to commit a crime. Later it was discovered that he had committed a similar crime in another city. Before appearing for preliminary hearing, he was released on bond. When the case was called he did not appear, and the bond was forfeited. Several months passed, and he was caught. Again a bondsman was found, and he was liberated. An interested civic agency pointed out to the court that the person who signed the second bond had no title to the property scheduled. The court ordered the defendant to be taken into custody again, but he was freed on the same day by another bond, signed before another judge by a new bondsman. He again failed to appear in court at the appointed time, and this bond was forfeited, too. He was once more caught by the police and held for the grand jury. The judge ordered that he be taken directly to gaol, but he was again released on still another bond by still another surety before still another judge. He then disappeared.

The case of this bold and resourceful young man illustrates in a very pointed way a problem which goes to the very heart of the administration of the criminal law in our large cities. He was able to use the legal device called bail to secure continuous liberty and ultimate freedom from trial. Judges, with blind confidence, accepted as bonds practically worthless documents secured by property which either did not exist or was insufficient to protect the state in the amount fixed. An investigation before the acceptance of the bond might have determined this fact, but no such investigation was made; perhaps because the judges had no facilities for making it. The fact remains that a practically worthless document was accepted, in spite of the fact that the man who had been arrested had shown on successive occasions that he did not intend to play fair with the state. He was repeatedly released by new judges. Apparently one judge could not know or had no way to know what another judge had done. No one seemed to care whether the bonds offered were adequate. Above all, the state seemed to lack the force, up to the time the indictment was returned, to insist upon an immediate hearing to determine whether probable cause existed. Thus at least a year's delay was secured prior to any semblance of a criminal trial. The device of bail was used to gain delay and ultimately to secure freedom.

I. *The History of Bail*

Yet this device which has so lent itself to deplorable abuses under the conditions existing in modern American cities has a long and honorable history. Legal historians trace its genesis to the medieval surety system.[1] The original provisions of that system were very strict. Bail implied a more stringent, mainprise a more lax, degree of responsibility. "English, Norman and French tradition seem all to point to an ancient and extremely rigorous form of suretyship or hostageship, which rendered the surety liable to suffer the punishment that was hanging over the head of the released prisoner. In Normandy these sureties are compared to gaolers, and a striking phrase speaks of them as 'the duke's living prison.' In England, when there is a release on bail, the sureties are often said to be bound *corpus pro corpore.*"[2] Under the less stringent provisions of mainprise, those who offered themselves as surety for the appearance of an accused person were no longer bound "body for body" but were liable to amercement only if the prisoner escaped. As Holdsworth points out, after the thirteenth century "it became usual, either to make the surety promise by recognizance to pay a sum certain in the event of non-production of the prisoner; or combining both the older idea with the new means to enforce it, both to make him promise by recognizance to pay a sum certain in the event of his

---

[1] See Holdsworth, *History of the English Law,* I, 13; Maitland, *The Domesday Book and Beyond* (1907), 284; Stubbs, *Constitutional History of England* (1875), I, 87.

[2] Pollock and Maitland, *History of English Law* (1899), II, 590.

non-production, and to commit the accused to the custody of the surety." [3]

The idea of bail did not grow out of any lofty ideal of freedom. The greatest classic in legal literature disposes of this bit of folklore. "It was not common to keep men in prison. This apparent leniency of our law was not due to any love of an abstract liberty. Imprisonment was costly and troublesome. Besides, any reader of the eyre rolls will be inclined to define a gaol as a place that is made to be broken, so numerous are the entries that tell of escapes. The medieval dungeon was not all that romance would make it; there were many ways out of it. The mainprize of substantial men was about as good a security as a gaol. The sheriff did not want to keep prisoners; his inclination was to discharge himself of all responsibility by handing them over to their friends." [4]

Nevertheless, the appearance of constitutional guarantees as to bail in a large part of the American system indicates that by the end of the eighteenth century bail had come to be regarded as a question concerning the more fundamental aspects of human liberty. In the Federal Constitution and in a number of states, there appears a negative type of guarantee, expressed by the Federal Constitution in the terms "excessive bail shall not be required." [5]

II. *Bail, An Impotent Legal Gesture*

Perhaps the most unfortunate aspect of administration of bail is the scattering of the power to accept it. In many instances the police may exercise the right to accept bail. Police magistrates and judges of inferior courts generally exercise the power in all cases coming within their jurisdiction, including felonies which have not yet been passed upon in preliminary hearing. In addition, there are all of the judges of courts of higher jurisdic-

[3] *History of English Law*, IV, 525-6.
[4] Pollock and Maitland, op. cit., II, 584.
[5] Weems v. U. S. 217, U. S. 349, contains a history of the adoption of the Eighth Amendment. New York has a provision identical with that of the Federal Constitution in Art. 1, Sec. 5. Other states having no constitutional guarantee of the right of bail are Alabama, New Hampshire, West Virginia, Virginia, Georgia, North Carolina, Massachusetts, Maryland.

tions. The serious aspect of this scattered responsibility is that one judge does not know what another judge is doing. He does not know, when he accepts a surety, whether he is granting a request which other and better informed judges have refused. There is no clearing house to which he can turn to determine how far the surety in question has already obligated himself on other bonds. He is called upon to accept the bond at the most irregular times and places.

Carelessness results in numerous improper admissions to bail. Sleepy judges routed out of bed at night to accept bonds are not likely to concern themselves with the demands of public justice, particularly when the exigencies of politics require polite assent. Hence persons are admitted to bail whose records show that they have repeatedly failed to respect the conditions of bail. Desperate criminals wanted for some much more serious crime than that most recently charged are often released on bail without proper investigation of their character or record. The most unsavory persons are accepted as sureties. In the *Missouri Crime Survey*,[6] numerous examples are given of this practice.

Startling evidence of the utter futility of the bail system as now administered is contained in the records concerning the amount of forfeitures as compared with the amount of money actually collected on these forfeitures. Forfeitures are frequently set aside by court on such inadequate grounds that bondsmen and defendants are encouraged to play fast and loose with their obligations. In Illinois, for example, the law does not permit forfeited bonds to be set aside without payment of costs, yet in Professor Beeley's book a remarkable amount of evidence is presented showing that this law is not adequately enforced.[7]

Examining bail records is laborious, but in two or three instances it has been done with rather startling results. The *Missouri Crime Survey* revealed that in St. Louis, Kansas City, and in thirty-eight other counties of the state, $292,400 in bail was forfeited in a single year. Of this approximately $20,500 was reduced to judgment and only $1,500 was collected. Collections were made in two rural counties where the obligation of bail is

[6] See my report on bail bonds, 211-213.
[7] *The Bail System in Chicago* (Chicago, 1927), 49.

still seriously recognized, but in St. Louis and Kansas City no one was able to remember when a collection had been made on a forfeited bail bond. Millions of dollars in forfeited bail have been outstanding in Chicago for years and the sum total is substantially augmented every year. The same thing is probably true in the majority of our other large cities. Bail, as administered in the United States, does not bind.

A great many persons who are charged with crime and released on bail disappear completely from the actual control of the court. They remain at liberty. It is impossible to determine exactly how many such cases there are in any specific jurisdiction; but of the 186 bail forfeitures in the year covered by the *Missouri Crime Survey*, 73 were not set aside, which means that in most of these cases the defendant did not return at all to stand trial.[8] The same report illustrates rather forcefully what this great leakage in the process of justice means in terms of persons charged with serious crimes who have, because of laxness in bail administration, entirely escaped from the custody of the court. Eighty-five felonies are listed in which, apparently, the prosecution failed because of the escape of the defendant. This fact should be considered in connection with the one already set forth, that except in two trivial instances the State of Missouri did not collect the amount of the bond, in spite of the complete and obvious failure of the sureties to fulfill their obligations.

Another problem is the grave injustice of the present administration of bail. A poor and friendless person cannot get bail at all, while a well financed but infinitely more dangerous professional criminal has ample resources and means to buy his release. Moreover, in most instances a court attempts to arrange its calendar so that the cases of those detained in jail will be tried first. This practice, which court parlance calls "emptying the jail," means that those at large on bail are not called for trial until last. Since all delay is an advantage to the defendant, the state thus penalizes those who are so unfortunate as to be unable to get bail, and gives an undeserved advantage to the adequately financed professional criminal.

---

[8] See *Missouri Crime Survey*, 201, for a table indicating the status of these forfeitures which were not set aside. New York has recently made bail jumping a crime.

Another form of injustice is involved in the cruel extortion of fees that professional bondsmen often practice in their dealings with ignorant people.

It is common knowledge that releasing professional criminals on bail very often gives them definite encouragement to commit further crimes. A sophisticated inspector of detectives once remarked, after a glance at his morning reports, which indicated that a number of crimes of violence had been committed on the preceding evening, "It looks as if the gang that we released the other day is collecting their bondsmen's and lawyers' fees from the public."

An interesting study of Police Department records made by the Grand Jurors Association of New York City points out the seriousness of this problem.

"The present unrestricted and haphazard practice of releasing arrested criminals on bail is probably the greatest single factor in nullifying effective work accomplished by the Police Department of New York City. During the first six months of 1925, for example, there were forty-two re-arrests, mostly for serious offenses, of persons out on bail; viz:

3 re-arrested for	homicide
2 " " "	assault and battery
6 " " "	robbery
11 " " "	burglary
1 " " "	felonious assault
9 " " "	grand larceny
3 " " "	carrying pistols
1 " " "	carrying dangerous weapons
6 " " "	miscellaneous crimes." [9]

III. *Professional Bondsmen*

A "professional" bondsman is one who accepts compensation for acting as a surety for a person accused of crime.[10] Wherever

[9] *Report of Grand Jurors Association,* November 16, 1925.

[10] Certain states have made statutory provision for the professional bondsman, defining him as a person who not only accepts fees for his services but writes more than a fixed number of bonds in a given length of time. The Code of Criminal Procedure of the American Law Institute, for example, defines a professional bondsman as a person who "has become a surety and has received compensation or promise of compensation therefor in more than two undertakings on neither of which he has been discharged from liability". See also the definition of professional bondsman in the New York *Code of Criminal Procedure,* Sec. 554 B.

there is a considerable amount of criminal litigation, his business flourishes. His habitat is usually the large urban community. He operates openly, distributes his business cards, advertises in the telephone directories, and often maintains a shop, proclaiming his business with glaring signs. At one time the Tombs Prison in New York was almost surrounded by these shops. At present many are located in the streets immediately adjoining certain magistrates' courts in New York City. Often professional bondsmen's advertising states that they are on call day or night, that their rates are reasonable, and that they are persons of standing.

It is difficult to determine the extent to which the professional bondsman dominates the business of bail. The records never show whether a bond has been signed for compensation, and often the bond does not bear the signature of the solicitor. Professional bondsmen not only sign bonds on their own responsibility, but frequently serve as agents for others. For example, they will solicit business for the small shopkeeper who is persuaded, for a price, to pledge his property on a bond. Needless to say, the solicitor always retains his share of the profits.

While it is usual for commentators to condemn all professional bondsmen, the fact persistently presents itself that those who are honest do perform a service of real importance. It is not the professional bondsman *per se* that is objectionable, but the almost inevitable conditions which attend his operations.

Because the obligation of bail is held so lightly under the law and its administration in most American cities, the bondsman who is familiar with conditions is able to operate on almost unbelievably inadequate resources. Perhaps the classical example of this is the case of Bondsman D. a professional, described in the *Missouri Crime Survey*.[11] Two statements filed by him more than a year prior to the investigation of his liability indicated that he claimed real property to the value of more than $20,000, but the records showed encumbrances on this property to an amount greater than its assessed value. His financial condition was rendered still more uncertain by the fact that he was delinquent in taxes to the amount of several hundred dollars, that the Fed-

[11] See my report on bail, 211.

eral Government had, in addition, a claim for income taxes pending against him, that $30,000 was outstanding in forfeited bonds, and that his police record indicated twelve arrests on minor charges. Even so, he had been accepted in the state courts of the city of St. Louis during the year preceding the investigation, for bonds aggregating $670,295. Of this total amount, $90,000 was outstanding on the date of the investigation. Another bondsman in the same city, whose property was probably not worth more than $10,000, had been accepted on nearly $100,000 in bonds. A third, whose property was assessed at $30,000, was permitted to have nearly $200,000 outstanding in bonds. In this case again, property taxes had not been paid.[12]

As a result of the publication of these facts, a St. Louis newspaper instituted a campaign against professional bondsmen in general and against Bondsman D. in particular. The judge who had been so liberal in accepting him was called to account by the newspaper, and the circuit judges attempted to discipline their lenient colleague. The latter vigorously defended himself, saying that the bondsman was his friend, that he felt the man could be trusted, and that this was the explanation for his apparent overgenerous attitude.

It is interesting to speculate upon the income of these astute gentlemen whose working capital represents liabilities rather than assets. It was said in the *Missouri Crime Survey* that Bondsman D's compensation for a good year's work ranged somewhere between thirty and a hundred thousand dollars. A professional bondsman in New York, according to the newspapers, "sports his pale green Hispano Suisa town car driven by his own chauffeur." The fees which yield these fat incomes often prove a heavy burden to the less fortunate victims of the law. Kate H. Claghorn tells of a bondsman who came to the house of a Lithuanian whose husband had been arrested for the loss of two barrels of wine from the truck he was driving. The bondsman took

[12] E. W. Sims, President of the Chicago Crime Commission, said before the American Bar Association at Cincinnati, August 30, 1921, that he knew a professional bondsman with an equity of only $6,750 in an apartment house who had been accepted as surety on bonds aggregating $269,500 and after a judgment on a forfeited bond had reduced his equity to $3,200, he was able to get the courts to accept $160,000 more in bail bonds.

$55, all the money the woman had, and said he would get her husband released for $55. The man was released on Sunday, and when the case came up on Monday, he was fined $18 and costs, $22 in all. "The bondsman paid the fine and kept the rest of the money, saying that he had paid a bribe to the judge and the police to release the man on Sunday." [13] This cruel extortion of unwarranted fees is a common practice of professional bondsmen in their dealings with ignorant people.

There is also the crime committed to get the money to satisfy the bondsman's exactions. Professor Beeley gives a moving example:

"In addition to the demoralizing effect of the professional bondsman, there is the increase in crime itself which the system directly induces. This is well illustrated in the case of Jimmy Smith, who shot and killed O'Connell in the hold-up while trying to raise $500 to satisfy a professional bondsman who had obtained his release from gaol on another charge. The account of this case reads as follows:

" 'My old mother had mortgaged her $2,500 home to raise $500 as part of the $1,000 this bird had demanded for going $40,000 to "spring" me from jail. I was to get out and "earn" the other $500 before October 7. I had only one week to go. How else could I raise $500? So Saturday I took my gun and went out on the "stick up". I'm sorry O'Connell is dead, I didn't mean to shoot him, but I was desperate.' "

It is almost imperative that professional bondsmen maintain rather close relations with the underworld. Their business requires fairly definite knowledge of the habits, haunts and plans of their customers. Consequently they all too frequently know more about the underworld than a law-abiding citizen can properly find out. They harbor many unwholesome secrets. In fact, it is not unusual to find that bondsmen are themselves possessed of somewhat extensive police records. "Gasoline Jack" Rubenstein, for example, a St. Louis bondsman, had a very serious police record.[14]

[13] *The Immigrant's Day in Court* (New York, 1923), 132.
[14] See *Missouri Crime Survey*, 208, where it is shown that of the five bondsmen used as examples, four had police records, two of which included a number of very serious crimes.

The relation between professional bondsmen and criminal lawyers is necessary and common. Frequently they occupy the same offices. An investigation made by the Grand Jurors Association of New York City indicated a most interesting series of relationships among public officials, criminal lawyers, bondsmen and political leaders based, it was evident, not only upon official and professional connections, but upon family ties as well. The records of this agency were full of the names of associated lawyers and bondsmen.

Much more serious is the relationship which arises between bondsmen and public officials. Professional bondsmen establish friendly and often questionable connections with clerks, assistant prosecutors and even with judges.

The professional bondsman is generally a good politician. An experienced St. Louis judge [15] says that the bondsman "is frequently active in ward politics and has a large following among the lawless, a very considerable class in the large cities; he contributes liberally at times to the campaign of some candidates, usually for an office having to do with administration of criminal law."

A Republican candidate for nomination as clerk of the Municipal Court was confronted by the Chicago Crime Commission, March 29, 1924, with the following reminder of his career as a professional bondsman:

"He has signed scores of bonds covering charges of non-support of wife and children, disorderly conduct, fornication, assault with a deadly weapon, burglary, robbery, larceny, receiving stolen property, possessing intoxicating liquor, confidence game and speeding.

"In the Criminal Court he has signed bonds for defendants charged with murder, assault with intent to murder, manslaughter, larceny, burglary and similar crimes.

"His record shows going surety on 43 cases and 55 cases in the Criminal Court in the short span of a few years."

An important variant of the professional bondsman is the surety company which specializes in criminal bail bonds. This type of corporation is not common in the United States. About the only city where an important part of the bail-bond business

[15] Judge Hugo Grimm, quoted in the St. Louis *Post Dispatch*, October 21, 1926.

is done in this way is New York. The nature of these companies is that of a corporation created under laws of the state, with agents in the various criminal courts who are authorized to solicit and arrange for the writing of bail bonds in the name of their respective companies. There are six important surety companies writing bail in New York City and their combined business is a sizable portion of the bonding business done in the courts, although the exact proportion has never been determined. However, the statistical bureau of the magistrates' court estimated during one year that forty per cent of the bail bonds were furnished by surety companies.[16]

A New York surety company employs brokers licensed under the provisions of the insurance law of the state, who act under powers of attorney for the company. It is well known that these brokers are often prominent in local politics and that occasionally they enjoy a not too favorable reputation.

The head of a leading New York surety company which refuses to furnish bonds for any questionable cases made the following rather significant statement to a representative of the *Evening World:*

"The peddling of bonds by men with criminal records and the system by which these peddlers exact high and unlawful rates from offenders has become a great public scandal. In the past few years these shady runners have become firmly intrenched and apparently it is impossible to dislodge them or to confine their fees to the legal limit."

The brokers who are employed and vested with power of attorney engage a species of agent, commonly known as "runners," who are the business getters for the company. These runners fairly infest some courts. The competition is keen and the runners often seek to increase their business by currying the friendship of court clerks. Court and gaol attendants in turn may tell bondsmen of the amount of valuables secured from the defendant when he was taken into custody, and in other ways

[16] On February 9, 1927, the New York *Evening World,* in the course of a newspaper campaign against prevailing bail-bond practices, said that a single surety company wrote $2,000,000 in bail. It indicated further that this company did the second largest business in the city. It is a fair inference from this that the surety companies are doing more than half of the bail-bond business of the city.

give unfair preferences. A striking example of this is in a report on the operation of the Municipal Court of Toledo, Ohio:

"The brazen shamelessness with which the firm having the bonding monopoly in Toledo operates is shown by the following incidents. They well illustrate why the professional bonding firm has a monopoly:

"Within recent weeks a Toledo lawyer called at the Clerk of Court's office at about three o'clock in the afternoon with a client. After loudly knocking on the locked door for several moments with no response, he became disgusted and walked down the hall. At the entrance of the Safety Building he noticed one of the partners of the bonding monopolists coming in. The lawyer followed him, watched him produce a key to the Clerk of Court's office, saw him unlock the door, and followed him in. There he saw employees of the Clerk of Court's office, and a policeman making out warrants for the next day.

"Earlier in the year another Toledo lawyer, after pounding on the locked door for some time, was admitted. There were employees of the Clerk of Court's office, together with a member of this same bonding firm, going over the warrants for the next day."

Report of Commission on Publicity and Efficiency, published in the Toledo *City Journal,* December 15, 1928.[17]

Yet the surety company does offer some improvement over the anarchy which obtains in other cities. A thoughtful student of the subject says: "And surely anyone who knows about the startling conditions that usually prevail in criminal courts where personal bail is the rule must realize that corporate suretyship marks a great advance. There would seem to exist in New York City and similar great centers of criminal practice an attractive

---

[17] The Brooklyn *Daily Eagle* ran a series of articles from February 14, 1926, to March 14, 1926, criticizing the operation of surety companies in New York City. These articles, however, drew a number of somewhat unfair inferences. They seemed to suggest that a surety was to be blamed for bringing about the release of a "criminal." Throughout the articles such words as "miscreant" and "felons" were used, thus creating the impression that all persons charged with crime were actually guilty of crimes. The fact is, of course, that the persons who were released on bond furnished by surety companies were presumably innocent of the charges against them and the surety company was operating within the expressed provisions of the law. The articles, moreover, failed to make a satisfactory case against the surety companies because they did not indicate clearly whether the releases brought about by the companies resulted in serious loss in efficient prosecution through the state and because they did not show that the defendants released on bail furnished by surety companies were more likely to escape than other defendants. The articles did, however, contain interesting data indicating the extent to which surety companies at that time dominated the bonding field.

opportunity for the surety companies to subordinate their individual activities to the public good, and contribute a joint service to the courts, to district attorneys, and to members of the bar in this important detail of judicial administration." [18]

But in spite of the superiority of the corporate surety over the individual professional bondsman, these corporations are not likely to assume such importance in the bail bond-business throughout the country as to place the giving of bail upon a sound, respectable basis. In fact, a good deal of criticism has been leveled at them in New York within recent years. The Association of Grand Jurors of New York County, while recognizing the advantages of corporate sureties, points out unsatisfactory conditions:

"We believe in corporate suretyship as the most practical and convenient criminal bail bond security, but it must be made available for the public through honest and responsible channels. However, so long as it is secretly peddled in our police stations and courtrooms, about the corridors and on the sidewalks surrounding the court buildings, in our prisons and in dingy lawyer-bondsmen offices, the abuses which spring from the traffic far outweigh its benefits." [19]

The same organization concludes that the remedy for conditions in New York is not to eliminate corporate bail "but to employ full time salaried and responsible representatives as substitutes for the existing itinerant surety agents."

On account of this criticism, some New York bonding companies have already announced that they will no longer give bail for professional criminals, and others have so limited their operations that they no longer meet the demand. Moreover, surety companies of other sorts have not been disposed to write criminal-bail bonds. They claim that such business would injure their prestige and that it is not profitable. Thus, in spite of the attempts on the part of the State of New York to recognize this type of suretyship and to provide for its regulation by

[18] E. C. Lunt, *Surety Bonds* (New York, 1922), 163.
[19] *Report of the Prison Committee* of the Association of Grand Jurors of New York County, October 18, 1926. In 1926 the Brooklyn *Daily Eagle* found that surety companies of the city of New York were employing about 332 bail-bond agents, 76 of whom were employed by one company. These agents in turn averaged from three to four runners each.

state law, it has not succeeded in eliminating the problems involved.

Clearly then, certain insistent problems have developed that render this aspect of criminal-law administration wholly unsatisfactory. They can be rather briefly stated.

IV. *Bail Reform*

Reformers have been very liberal with suggestions to remedy the bail-bond situation. Some of these have been tried with indifferent success, and all of them possess the common defect of remedies which will operate well if efficient and forceful officials are administering them. These remedies fall into three groups: (1) vigorous clean-up programs by which, under the existing law, bondsmen are held more strictly responsible for their derelictions, (2) new laws regulating the obligations of sureties, and (3) new administrative devices through which judges and administrative officers may have more information as a basis for action.

Many a city has witnessed spasms of vigorous activity to correct bail-bond evils. Prosecutors and judges occasionally issue lists of proscribed bondsmen and declare that on account of their reputation or their failure to live up to their obligations they will no longer be permitted to frequent the court. Prosecuting officers frequently institute vigorous proceedings to reduce forfeited bonds to judgment and to collect uncollected judgments. They also attempt in certain instances to bring criminal actions for perjury and the like. But usually these measures to secure strict enforcement of existing law are only as long-lived as the energy of the particular officials who sponsored them.

Various legislative measures have been recommended to effect a more complete protection for the state in the matter of bail bonds. In some places, the bail bond has been made a lien on the real property of the surety, thus preventing the surety from disposing of his real property after he has qualified through ownership. But this means that an innocent purchaser might accept property to which such obligations were attached and upon which the state might at any subsequent time realize legitimate rights.

Since this tends greatly to encumber property titles, real estate interests have always been opposed to the idea. Not long ago the real estate interests of Illinois brought about the repeal of the legislation in that state, and, it should be added, thus seriously augmented the bail-bond problem in Chicago. Another legislative measure often suggested is to make bail jumping a crime, just as breaking from prison is a crime under the laws of most states. Other legislation would provide for the registration of professional bondsmen and a strict legal limit upon their fees.

Abuses of bail in New York City were widely discussed in 1926, and as a result the legislature passed four bills, chiefly designed to deny bail to professional criminals. They provided that no defendant charged with a felony or with certain designated major misdemeanors should be admitted to bail until he had been finger-printed and his previous record had been submitted to the official authorized to accept bail. It was further provided that in case the defendant's record indicated a prior conviction of a felony or two convictions of the specified misdemeanors, the bail could be accepted only by a judge of the trial courts. This specifically made it impossible for a minor judge to accept bail in the case of a professional criminal. It also required that the judge know clearly the kind of person who was being released on bail.

Much more hopeful has been the suggestion for more adequate administrative devices to regulate bail. The most interesting example of such an administrative device is a plan devised by the Chicago Crime Commission for the State Attorney's office in Cook County. The system, which was installed there some years ago, provides a Bail Bond Bureau for the office, in which a complete record is kept of all bonds and of all bondsmen who do business in the criminal court. A ledger shows at a glance the status of a given bondsman. At any time it can be determined whether he has exceeded the limit of his probable financial responsibility. Moreover, the Bureau is supposed to investigate every bond, both as to the financial standing of the surety, and the criminal record of the defendant. The Bureau makes recommendations with regard to each bond offered the court, and the judge's acceptance is based upon the report from this Bureau. To be sure, the Bureau has no power to compel a judge to accept its recommendation, but because of the vigilance of the Chicago Crime Commission judges are very reluctant to accept bonds that do not have the approval of this office. This administrative device, however, applies only to the Criminal court and does not extend to the other courts of the city; therefore it is still possible for bondsmen to exceed their financial resources by distributing their business among the various courts. There is no organic connection between the Municipal and Criminal courts of Chicago, and the evils of bail bonds are still present. On many occasions a Central Bail Bond Bureau for the City of New York has been suggested because the scattering of responsibility is even more serious there than in Chicago.

The bail-bond court has also been suggested as a means of centralizing responsibility for acceptance of bail. An example of this is a new bail-bond branch established in 1927 in the Chicago Municipal Court, in charge of a judge of that court. It investigates bail bonds offered in the various branches of the court. The value of this branch depends entirely upon the coöperation which the other judges of the Municipal Court offer, and while its establishment marks the beginning of an improvement in the bail-bond business as transacted in the Municipal Court, much still remains to be done to bring about complete coöperation and centralization of responsibility.[20]

After a rather intensive study of the gaol population of Chicago, Professor Beeley,[21] was convinced that a great many defendants are kept in gaol merely because they have no friends and no money to procure the services of professional bail bondsmen. Many of these, in fact a great majority, could safely be released on their own recognizance, thus relieving the gaol of their care, and equalizing the application of the law so that the poor and friendless might have the same advantages enjoyed by the more fortunate. The study further suggests that an attempt be made to individualize the form and amount of bail after an investigation of the defendant made, perhaps, by a probation officer.[22]

[20] See my report on the Municipal Court of Chicago in the *Illinois Crime Survey,* 410-413, for a description and detailed criticism of this court.
[21] *The Bail System in Chicago* (Chicago, 1927).
[22] *Acts and Resolves* of Massachusetts. 1926. Ch. 320.

Notwithstanding all due allowances made for the very many cases of prisoners who can be released on their own recognizance, there will probably always be a substantial number of cases requiring a surety, and bondsmen, professional and otherwise, will have to be accepted. The administration of these cases—and the problem is, after all, mainly administrative—should be centralized and equipped with the necessary facilities for gathering accurate information concerning sureties who are accepted. Under such a system judges can intelligently exercise their discretion in the acceptance of bail. Whether they permit this discretion to be governed by political or other types of preferential treatment will, of course, depend upon the personal characteristics and relationships of each individual judge. No system will rise higher than the judges who govern it. Here, as elsewhere in the administration of criminal justice, the answer is not more legislative and administrative machinery, but more judges who are courageous, intelligent and independent.

The bail problem is, however, a symptom rather than a cause of the general inefficiency of the administration of criminal justice. If cases were tried more promptly, it would be unnecessary to provide for the release of many defendants on bail. The absence of a bail-bond problem in England is probably due to the promptness with which cases are brought to trial. With reasonably prompt action to determine their guilt or innocence, it would be possible, in the absence of constitutional difficulties, to deny bail entirely in many cases, particularly in those which involve habitual and well-known offenders. There would seem to be no common-sense reason for releasing such cases on bail if detention were a matter of only a few days. The bail-bond problem, then, will probably await satisfactory solution until the American criminal courts are able to perform their duties more promptly. An examination of the English system shows this rather clearly.

V. *The Bail System in England*

A comparison of English experience and our own with regard to bail provides, as in most other features of criminal justice, a striking contrast. If a problem exists there, it is quite unlike our own.[23]

English legislation has succeeded in freeing judges and other officials who administer bail from the many restrictions involved in the "right" of bail. In felony cases the judges of the court with jurisdiction to try the offense may refuse bail.[24]

In case of misdemeanors (in spite of Blackstone's assertion that to refuse bail in cases where, under the common law, the offense is bailable, is in itself an offense, and in spite of legislation of similar import) [25] no action will lie against a magistrate who refuses bail unless his act springs from corrupt, oppressive or partial motives.[26]

That courts have been in the habit of denying bail is shown by the recent acts of high authority to enforce more liberality. In 1906 the Home Secretary addressed a forceful letter to magistrates, urging a freer use of their discretion as to the admission of defendants to bail. In 1921 Lord Birkenhead and the Home Secretary initiated an inquiry to find out why bail was so frequently denied, and in 1922 a report was issued setting forth the extent to which innocent persons had been detained and strongly urging greater leniency. This report contains statistics indicating that from 1911 to 1921 from thirty to fifty per cent of the persons who were ultimately acquitted had been held without bail. More legislation followed this report, intended to encourage bail, but denial of bail still seems to be quite common.[27] Thus the import of practically all of the investigations and public criticisms of bail in England has been quite contrary to those which have characterized American discussion of the subject. Here the judges and magistrates are scored for excessive leniency; in England, for lack of leniency.

Another contrast is the practical absence of professional bonds-

[23] For data and conclusions concerning English practice I am indebted both here and in Section I of this Chapter, to Miss Elsa de Haas of Hunter College, who has in preparation a monograph on the *History, Law, and Practice of Bail in England;* also to Professor E. Pendleton Howard of the Law School of the University of Idaho, who has under way a monograph on *Prosecution in England.*

[24] Short and Mellor, *Crown Office Practice* (2nd Ed., 1908), 280.

[25] 31 Car. 2 Ch. 2 (1679) and 1 W. and M. Ch. 2 (1689).

[26] Short and Mellor, op. cit., 281.

[27] See the Report of the *Royal Commission of Police Powers and Procedure.* March 16, 1929, Cmd. 3297, 117.

men and corporate sureties in criminal bail. Moreover, it is strictly criminal for a bondsman to enter into an agreement by which he will be indemnified in case of forfeiture.[28] In the United States it is not usually regarded as contrary to public policy to indemnify or to promise to indemnify a surety.[29]

Another striking difference is the amount of bail required. For offenses of a similar nature and for similar risks the amount required in England seems to be much smaller. For burglary twenty pounds is not uncommon, while for even more serious crimes amounts of from two to five hundred pounds are not unusual. The amounts usually required in the state courts of the United States are much larger.

In case of forfeiture (or estreating) the penalty seems to be prompt and severe. In case the amount pledged cannot be collected, imprisonment is in order. As a result of the combination of the restricted granting of bail and the rigor of the penalty, the number of absconders is small. The published data indicate that in indictable offenses not more than one in two thousand abscond. Available data in the United States indicate a much higher ratio.[30]

The American reformer who expects to find in England some legislative formula by which the baffling problem of bail can be solved will be disappointed. The legal practice and restrictions are, as we have shown, not radically unlike our own except in regard to indemnification, which has never been a problem with us. The difference in result is attained by strict examination of sureties, free use of the right to deny bail entirely, vigorous action after forfeiture, and, above all, more speed in bringing cases to trial. These characteristics are not derived from law. They are due to the fact that justice is administered by trained, efficient and non-political public servants.

[28] Rex V. Porter, 1 K.B.D. 369 (1910). Also see Alexander, *The Administration of Justice in Criminal Matters* (London, 1915), 33.

[29] Leary v. U. S., 224 U. S. 567.

[30] See my report in the *Missouri Crime Survey*, 197-200.

CHAPTER IV

THE GENTLEMEN AT THE BAR [1]

THE administration of criminal justice is greatly handicapped by the fact that the members of the bar who give their chief professional attention to criminal cases are as a class neither the most highly respected nor the most capable of their profession. The practice of criminal law, in spite of the unquestioned human values involved, has lost caste. As Dean Pound phrases the transition:

"The first is marked by the leadership of the trial lawyer. The great achievements of the Bar were in the Forum and the most conspicuous success was before juries in the trial of criminal cases. . . . In the second stage leadership passed to the railroad lawyer. The proof of professional success was to represent a railroad company. . . . Criminal law became the almost exclusive field of the lower stratum of the Bar."

The problems involved become still more complicated when it is considered that the persons caught in the criminal law as defendants are for the most part poor, ignorant and without helpful friends. While the theory of the law requires that these should stand equal with others the fact is that they do not. Some progress has been made through the public defender movement which challenges interest largely as a means by which the disposition of a criminal case may become rather a coöperative search for corrective and preventive care than a contest of skill.

I. *The Practice of Criminal Law*

The lack of prestige associated with the criminal practice to-day among the legal profession as a whole is reflected in statistics obtained in the *Cleveland Survey of Criminal Justice*. Of

[1] This chapter is contributed by Miss Sienna Delahunt of the Editorial Board of the *Columbia Law Review*.

the 386 lawyers who replied to a questionnaire sent to 1400 members of the Cleveland bar, 128, or almost 40 per cent, accepted no criminal cases at all, and only three per cent took them regularly.[2] One of the reasons most frequently assigned for refusal to take criminal cases was a feeling that it was detrimental to financial success in civil practice. That feeling is not confined to lawyers of Cleveland, and is probably well founded. However, one of the reasons why the taking of criminal cases is detrimental to financial success in civil practice is, undoubtedly, the disrepute of the criminal lawyer in the eyes of the public. This disrepute is, in some measure, at least, caused by the refusal of the Bar to face the fact that there is a difference between traditional professional ideals and actual standards of practice.

Thus, the criminal branch of the legal profession has become highly specialized. On the whole it is comparatively unremunerative, since it is impossible to build up a clientele except among professional criminals. In theory, and in tradition, the criminal lawyer is an agent of society to see that justice is done to his client. But the criminal lawyer, like the prosecutor, builds up his reputation by winning cases. Thus if there is a trial (which is not the garden variety of criminal cases) [3] it is a battle between two men, the lawyer for the defense, whose economic and professional career is involved, and the prosecutor, whose record is waiting for an entry of a conviction. The trial room becomes an arena, and the judge frequently merely an umpire.

A survey of the procedure taken by the attorney for the client who understands explains why the best attorneys are not commonly found in criminal practice. The steps taken by such an attorney succeed better than those which a learned, high-priced lawyer might use. The dickering character of the work is not pleasant and the element of human interest, formerly the strongest attraction of the criminal case, is entirely gone. Moreover, the guilty defendant does not seek a lawyer because of his legal ability. It is the man who knows the "boys" who can get

[2] *Criminal Justice in Cleveland,* 218.
[3] The ordinary criminal case is a mere "dickering" job—dickering with the district attorney to get a "light rap" (or sentence) for his client "by taking a plea."

things done for him. "Were the system as invulnerable as Achilles these political lawyers would find the penetrable heel." [4]

Because of the odium attached to this branch of the profession, a large part of the lucrative practice in the criminal courts goes to a small number of specialists. "Considering all the Common Pleas criminal cases begun in 1919, we find 244 lawyers appearing in a total of 363 cases, no single lawyer appearing in more than three cases, against 89 lawyers appearing in a total of 842 cases (exclusive of cases where counsel was appointed by the court to aid indigent prisoners and cases in which more than one lawyer appeared for the defense), no one appearing *fewer* than three times. About one-fourth of the privately retained lawyers appeared in more than two-thirds of the cases. Twenty-eight lawyers appeared ten or more times each in 1,492 cases, or one-twelfth of the lawyers in considerably more than one-third of the cases." [5]

II. *Defending the Indigent*

The foregoing shows the participation of the bar in aiding known criminals. In most of these instances the client goes to the lawyer. What about the fellow who is arrested and who has no prearranged connections with a "mouthpiece"? He will find plenty of unofficial public defenders anxious to take his case.

The situation in Chicago may not be typical of large urban communities, but it has been described thus:

"Many of the branches of the Chicago Municipal Court seem to tolerate a condition in connection with attorneys for the defense which is even more serious than the lack of prosecution already described. It seems to be customary for certain lawyers to assume a proprietary attitude toward defense cases. These privileged characters come to the court daily, deposit their coats and hats immediately upon arrival, and participate in the activities exactly as if they were paid attendants. They solicit business through the assistance of clerks, bailiffs and assistant prosecutors, and occasionally through the judges themselves. They also mingle freely among the unfortunates who are hailed before the court, and so get business first-hand. The continuous presence of a "permanent defense lawyer" in the courtroom means that pleasant and sometimes profitable relationships are

[4] *Criminal Justice in Cleveland*, 234.
[5] *Ibid.*, 233, 234.

established between him and courts attachés. Such lawyers have been known to divide their profits with the kindly officers who throw business to them. Indeed, it is stated on good authority that occasionally the lawyers buy such a position in a given branch court. Either on a percentage basis or as an initial fee, he pays for the privilege of preying upon the victims of that particular neighborhood. The names of the men who operate in a given court are not difficult to secure. The survey has a practically complete list of the 'regulars'.

"In the Harrison Street branch one may observe almost every day at least half a dozen attorneys who appear in the majority of cases wherein defendants are represented by counsel. They are commonly known as 'regulars' and their hats and coats are left some place about the building. It is apparent that there must be some sort of understanding among the attorneys, the lock-up keeper, the police, the bailiffs and the professional bondsmen. Often defendants are still in custody, being brought in from the police station, but they are, nevertheless, promptly represented at the trial by one of the 'regulars'. These defendants are probably unable to pay more than a couple of dollars, but the attorneys in question freely accept this, as the work of defending them is light and the 'regulars' are present anyhow. While direct evidence is probably not easy to obtain, an opinion may be ventured that there is some kind of connection between those lawyers and the custodians of the defendants.

"The criminal branches of the Municipal Court have at least one, and some have two or three, of these 'regular' attorneys. Harrison Street has about seven. The ease with which they secure favors in a given court, and the greater degree of success which they seem to have in their cases, indicate the presence of what may be a well-defined 'ring' within certain courts, or what may be a less definite, but nevertheless potent, understanding between them and the officials of the court. Where such a 'ring' exists the defense lawyer holds his status by giving favors, if not money, to those who assist him. We are now speaking plainly, but we are certain of the presence of such arrangements. When a vacancy occurs in a 'regular's' position in a given court, a new attorney is admitted if he meets with certain requirements. In one instance certain city officials made a proposition to a young lawyer and the assurance was given that the cases in which he was interested would not be vigorously prosecuted, provided he accepted the status. He was told that no 'split' was necessary but that from time to time he would have to take care of the lock-up keeper and the bailiffs. It was also said that he would have to be acceptable to the bondsmen who operated in that court.

"It is difficult to determine how much these 'regulars' collect in fees. It is certain, however, that most of them make a very good living. Many of them do not even maintain a Loop law office but make their headquarters at the police station and the courtroom, thus cutting down overhead. Altogether we have in the presence of these men an unofficial but well-defined occupation. They are as definitely a part of the court machinery as the bailiff, the clerk, the prosecutor or the judge.

"The dubious relationships between these men and court officials suggest a condition which is dangerous and reprehensible in the extreme. It is, however, a situation which probably cannot be met by direct negative action. In other words, it might be possible to drive out of the courtroom certain of these parasites, but their function would be fulfilled in some other way. We may as well face the fact that these men are playing a necessary part in the court but are doing so in a very objectionable manner, and under a status that is highly undesirable.

"Some modified form of the public-defender system might be helpful in ridding the Municipal Court of the undesirable aspects which we have described. An office might be created under the jurisdiction of the chief justice to defend the indigent and to institute a system of inspection throughout the branches of the court for the purpose of eliminating the solicitation of business by certain lawyers, as well as to advise all defendants of their rights and duties in the employment of counsel and the compensation therefor." [6]

Justin Miller, Dean of the Law School of the University of Southern California, has described similar conditions elsewhere.[7] Often the unrepresented defendant is tipped by the gaoler, confederate of the shyster, or a "tout" or "capper," to hire "so and so" to defend him. Meanwhile a rapid investigation has been made with respect to the wealth of the accused and of his relatives and friends. If the shyster takes the case there is a continued extortion from people who know no better than to permit themselves to be made victims.[8] The attitude of such counsel in wringing the last dollar from an ignorant or frightened relative of a defendant does not differ greatly from that portrayed in a recent play,[9] in one scene of which the defendant's attorney is wrangling with the husband of the accused for his retainer

[6] Moley, Report of the Municipal Court of Chicago in the *Illinois Crime Survey*, 408-410.

[7] "Guilty or Not Guilty," *No. Am. Rev.*, 361, March, 1929.

[8] In the case of foreigners the court interpreter is frequently a confederate of the shyster. Justin Miller tells the story of a boy, arrested and charged with assault. The district attorney assured his mother that he would examine the evidence carefully and advise her before he proceeded with the prosecution. Meanwhile a shyster frightened her into agreeing to give him a mortgage on her house to raise money to get her son out. When the evidence revealed that the boy had struck in self-defense the case was immediately dismissed and the shyster went to the district attorney and upbraided him for dismissing the case before the shyster had been able to secure a fee.

[9] *Chicago* (New York, 1927), 40-41.

in advance of trial. The husband has offered to pay on the install-ment plan. The reply is, "When you came to me yesterday . . . I said: 'Have you got $5,000?' And you said 'Yes.' . . . You dirty liar! . . . and I took your case and I'll keep it, but she'll rot in jail before I bring it to trial."

III. *The Public Defender*

One method suggested for ridding our courts of these self-appointed extortioners is the creation of the office of public de-fender to represent those who are accused of crime and are un-able to pay for competent legal representation. Most states rec-ognize the right of the accused to counsel by providing that a defendant without means to hire a lawyer may have counsel as-signed by the court. However, only ten states provide for com-pensation by the state for defending all such cases, and nineteen provide for compensation in capital cases only. That this method of dealing with the indigent accused is not adequate to protect rights to which he is entitled by law is shown by numerous examples of its operation.[10] No pay is provided in most states. The court, of necessity, usually appoints young and inexperienced attorneys who are anxious to gain experience and who cannot possibly meet defense expenses for the client, or old shysters who hang about the courts and use such assignments as a means of extortion. A good attorney may be appointed, but he is usually too busy to give proper attention to the preparation of the de-fense. Moreover, since in most cases counsel is not assigned until after indictment, there is ample opportunity for "capping" to have taken place between the time of arrest and the time when counsel can be appointed. Justin Miller gives an excellent picture of the difficulties of the poor man accused of crime:

". . . Those who think of the accused as one at an unfair disadvan-tage with all the powers of the state arrayed against him . . . if they think intelligently and not merely as emotional romanticists . . . think of that half-concealed, unsupervised procedure which precedes the appearance of

[10] Cf. Smith, *Justice and the Poor* (published by the Carnegie Foundation for the Advancement of Teaching, 1919); Goldman, *The Public Defender* (New York, 1917); Maguire, *The Lance of Justice* (Cambridge, 1928), 244 et seq.

the accused in the court of record. Here it is that we find the third degree, the bail bond broker, the stool pigeon, the crooked interpreter, the shyster lawyer, the lame-duck magistrate, and all the rest of the motley of underworld characters and methods. The poor man . . . often is the victim of a grotesque burlesque on the administration of justice."

Such conditions have led to agitation for the creation of the office of public defender. Three main types of public-defender plan have been worked out in this country. The first, represented by the Voluntary Defenders Committee in New York, is that provided and supported by private agencies. The second and third types, variations of a publicly maintained defender, are represented by the Los Angeles and Connecticut plans, respectively.

The Voluntary Defenders Committee,[11] organized in 1917, has become the criminal branch of the New York Legal Aid Society, and operates in New York County exclusively. Through the courtesy of the municipal authorities it has been given an office in the Criminal Courts Building. It has, in addition to a social worker, four investigators and two secretaries, a staff of four lawyers, paid by the society to devote their entire time to the defense of indigent accused in the Court of General Sessions. This work is handled far better by the lawyers of the Committee than it is by the average assigned counsel and with a far greater degree of coöperation with other court agencies. In addition to this work the staff performs valuable social work, such as getting jobs for defendants and prisoners whose discharge they have procured, and looking after the families of the accused.

The Voluntary Defenders Committee, however, while a notable improvement over the old system of assigned counsel, has not proved itself entirely adequate to meet the problem of the indigent accused. It has always been handicapped by lack of sufficient funds. Although it has been estimated that each year about 1,500 defendants in the Court of General Sessions of New York County are without means to retain counsel, the Committee in

[11] For a detailed account of the history and operation of the Voluntary Defenders Committee see Maguire, *The Lance of Justice*. See also Embree, "The New York Public Defender," 8 *Journal of Criminal Law and Criminology,* 554 (1917).

1927 with a staff of two lawyers represented only 558 of them. In 1929 with a staff of four lawyers the Committee represented about 1,000. Even taking into consideration the fact that the Committee does not handle first degree murder cases [12] these figures give some indication of the limited scope of voluntary defense activities. It cost the Committee $18,000 to handle 558 cases. It cost them $26,000 in salaries alone to handle 1,000 cases in 1929. Moreover, the Committee cannot cover the magistrates' courts to give the necessary protection to the defendants there.

The second type of public-defender system in operation in this country is that which is financed by the state. This type, roughly speaking, has two variations, the Los Angeles plan, and the Connecticut plan. Based upon these two as models, Minnesota, Nebraska, Tennessee and Virginia have fashioned their own public-defender projects. Generally, however, the assigned counsel system prevails throughout the United States.

The first official public defender was created by charter in 1913 in Los Angeles County, California. The holder of the office was, and is, appointed after a competitive civil service examination, by the Board of Supervisors of the County, who fix his salary and make rules and regulations governing such of his duties as are not delineated in the charter. The scope of his work as prescribed in the charter is as follows:

"Upon request of the defendant or upon the order of the court, the public defender shall defend, without expense to them, all persons who are not financially able to employ counsel, and who are charged in the superior court with the commission of any contempt, misdemeanor, felony or other offense. He shall also upon request give counsel and advice to such persons in and about any charge against them upon which he is conducting the defense, and he shall also prosecute all appeals to a higher court or courts of any person who has been convicted upon any such charge, where, in his opinion, such appeal will or might reasonably be expected to result in the reversal or modification of the judgment of conviction."

As originally outlined, the work of the public defender was limited to the higher courts, but in 1915 a Police Court Defender was created whose salary was to be paid by the city. After an

[12] For the defense of these cases the state allows a fee of $1,000, and they are therefore "plums" for which there is a great demand.

experiment of nine years in Los Angeles County the legislature passed a law authorizing any county to have a public defender. The need of such defenders in the police courts has been pointed out as a means to eliminate gaol lawyers and "cappers," etc.[13] A report to the Los Angeles Crime Commission in 1923 indicates that these undesirable factors have not been eradicated, but the abuses referred to have been materially reduced. Replies to inquiries sent to those who have closely observed the system in operation in Los Angeles indicate that it has proved far more efficient than the old assigned system and that perjury, spiriting away of witnesses, and similar abuses are unknown where defendants are represented by public defenders rather than by privately retained attorneys.

The Connecticut plan of public defender varies in detail from the Los Angeles plan, and is not subject to the danger which cropped up in some cities, where the Los Angeles plan was adopted, and where the office was abolished because the personal political views of the Public Defender were not in accord with those of the administration in power.

Under the Connecticut plan, the superior court of each county appoints an attorney of at least five years' standing to act in behalf of any person charged with crime in the higher courts of the county. Although the appointment is nominally for one year only, the practice has been to continue the appointee in office as long as his services prove satisfactory. Under the rules adopted by the judges, he may appear at preliminary hearings and before committing magistrates, in order that he may represent a defendant from the time of arrest to the end of the action. The services of the public defender are, of course, gratuitous, but if the accused has some means, he must pay a reasonable fee into court for the use of the state. At the close of each term the defender submits a bill for reasonable compensation, which the court is authorized to allow.

The relative advantages of the Los Angeles and Connecticut plans, the former under the control of the governing board of the county, and the latter under the supervision of the courts, have been debated. We have at least one example of each type

---

[13] Cf. Miller, *op. cit.*

that has been an outstanding success, but sufficient data are not yet available upon which to judge their comparative merits. It would seem that if politics did not intervene, the official public defender system could claim very definite advantages over the voluntary defender type. The status of the "official" public defender, it has been contended, would place him on a plane with the prosecutor, like him, paid by the state, and, like him, having the same privileges of employing experts where needed. It is likewise contended that since both attorneys in a criminal case would be, in fact, officers of the state, the wide divergence in purposes which now exists between the prosecutor and the defense attorney would be partially eliminated and there would be a singleness of purpose to see that justice is done.

IV. *The Criminal Lawyer as a Statesman*

Those who fear that legislative action, under the stress of popular demands, will go too far in amending procedure and deny the defendant necessary and just rights, lose sight of an ever-present protective force, the criminal lawyer legislator. In many states the complaint is heard that programs of reform have been defeated because of the lawyer group in the legislature. It is well known that legislatures have a generous number of lawyers. In New York State, for example, the proportion is about one-half, the proportion from the City of New York running much higher.

The practice of criminal law is always closely related to the practice of politics, and the lawyers who are chosen for the state legislature by political organizations are usually criminal lawyers. On account of the fact that they are lawyers, moreover, they come to fill the committees of the legislature to which most measures for procedural reform are referred. When such measures are under consideration it is, of course, difficult for these criminal lawyer-legislators to consider such enactments without bias. If, as in many instances, these measures change the relative position of defendant and state, they are likely to be prejudiced against the proposed change. When the "accomplice rule" was voted upon recently in the Legislature of New York, twenty-one of the twenty-three representatives of New York County voted against the change although it had been approved by the Bar Association of the City and State of New York. The lover of liberty may rest assured that so long as such a liberal representation of lawyers from the great cities is sent to the legislature the rights of the defendant will suffer no drastic reduction.

This is sustained by present evidences that the reaction toward a curtailment of the defendant's present advantages in criminal procedure quite marked in various reform proposals is already on the wane. Not only are the lawyer-legislators who favor the retention of the present status still active but apparently public opinion is drifting away from the belief in more severity. The New York Legislature, which in 1926 enthusiastically enacted the Baumes Laws, has in 1930 rejected practically the entire program of the Crime Commission. Some of the proposals for procedural modification defeated are a bill to permit a district attorney to comment upon the fact that a defendant in a murder case had failed to take the witness stand; another to permit judicial comment upon the character of the evidence; the bill to reduce the number of peremptory challenges and, finally, the measure which would permit a district attorney in a criminal case to impeach his own witness; a proposed constitutional amendment to permit a defendant to waive trial by jury and a bill abolishing all jury exemptions.

PART II
THE LONG DAY IN COURT

CHAPTER V

MACHINERY

DURING the past twenty-five years there has been a distinct drift toward the reorganization of state and local governmental machinery. The rising cost of government occasioned by the assumption of new functions turned the attention of political leaders and other students of public affairs to the devising of means by which government could carry the new burdens without too greatly increasing the tax rate. "Efficiency and economy" became the watchword and numerous commissions were created to plan for the reorganization of the administrative structure.[1] This movement resulted in the rearrangement of the administrative machinery in many states, notably New York and Illinois. The reconstruction has been more a rearrangement of bureaus, departments, boards and commission than a thorough reintegration. Its method, adhered to almost fanatically at times, has been that of centralizing responsibility for administrative work in someone at the head of a department and with this centralization to achieve control over him through direct contact with the chief executive. This enables the governor of the state to assume specific responsibility for what happens in state departments and justifies the electorate in judging him on this basis. The effect of this drift toward a federal system, which seems to have been contemplated in the creation of the national Constitution itself, has been felt by the courts, and a large part of the discussion concerning the reconstruction of the mechanical side of judicial administration has centered about the idea of a chief justice with large powers of administration. After the creation of the Chicago Municipal Court a number of

[1] For the early history of this movement see Moley, *The State Movement for Efficiency and Economy* (New York, 1918), and for the period since 1918 see Buck, *Administrative Consolidation in State Governments* (New York, 1924).

other city courts of similar nature were established. A great deal has been written to urge upon states the necessity for an application of this principle to the entire state judiciary.

No state, however, has undertaken such a plan, and in general the county and judicial district system has remained. The chief development in the state judiciary as a whole has been the creation of judicial councils, varying from merely paper committees of judges and lawyers to actual administrative agencies with considerable power such as is possessed by the California Judicial Council.

The movement for a judicial council is only incidentally related to the immediate problem of criminal justice and for that reason is not properly within the scope of this book. The two questions which are much more pertinent to the subject matter of criminal justice are: first, the extent to which the courts of a city or judicial district should be subjected to control by a single administrative head; and second, whether it is desirable that a single court be created which is essentially a criminal court. The value of these changes must be measured in terms of what specific courts have achieved. Consequently, most of our attention is directed in this chapter to a consideration of two courts, the Municipal Court of Chicago, and the Recorders' Court of Detroit, which strikingly illustrate the two principles of centralization and specialization. We are in this treatment seeking to measure the value of administrative change as compared with the human element involved in judicial personnel. The fact that we show a declining efficiency in both courts in spite of mechanical excellence does not belittle mechanical change, but it emphasizes the greater importance of personnel.

I. *The Reform of Court Organization*

The most valuable guide to the movement for the reform of Judicial Administration in the United States is *The Journal of the American Judicature Society*. It contains a great many arguments and plans, and the results of the entire agitation for the reform of judicial administration in the United States. It has since its beginning in 1915 performed the service of bringing to the attention of members of the bar the need for reform of this character. The subject matter with which it has dealt can best be indicated by the classification of its various articles and editorials, in its cumulative index: bar organization, commerce arbitration, conciliation and small-claim procedure, court organization, city courts, federal courts, federal courts and procedure, legal education and admission to practice, procedure in civil cases, procedure in criminal cases, and selection, tenure and retirement of judges.

An examination of the files of the *Journal* with reference to matters of court organization shows that those who are interested in reform of this character are actuated by a number of principles or dogmas. These can be stated in the following terms:

(1) So far as possible, jurisdictional lines between the various state courts should be limited and there should be some sort of organic unity among all the courts of a state. Such unity should permit a general "judicial superintendent" or "judicial council" at the head of the state system with certain limited powers over the distribution of cases among courts and in the assignment of judges. Within cities and counties where a number of judges are necessary there should be established a similar kind of unity.

(2) In the reorganization of the courts a greater degree of specialization should be recognized. *The Journal of the American Judicature Society,* for example, very enthusiastically praised the principle of the Detroit Recorder's Court, established in 1921, which was a consolidation of the criminal jurisdiction of the city in a single court. With this general tendency toward specialization has come a support of specialized courts of various kinds, such as domestic relations, courts dealing with sex delinquency, traffic courts, and other specialized types of criminal litigation. There is no essential conflict between the movement for unification and the movement for specialization because, as the advocate for reform would point out, it is possible to create specialization of function within a court system while at the same time maintaining a general administrative control.

(3) An element almost universally insisted upon by reformers has been a chief justice, not only of local centralized courts,

but of circuit and state systems. This administrative position seems to be a product of two concepts. The first is that of the traditional presiding judge of a court similar in character to that of the Supreme Court of the United States. The second is that of the chief administrative officer in public or in private administrative supervision and direction. Powers of such a chief justice have been variously described in the legislation creating the office. In some instances, such as in the Chicago Municipal Court, his power is very broad, and the control over the assignment both of cases and of judges, direction of the administrative staff, and the control of records and reports. In some instances the office is, however, little more than that of a presiding judge who is merely a moderator at the general meetings and conferences of judges.

(4) A great deal has been said concerning the need for a shift of the rule-making power from the legislature to the courts themselves. Under some of the more ambitious programs for the reform of state judicial administration, it is provided that the power to make rules of procedure should, within certain limitations, be vested in the judges themselves acting jointly, or in a committee of them, or in a judicial council, or in the chief justice himself.

(5) Another proposal for the improvement of administration applies to the administrative staff of the court. A number of changes has been suggested here, among them the creation of new agencies such as probation departments, bail bond bureaus and clerical offices of various sorts. In addition to probation departments a strong suggestion has been made that courts employ clinics of various kinds for their work.

(6) In some cities there has been a strong movement to centralize the various courts physically. This is particularly true in New York City, where there has been a proposal widely approved in the newspapers to provide a central building for the magistrates' courts to the end that administrative services be concentrated in one place. That would enable the public more effectively to follow and understand and, if necessary, to disapprove of certain practices that might be unnoticed in a branch court located off the beaten track.

II. *The Chicago Plan of a Strong Chief Justice*

In Chicago the administration of criminal justice in state offenses is almost wholly vested in two courts. The trial court is called the Criminal Court and is composed of judges of the circuit and the superior courts assigned to the Criminal Court for short periods of service. The powers of the chief justice of the Criminal Court do not extend beyond those of a mere presiding judge. The Municipal Court, however, which has wide civil jurisdiction, also, has jurisdiction over all preliminary hearings in state cases and all misdemeanors and violations of city ordinances. The following description of this court quite properly stresses the importance of the chief justice and includes not only a description of his powers but the conclusions which seem to be warranted by a detailed study of the work of the court.[2]

In November, 1904, the voters approved a constitutional amendment which permitted the creation by statute of a Municipal Court in Chicago. At that time Chicago had a curious assortment of courts with confused and often conflicting jurisdictions. It had a county court with one judge and a jurisdiction involving insanity proceedings, taxation and elections, a probate court with one judge, courts of general trial jurisdiction called the Circuit and Superior Courts with twenty-six judges altogether. The latter had general civil jurisdiction and criminal jurisdiction in cases involving felonies. The inferior civil and criminal jurisdiction of the city was vested in fifty-four Justices of the Peace. It is unnecessary to say that the Justices of the Peace system was not wholly unable to cope with the amount of business which came to its attention but was susceptible to grave abuses. The justices were not elected, as in most other jurisdictions of the United States, but were appointed by the judges in the Circuit and Superior Courts. This was a fairly satisfactory feature, but any benefit that might come from this mode of election was lost on the criminal side by the fact that those justices who sat as police court judges were designed for this work by the mayor at the suggestion of aldermen. Politics, crime and the judiciary were thus closely linked together. The Municipal Court was created largely to take over part of the work of the Circuit and Superior Courts, which were then seriously overloaded, and to eliminate the conditions of the justice courts in small civil and criminal cases.

In 1905 the legislature passed an act creating the Municipal Court of

[2] The passage which follows is quoted from my report on the Municipal Court of Chicago, published in the *Illinois Crime Survey*, 394-398.

Chicago. It gave this new court jurisdiction in contract cases concurrent with the Circuit and Superior Courts within the city's boundaries, and in tort actions, jurisdiction over cases involving not more than one thousand dollars. It transferred all of the civil and criminal jurisdiction of the Justices of the Peace to the new court and thus abolished these anachronistic survivals. It provided twenty-seven new judges, including one chief justice, and it provided that these judges should serve for terms of six years. These judges were to be elected by the voters of the city.

A strong centralization of power was provided in the court by the creation of the office of chief justice, whose duties will be presently described. It was provided that there should be meetings of the judges over which the chief justice should preside, and that the court through its judges, should have wide power in making rules of procedure for its own guidance. The Municipal Court is by statutory enactment a court of record.

In the beginning, jurisdiction was conferred upon it to extend to "all classes of cases, civil or criminal, at law or in equity, by transfer from other courts". This seemed to give the court power to try felony cases, and it started to exercise such power. But in the case of Miller v. the People (230 Ill. 65) it was decided that this power to try felony cases could not be exercised. Jurisdiction in felony cases, therefore, was and is limited to preliminary examinations. It also has jurisdiction of misdemeanor cases and violations of city ordinances as well as quasicriminal actions, such as bastardy cases, proceedings for the prevention of crime, proceedings for the arrest, examination, commitment, and bail of persons charged with criminal offenses, and all proceedings pertaining to searches and seizures of personal property by search and search warrants.

Municipal Court trials are by the court without a jury, or with a jury on demand of the litigant, and are official in the sense that there can be no trial *de novo* in another court. Appeals are taken direct to Appellate and Supreme Courts in Illinois. At the present time, by a recent action of the legislature, the number of judges has been increased to thirty-seven. The chief justice and the associate justices are elected for terms of six years, with provision for the election of twelve associate judges every two years. The salary of the chief justice is fifteen thousand dollars and that of the associate judges ten thousand dollars. There is provision that a justice of the court must be as least thirty years of age, a citizen of the United States and must have resided in Cook County and there been engaged in active practice as an attorney or in the discharge of duties of a judicial office for five years preceding his election. He must be a resident of the city of Chicago.

The law provides for the separation of the work of the court into branches and vests with the chief justice the large powers of determining what these branches shall consider. The character of these branches changes from time to time, but there are usually about seventeen criminal branches and the remainder civil. Of the criminal branches, twelve are unspecialized courts in the various Municipal Court districts into which the city has been divided and the others are specialized courts located in the courthouses. There are special branches handling traffic cases, domestic relations cases and bail-bond matters. There are also the Morals Court and the Boys' Court. In 1926 a branch was created called the Delinquency Branch to which are assigned sex offenses formerly heard in the domestic relations branch.

The Boys' Court is not considered in detail in this report because it has recently been subjected to a very detailed study by the United States Children's Bureau, the report of which is presumably to be made public. An advance copy has been available to the author of this report and with its general conclusions we are in substantial agreement.

For convenience in describing the various branches of the Municipal Court of Chicago which deal with criminal cases, let us divide them into two groups. First, what we may call the headquarters courts, which are located in the city hall and courthouses and which perform certain specialized functions. The second group includes the district courts established throughout Chicago and dealing with a general line of criminal cases. The following tabulation indicates the number of each of these branches, the name commonly attached to the court, and the number of felony cases disposed of in each of these branches during the year ending December 4, 1927. We can in this way see at a glance the relative importance of these courts in the trial of felony cases:

BUSINESS OF BRANCH COURTS

1927

Branch Number	Name of Court	Felony Cases Disposed of in 1927
1	Bail Bond	....
3	Quasi-Criminal, etc.	5
8	Bastardy and Delinquency	359
10	Domestic	10
19	Perjury and Vagrancy	60
20	Morals Court	25
22	Boys' Court	3,532
25	Fillmore Street (4001 Fillmore St.)	953
27	Harrison Street (625 S. Clark St.)	2,345
28	Desplaines Street (120 N. Desplaines St.)	808
29	East Chicago Avenue (113 W. Chicago Ave.)	605
30	West Chicago Avenue (731 N. Racine Ave.)	542
31	Maxwell Street (943 Maxwell St.)	755
32	Town Hall (3600 N. Halsted St.)	1,238
33	Shakespeare Avenue (2138 N. California Ave.)	1,104
34	Wabash Avenue (4802 Wabash Ave.)	1,273
35	Stock Yards (811 W. 47th Pl.)	597
36	Grand Crossing (834 E. 75th St.)	1,049
37	Pekin (2700 S. State St.)	909
38	South Chicago (8855 Exchange Ave.)	629

When the Municipal Court was established, one of its most striking innovations was the creation of a chief justice vested with large powers to superintend the administrative work of the court. This conception of a judicial superintendent was probably more a result of the influence of business methods upon the thinking of those who created the court than any idea embodying the traditional power of a chief justice as it had been known in the State Supreme Courts and in the Supreme Court of the United States. In fact, the powers of the chief justice of the Municipal Court of Chicago are much more striking and significant than those of the head of any of the state or federal courts of the United States up to the time when the Chicago court was established. His chief powers are thus described in the language of the Act creating the court:

"The chief justice in addition to the exercise of all the other powers of judge of said court, shall have the general superintendence of the business of said court; he shall preside at all meetings of the judges, and he shall assign the associate judges to duty in the branch courts, from time to time, as he may deem necessary for the prompt disposition of the business thereof, and it shall be the duty of each associate judge to attend and serve at any branch court to which he may be so assigned. . . . The chief justice shall also superintend the preparation of the calendars of cases for trial in said court and shall make such classification and distribution of the same upon different calendars as he shall deem proper and expedient. Each associate judge shall at the commencement of each month make to the chief justice, under his official oath, a report in writing of the duties performed by him during the preceding month, which report shall specify the number of days' attendance in court of such judge during such month, and the branch courts upon which he has attended, and the number of hours per day of such attendance."

Thus the chief justice has two significant powers. He may assign the associate judges to duty in the branch courts, and he also controls the calendars and may make such classification and distribution of cases as he deems necessary. In addition, he is empowered to require the judges to submit reports to him. These two powers enable him to create new branches of the court by the simple method of assigning certain classes of cases to a certain judge and to distribute judicial personnel in whatever way he desires. He has, in addition, the very important power of indirect coercion over the judges by requiring from them reports as to their work and by having the power himself to publish the results of such reports.

Summing it all up, while he is not able to secure the removal of an objectionable judge, and, of course, is not able to control the selection of new judges, he is able to exercise strong coercive power over the judges. He may, if he so desires, assign a judge to very unimportant work; he may prevent judges from securing assignments which will be of assistance to them politically; he may bring indirect pressure upon judges by the publication of reports. The power of assignment is therefore exceedingly significant. It is a fact to be taken for granted that certain judges are able to do certain types of work exceedingly well and a wise chief justice may draw upon this exceptional ability in ways very helpful to the general business of the court. He may, moreover, assign weak judges to branches where their frailties may bring about no very serious consequences to the community.

In any attempt to reach a general conclusion as to the net achievement of the present chief justice as administrative head of the court since its beginning more than twenty years ago many factors must be passed in review. There have been and are, as we indicate in this report, many instances of inefficiency, weakness and bad taste in the work of individual judges. The chief justice may, under the law, and does in actual fact, terminate or mitigate such undesirable conditions by the use of his powers. There are limits to the exercise of his powers, however. The judges are not of his selection, nor does their retention rest within his discretion. He may assign them at will, but he must in practice assign them to something. With the declining caliber of personnel with which he has had to deal, it is increasingly difficult to find sufficient good judges to cover the more important assignments. He must, moreover, limit himself in the exercise of his powers because it is necessary to maintain some degree of harmony in the official family. A majority of judges may embarrass him seriously in the administration of the court because the judges as a body have certain important powers. Finally, there are the limitations imposed upon any administrative officer by his inability to know all that is going on throughout a large organization. Considering these factors, and at the same time balancing the good and the bad in the work of the criminal arms of the court, only one conclusion is possible as to the value of the contribution of the present chief justice.

It is to be said in favor of the present chief justice, that he has exercised his large powers as chief justice of this court with very remarkable skill and force. In spite of the general breakdown of the administration of criminal justice in the city of Chicago, the Municipal Court has probably survived with less discredit than most of the other agencies of law enforcement, due to the high standards and vigilant watchfulness of the chief justice. It should be said, in addition, that he has been an able exponent of the idea of judicial reform in municipalities throughout the United States. He has, through writing and speaking, performed a distinct public service to other states and cities.

III. *The Detroit Experiment in Specialization*

In 1920 the Legislature of Michigan provided by special act for the reorganization of the criminal courts of the City of Detroit. The Police Court with inferior criminal jurisdiction was merged with the Recorder's Court under the name of the latter. The new court was to exercise both inferior and trial jurisdiction in all criminal cases. The act also provided that a presiding judge be elected by his associates with a vaguely defined grant of power to superintend the business of the court. The act also provided for a psychiatric clinic. The number of judges was fixed at seven, but by amendment in 1924 it was raised to ten. A probation department was created.[3]

The Detroit Recorder's Court was from the beginning placed under the handicap imposed by the extravagant claims of its friends. *The Journal of the American Judicature Society* predicted that "if Detroit accepts this act it will within two years become the best governed city in the United States from the standpoint of criminal law enforcement; that it will reduce the volume of crime at least fifty per cent; that it will rid the city of professional crooks; and that it will set a standard and point a route for all other cities of this country." Later, it said that the new régime would "kill off bail troubles," reduce perjury, and drive away shysters.

The court began its operation and elected its first judges at a time when Detroit was passing through one of those periods of temporary good government and public "righteousness" so characteristic of American cities. Of the first seven judges elected, at least four were of superior ability and independence. For three years these men dominated the court. Many unusual administrative changes and innovations were made. The probation department and the psychiatric clinic were manned by persons of extraordinary competence. The clerk's office was brought to a degree of efficiency uncommon among American courts. Excellent reports were published.

Many of the predicted and claimed advantages may be conceded, although it is difficult to verify them. "Efficiency" cannot be "proved" except by general impressions. The justice of the decisions likewise eludes measurement. Of the quality of personnel something should be said later. The speed with which cases are tried, however, can definitely be determined and in this the Detroit court has taught some interesting lessons. After it had

[3] For a description and account of the Detroit Court see Mandel, "Appraising Detroit's New Criminal Court," *National Municipal Review*, X, 550-553; *Public Business*, published by the Detroit Bureau of Governmental Research, Nos. 63 and 72; and several articles in the *Journal of the American Judicature Society*, III, 5, and 177; IV, 14 and 38; V, 93, 163, and 173; VI, 18.

been in operation a year, Mr. Arch Mandel of the Detroit Bureau
of Governmental Research made a comparative study of the speed
with which cases were tried in the new court and in the courts
which it had succeeded. The following year he added to his
study the results of the second year of its operation. These two
pieces of research are important not only because they provide a
quantitative test of a new departure in court machinery, but
also because the method followed was an illustration of an excellent way of measuring one aspect of court efficiency. These
studies apply only to felonies. The following is a statement of
Mr. Mandel's results:

"A study of 1,965 felonies originating in the new court during the first
six months of its operation reveals the fact that 38 per cent were disposed
of within seven days, that is, from the arraignment on the warrant through
the final trial; 52 per cent were disposed of within fourteen days and 93
per cent within ninety days," [4]

In the following year Mr. Mandel made a comparison of the
time used in disposing of cases in 1921, the second year of the
new court, as compared with 1919, the last year of the old system. The comparison was again favorable to the new court, and
to an even greater degree. The following table combines Mr. Mandel's two studies—including, for the sake of condensation, only
percentages:

PERCENTAGE OF FELONY CASES DISPOSED OF, BY WEEKS, IN 1919, 1920 AND 1921

Weeks	Cumulative Percentage of Cases Disposed of:		
	1919	1920	1921
1	2	38	66
2	5	52	72
3	10	61	77
4	15	68	84
5	21	74	90
6	27	79	94
7	34	83	96
8	40	86	97
9	59	87	98
Over 9	100	100	100

This statistical measurement of court efficiency demonstrates
a genuine improvement. It does not, to be sure, take account of

[4] Mandel, "Appraising Detroit's New Criminal Court," *National Municipal Review*,
X, 550-551.

the methods used in disposing of these cases, whether by plea or by trial, nor does it measure the justice of the dispositions. However, after all due allowances had been made the observer of the experiment would be compelled to grant to the new court and its judges credit for an amazing improvement in the work for which it was created.[5]

In order to determine the extent to which this efficiency continued to be a feature of the court after a few years had passed and several of the original judges had been displaced, I made a similar study in 1927 with funds provided by the Council for Research in the Social Sciences of Columbia University.[6] The period used by Mr. Mandel for his studies of 1919, 1920, and 1921 had been the cases initiated between April 20 and December 31. I used the same period for 1926. The same methods, in every detail, were used as had been developed by Mr. Mandel. The results are, therefore, wholly comparable. The data of my study, combined for comparative purposes with Mr. Mandel's statistics, are embodied in the following table:

TABLE

TIME REQUIRED FOR THE DISPOSITION OF FELONY CASES IN DETROIT IN 1919, 1920, 1921 AND 1926

Weeks	1919 No. Cases	Pct.	1920 No. Cases	Pct.	1921 No. Cases	Pct.	1926 No. Cases	Pct.	Cumulative Percentages 1919	1920	1921	1926
1	31	2	748	38	2189	66	479	10	2	38	66	10
2	61	3	267	14	203	6	596	13	5	52	72	23
3	95	5	172	9	154	5	435	10	10	61	77	33
4	105	5	135	7	252	7	315	7	15	68	84	40
5	114	6	119	6	197	6	289	6	21	74	90	46
6	123	6	92	5	138	4	269	6	27	79	94	52
7	132	7	76	4	64	2	191	4	34	83	96	56
8	128	6	71	3	42	1	143	3	40	86	97	59
9	371	19	27	1	31	1	127	3	59	87	98	62
65- 90 days	137	7	113	6	over		207	5	66	93 }	100	67
90-270 days	265	14	145	7	9 wks.		1487	32	80	100 }	100	99
270-610 days	386	20			68	2	44	1	100			100
Total	1948	100	1965	100	3338	100	4582	100				

[5] This was the conclusion which I reached after a somewhat intimate study of the operation of the court and of Mr. Mandel's methods of measurement.

[6] In making this study Mr. Thomas Dabagh collected the data from the records of the court and Miss Elizabeth Dublin coded, calculated and tabulated the cards.

The decline in efficiency which is the unquestionable lesson of these figures is also shown in the number of cases pending at the end of each year, as shown by the annual reports of the court.

FELONY CASES, DETROIT. RECORDER'S COURT

	Pending	Total Cases Filed
Dec. 31, 1920	1208	4840
" " 1921	1049	6180
" " 1922	1195	6558
" " 1923	1511*	6149
" " 1924	1865	6510
" " 1925	3300	7485
" " 1926	3956	9510

* Election year. This table includes only the years before and after the changes in personnel. The more recent reports show some decline from 1926 but the early standard has not been regained.

Three possible explanations can be made for the decline in efficiency of the court between 1921 and 1926. The first is the increase in the number of cases from 3,338 in 1921 to 4,582 in 1926. This increase, amounting to thirty seven per cent, was cared for by adding three judges to the court; so that the increase in judicial personnel was greater than the increase in cases. The second explanation is more important. After the elections of 1923 the rules were changed to provide that the term of the judge serving as presiding officer be one month instead of a year and that the office rotate among the judges. This probably interfered with the administrative efficiency of the court, but certainly not enough to explain the figures which we have given. The really important reason was undoubtedly a change in the personnel of the court. In the judicial campaign of 1923, a violent newspaper attack was made upon four of the judges then sitting. These judges, popularly called "the big four," were young, independent, vigorous and enthusiastic. In the campaign of 1923, the sensational press accused them of "autocracy" and succeeded in defeating two of them. This ended the vigorous administration of "the big four" and as a part of the reaction the change was made in the rules limiting the tenure of the presiding judge. The return of the court to the old type of judges marked a decline in efficiency which is clearly shown in the figures above. If this evidence reveals anything fundamental, it is the fact that judicial business can be expeditiously performed if we have energetic judges. It indicates that the true objective of judicial reform should be to secure better judges.

IV. *Structural Reform and Criminal Justice*

It is not within the province of this book to consider in any detail the general problem of judicial administration, which is largely concerned with civil jurisdiction.[7] The fact, however, that the main theme of this book, and particularly the two foregoing sections of this chapter, stresses with so much emphasis the paramount importance of personnel, necessitates making clear here that structural matters are of importance also. A number of conclusions, which are in the main purely personal impressions rather than demonstrated facts, may be ventured. They relate not to judicial administration generally, but only to those aspects which have a bearing upon the administration of criminal justice in felony cases.

It is impossible to pronounce approval of the general proposition that "centralization" of courts under a strong chief justice is desirable. The question must be answered as it applies to a concrete situation. To combine, as in Chicago, the minor civil jurisdiction, the preliminary hearings and the trial of misdemeanors has definite advantages. To press the centralization to include courts dealing with jurisdiction over juveniles and probate matters is highly questionable. Here are specialized interests requiring most unusual temperament and experience. They require, as well, continuity of tenure because their "cases" are not to be disposed of in a short time, but remain a permanent responsibility for a long time. The juvenile judge or the surrogate acts for the state in certain of its most delicate concerns. Here "efficiency" is secondary to permanence, independence and specialized competence.

To propose, moreover, that "centralization" be upon a state-wide basis, with a state chief justice in command over district and county judges, is to raise the question as to what the central

[7] The most informative, tempered and reasonable discussion of the structural aspect of judicial administration is by Professor Walter F. Dodd of the Yale Law School in his *State Government* (Revised, 1928), Chapters 10-12.

power should control. If such control means merely to require reports, or to shift judicial personnel temporarily from one county or district to another to meet emergencies, the argument is still good. But to try persons charged with criminal offenses under judges brought from other jurisdictions is to raise serious problems. It raises the question of whether a community should determine for itself the extent to which a flexible criminal law is to be enforced. It gets itself into the vexatious question of home rule.

The Detroit experiment justifies a number of conclusions as to the value of a court system limited to criminal jurisdiction. In the first place, there is the question of whether minor and major criminal cases can be tried in the same court. The enthusiastic supporters of this court said many brave things about the "human values" in minor cases which judges of superior qualities would be proud to try. *The Journal of the American Judicature Society* said: "The objection raised to a unified criminal court, that of requiring its judges to participate in the mean and petty work of the Police Court would degrade the entire court, is absolutely exploded. There is nothing more degrading in enforcing traffic laws or trying assaults and battery, bootlegging or vagrancy cases than trying burglary, robbery and murder cases. All this work is disagreeable and wearing on nerves; all of it is honorable in that it affords the only protection to the public and is not surpassed by any other work in importance, either legally or socially." The honorable character of such work would be freely conceded by the ablest men of the bar, but they would probably permit their younger and less experienced colleagues to run for the judgeships. In fact, a sort of a Gresham's Law has been in operation in the Detroit court during the ten years of its existence. The combination of minor and major jurisdiction in one court has not resulted in drawing superior judges to the trial of inferior (though "honorable" and important) cases; it has leveled the quality of judges so that inferior judges now try major cases. A final evidence of the decline has occurred within the past two years when the ablest judge of the original bench has accepted an appointment to the civil bench, apparently indicating his own notion that civil trial work is more to his liking than service in the Recorder's Court. While it is easy to claim that inferior criminal work is as important as the trial of major crimes, it is difficult to make able trial judges act upon such a principle. Many judges of long experience have testified that while short periods devoted to criminal work are stimulating, it would become a heavy psychological burden to remain in such work permanently. This question involves subtle temperamental characteristics which do not permit easy generalizations. Some persons can unquestionably sustain flexible and enthusiastic interest in the sordid and abnormal, others grow hard and callous, still others break under the strain. These questions cannot be answered by soft generalizations about the "honorable" character of such work. They require the taking of an honest inventory of things as they are.

Lest there be misunderstanding, it should be said in conclusion that the main purpose of this chapter is to say that such success as American cities and states have already achieved in structural reform is mostly on the surface. It will be answered that centralization, with strong chief justices and the rest, is admittedly only a preliminary step, necessary to bring about other changes. Efficiency of administrative routine, the creation of specialized courts and other actual improvements can best be done through an administrative mechanism of a centralized nature. But the Municipal Court of Chicago has been in operation nearly a quarter of a century and it is still as inefficient and confused and political as most of the unreformed police courts in other cities. It has been widely advertised, it is true, and that accounts for the widespread impression of a new era. But the thing the honest and decent citizen wants, namely the getting of cases heard and tried with intelligence, justice and freedom from politics, is not being done. In Detroit the administration is better, but so it is in Milwaukee without well advertised reform. Quite pertinent here are Pope's worn words about "forms of government":

"That which is best administered is best."

and that which is best administered is that which has most brains and most courage in high places.[8]

---

[8] A very informative article on the mechanical aspects of the English judiciary is Kales, "The English Judicature Act," *Jour. of the Am. Judic. Soc.*, IV, 133 (1919).

CHAPTER VI

RULES

THE defendant's day in court has captured the attention of many of those who are contributing to the growing literature of criminal justice reform; particularly of those members of the legal profession who have thought of the problem. To them the day in court seems shaped and determined by set rules; rules that are defective, that are outworn and overtechnical—rules that permit delay and inefficiency. These rules, they say, are in immediate and urgent need of reform. Such reform should simplify them, make them less advantageous to the defendant and provide for more expeditious proceedings before, during and after trial. Such reform as this point of view urges would, according to one of its most experienced and eminent exponents, make the trial of a criminal case "less of a game of contest of skill, cunning and endurance between opposing lawyers and . . . more of a judicial investigation under the trained and impartial direction of a judge to ascertain the truth." [1]

I. *Two Centuries of Procedural Change*

The history of Anglo-American criminal justice since the close of the seventeenth century justifies this view of the need to reconsider the rules. Procedural reform in England grew largely out of a realization that existing rules were the survivals of a day when the severity of the criminal law was mitigated by clever devices invented to protect defendants from disproportionate punishment. The enormous number of capital crimes in England in the eighteenth century—more than two hundred—and the severity of the punishments inflicted for minor offenses led to the

---

[1] Former Governor Herbert S. Hadley of Missouri in *Am. Bar Assoc. Jour.*, XII, 690 (1926).

use of ingenious subtleties to protect minor culprits from disproportionate punishments. Some judges and many juries evaded their clear duties under the law. Called to fix the value of goods stolen, for which theft the penalty might be death, juries made absurd undervaluations to avoid the hard penalty and judges approved the fiction. Procedure, too, was hard on the defendant even at the dawn of the seventeenth century. The grim Jeffreys himself said in 1684:

"I think it is a hard case, that a man should have counsel to defend himself for a two-penny trespass, and his witnesses examined upon oath; but if he steal, commit murder or felony, nay, high treason, where life, estate, honour, and all are concerned, he shall neither have counsel, nor his witnesses examined upon oath."

The instincts of humanity were stirred by these hard laws, and slowly the law yielded to public opinion. But as with many other legal reforms, the process of change did not substitute new for old. It retained the old forms but rendered them impotent. In the administration of criminal law, in the seventeenth and eighteenth centuries, technicalities came to be used solely to mitigate the severity of the penal law. An artificial and tautological form of indictment developed. Certain rights and presumptions designed to protect the accused against harsh prosecution became established principles of the common law. Some of these were the presumption of the innocence of the defendant; his right to be confronted with the witnesses against him; his right not to be compelled to be a witness against himself, and the right to a verdict by a jury of his peers. The American states, besides preserving the above principles in most of the state constitutions, added two of their own, based on the fear of oppression which followed the Revolutionary period of American history, the inferior position of the judge in the conduct of the trial, and the rights of appeal allowed the defendant.[2]

The age of Bentham ushered in an era of fundamental legal reconstruction in England, and the rigors of the criminal law were modified to conform with the new state of the public mind.

[2] Report to the Council of the American Law Institute of a special committee on *A Plan for the Preparation of a Code of Criminal Procedure*, November 20, 1925.

This made necessary the reconstruction of criminal procedure, which was accomplished during the nineteenth century. It culminated in the Judiciary Act of 1873, which swept away the English system of common-law pleading. It is an interesting and somewhat disquieting fact that although the renascence in the field of procedural law had its inception in the United States, with the launching of the New York *Code of Civil Procedure* of 1848 the very state which originated the reform movement slipped back into the artificialities that reform was designed to remove, while English procedural law became more and more untrammeled. A federal judge is quoted as saying, "The criminal procedure which we have in our courts today, instead of speaking to us of the present time, takes us back to the time of the Stuarts in England. We have long since passed the time when it is possible to convict an innocent man, and the problem which confronts us today is whether we can convict a guilty man." [3]

II. *Rule Reform*

The contemporary attack upon procedure is quite general. Many criticisms apparently have no specific rules as their objective but proceed against an altogether indefinite and generalized conception of a "system." Upon cross-examination some critics would probably find it difficult to be specific. Yet, quite obviously, not all the rules of criminal procedure can be useless and antiquated. The rules which govern procedure in criminal actions are legion. Collected in compact codes in states like New York and California, they fill scores of printed pages. If subjected to intensive scrutiny most of them would find no critics. The attack, it may be assumed, is provoked by specific rules. What, then, are the rules which cause the trouble?

One of the most convenient methods of reaching an answer to this question is to examine the most important of recent proposals for reform. By disregarding those made by individuals,

[3] Hepburn, C. M., *The Historical Development of Code Pleading in America and England* (Cincinnati, 1897), 116. Field, D. D., *Law Reform in the U. S.*, 25 Am. L. Rev., 515 (1891), Stephen H., *Criminal Law Reforms Since 1822*, 57 The Law Jour., 419 (1922). Since Hepburn wrote, however, great legislative changes have been made in New York.

and limiting ourselves to those which represent the conclusions of responsible groups, and then selecting from such lists a few of the most characteristic, it is possible to determine fairly definitely what are the most commonly criticized aspects of procedure and what have been the more common proposals for reform.

There are eight such lists, published during the past twenty years, which will serve this purpose. The first, and perhaps the most important, is the report issued by a committee of the American Institute of Criminal Law and Criminology which was made public in 1917. Others are a report of the Committee of the National Crime Commission headed by former Governor Herbert S. Hadley, the various reports of the New York State Crime Commission, the California Crime Commission of 1927, the Missouri Association for Criminal Justice, California Crime Commission of 1929, New York Crime Commission of 1930, and the Illinois Crime Survey of 1928. The recommendations made in these reports are quite similar. Certain of the suggestions are made in all of them.

An examination of the proposals for changes in procedure made by these various organizations shows a great variation in the importance of suggestions to amend the rules singled out for attack. Some of the recommendations are of fundamental importance. Others concern trivial matters of detail. In order to discriminate it is advisable to consider them with relation to what seem to be three very well-defined objectives and to group the recommendations in three classes. The first includes a series of the rules which take away from the defense some advantages which he now possesses and, as a consequence, strengthen the position of the prosecution before the court. The second seeks to expedite the final determination of guilt or innocence. The third group includes various changes designed to readjust and redistribute the powers of judge, jury, prosecution and other agencies.

A convenient way to show the nature of the rules most frequently criticized is to list all the proposals for reform and to show the frequency with which each recommendation has been made. In the list which follows, letters indicate the agency making the recommendation in each case. The key to these letters is:

A. American Institute of Criminal Law and Criminology
B. National Crime Committee
C. New York State Crime Commission, 1927
D. California Crime Commission, 1927
E. Missouri Association for Criminal Justice
F. California Crime Commission, 1929
G. New York State Crime Commission, 1930
H. Illinois Crime Survey

The recommendations are:

GROUP I. Measures providing for the modification of safeguards for the defendant:

1. That the defendant be required to give notice, by plea or otherwise, of the nature of his defense—e.g., insanity, alibi, etc.
   A, D, E.

2. That the relative number of peremptory challenges allowed the defendant be reduced.
   B, D, E, G.

3. That the right to take the depositions of witnesses be extended to the state equally with the defendant.
   A, B, C, D.

4. That the presumption of the innocence of the defendant be limited to the duty of the state to prove him guilty beyond a reasonable doubt.
   B, C, D, E.

5. That comment on the failure of the defendant to take the stand and testify in his own behalf be permitted.
   A, B, C, D, E, G, H.

6. That the right of appeal be extended to the state equally with the defendant—except where there is a judgment or verdict of not guilty.
   A, B, C, D, E.

7. That the right of appeal be extended to the people in habeas corpus cases.
   A, D, H.

Most of these suggested changes require no explanation, with the possible exception of 6. Governor Hadley explains this suggestion as follows:

"Under our present practice practically all of the appeals have been taken by the defendants and consequently all of the questions that have been presented to the appellate courts for decision have been questions in which it is claimed the rights of the defendants have been unfairly dealt with. Thus the rights of society have been 'whittled away' by the decisions of the appellate courts because the complaints that the prosecution might have presented to the appellate courts as to adverse rulings by the trial court have not arisen for decision. Therefore in any appeal that is prosecuted by the defendant the state should have the right to ask for a ruling by the appellate court upon any adverse decisions during the trial, as it should also enjoy a right of appeal from any verdict or judgment other than that of 'not guilty'." [4]

It should be noted here that while in the above passage Governor Hadley has suggested, somewhat indirectly, it is true, that rulings of the court that are made in cases resulting in a verdict of not guilty may be appealed by the state in order to have matters of law settled for the benefit of future trials this extension of the right of appeal is not suggested by the other commissions and committees named above. There is fairly definite agreement among them, however, that such an appeal by the state shall be possible in cases in which a judgment or verdict of guilty has been rendered.

Recommendation 5 is designed to remove from the prosecutor the inhibition restraining him from commenting upon the failure of the defendant to take the stand. A former judge of the New York Court of Appeals, Frank H. Hiscock, has stated the purpose and substance of this suggestion:

"The repeal of this provision would cure what is frequently a species of legal hypocrisy whereby courts and jurors are compelled to assume an appearance of disregarding and forgetting something which it is practically impossible for either of them to disregard or forget; and it would also remove the danger, by no means an inconsequential one, that a conscientious district attorney in the heat of a trial may, with honest inadvertence, say something which may be regarded as an intrusion into this prohibitive field of comment and thereby furnish a claim for a reversal." [5]

[4] *Missouri Crime Survey*, 368.
[5] *Columbia Law Rev.*, 253 (1926),

Judge Hiscock has probably stated all that may reasonably be expected of such a change in the rules. Other commentators, however, are much more enthusiastic. The impression seems to prevail that to permit comment upon the failure of the defendant to testify would appreciably increase the proportion of convictions in the American courts. It is difficult to find a substantial basis for such a belief. It is fair to assume that juries inclined to be influenced by the defendant's failure to take the stand will be likely to consider this failure, even in cases where it is not brought to their attention. Unquestionably, as Judge Hiscock states, it is doubtful whether such a modification would "change the result in any great percentage of criminal trials." This has been demonstrated by the experience of Ohio, which in 1913 adopted a rule permitting comment by the prosecution on the failure of the defendant to take the stand.

Inquiry among judges and lawyers who have had practical relations with the courts before and after the change reveals a prevalent opinion that the change has had little effect upon the outcome of cases. It certainly has not justified the hope of many of those who urge its adoption in other states. A wise and experienced Cleveland judge, George Baer, who has served on the bench for twenty years, says of this rule:

> "It is my observation that when the defendant takes the stand, it gives him the opportunity of making an explanation to the jury that often results in an acquittal. The prosecutor's comment on the failure of the defendant to take the stand does not add anything to what the jury would know and take cognizance of."

GROUP II. Measures designed to expedite and facilitate the process of justice:

   1. Reforms relating to indictments: simplification of the form of indictment or information; provisions to facilitate the amendment of defective indictments and the curing of defects by order of court.
   A, B, C, D, E, H.

2. Extradition of witnesses wanted in other states, similar to the extradition of persons accused of crime. The purpose is to help other states which require such witnesses in enforcing their criminal law.

C, D, G.

3. Regulation of bail bonds.

A, B, C, D, E, F, H.

4. Joint or separate trial of joint defendants, in the discretion of the court.

B, E.

5. Provides for rendition of jury verdicts by five-sixths vote of jury, except where the crime charged is, or may be, punishable by death.

G.

6. Scope of new trial when the verdict or judgment is set aside: that the accused be retried on the original charge, though convicted of a lesser offense.

A, B, D, G.

7. Appeals:

A. Prejudicial error: that there be no reversals on appeal for error except in case of miscarriage of justice.

A, B, C, D, E, H.

B. Rules for speeding up proceedings on appeal.

A, B, C, D, E.

C. Extension of power of the court to modify judgment, sentence, etc., on appeal, without necessitating the granting of a new trial.

A, B, D, E, H.

D. Simplification of the charge to the jury, to lessen the possibility of error.

F, H.

The reforms suggested in this group are intended to expedite trials through the elimination of so-called technicalities. The purpose of and the necessity for these are quite obvious, with the exception of 3, which has already been discussed in Chapter III.

GROUP III. Measures designed to redistribute the powers possessed by various agencies involved in the criminal process:

1. The alternative use of indictment or information.
   A, B, C, H.
2. Enlarged control of the trial by the judge.
   A, B, C, D, H.
3. Waiver of jury trial by the defendant.
   B, C, D, F, H.
4. Control of selection of the jury by the court.
   B, C, D, H.
5. Proceedings in cases involving insanity.
   B, C, D, E, F.
6. Regulation of granting of probation, pardon and parole.
   B, C, D, E, F.

The proposals embodied in Group III are of distinct importance. They tend toward reorganization of the whole criminal process. Taken in the aggregate, they display a tendency to reduce the importance of the jury through increasing the powers of the judge. They are, of course, much more than the usual modifications in the rules of criminal procedure. For this reason they should be reserved for specific consideration and treatment. No. 1 has been discussed elsewhere,[6] and the others are considered in subsequent chapters.

III. *The Importance of Procedural Reform*

Any candid examination of the foregoing summary of reforms must raise serious doubts as to the fundamental importance of an attack upon the shortcomings of American criminal jus-

[6] In my *Politics and Criminal Prosecution*, Chapter VI.

tice, limited to such procedural details as the ones named. These changes merely readjust the details of the game; they do not make it any less a game. They do not constitute a particularly formidable or far-reaching reorganization of procedure. They represent, at most, piecemeal reform. They show no disposition on the part of legal reformers to depart very far from the present norms of the traditional criminal process.

They do not notably aid in bringing the processes of criminal justice into harmony with our advancing scientific knowledge of crime and criminals. They constitute a few details in the methods pursued in a legal conflict between the state and the defense, and provide, in this contest, certain advantages for the state. Their adoption would probably result in making conviction easier; but that does not necessarily mean that more criminals would be convicted. As has been shown elsewhere, the criminal process is largely conducted outside of the courtroom, and an accurate measurement of it is achieved not through a determination of the number of convictions but through a consideration of the concessions which one side or the other is compelled to make. It is quite probable that if it were not so easy to secure an acquittal before a jury, the proportion of those who plead guilty would be somewhat larger and of those who do plead guilty a few more would plead guilty to the offense charged rather than to a lesser offense; but it is easy to see that the changes that would be brought about by an adoption of all of the reforms above suggested would not be a serious change in the relative positions of the two parties.

Moreover, the long perspective necessary in viewing the criminal process in order to discern the reasons why it operates so imperfectly shows rules of procedure falling within a rather diminished area. The advantages possessed by the defendant under the present criminal codes account in only a small degree for the fact that the state punishes so few criminals. It is well known that thousands of crimes are committed for which no one is arrested. Hundreds of persons known to be desperate criminals are repeatedly arrested and are released because no one can, or will, get evidence against them. One of the best known criminal leaders of Chicago has as his police record only two arrests, both of which resulted in dismissals. It is also well known that many persons who could be convicted will not be because police and prosecuting officials do not want to do their duty.

There is no way of proving that prosecutors who now permit the compromise of so many criminal cases before trial will be any less lenient if they are given more advantages in the trial. There is no good reason to suppose that giving them greater advantages in trials will result in anything more than the release of a greater proportion of their energies for their interesting extra-official political pursuits. What is more, the changes in procedure mentioned do not cover the whole range of opportunity for the defendant. It has repeatedly been shown that to close one procedural advantage promptly results in the opening of another.[7] The labor and the effort involved in securing the acceptance by a reactionary legislature of a minor change in procedure may finally come to absolutely nothing.

In some of the speeches and articles criticizing the "technical" nature of criminal procedure and stressing the need for "simplification" the rules are held out as the sole reason for the failure of criminal justice to serve its proper function. Certain critics of criminal procedure may be entirely unconscious of it, but the import of what they say is that criminal justice fails because the rules are antiquated. This statement carries with it very little genuinely convincing evidence. It is presented without any indication that cases are actually lost in large numbers through those same rules of which they complain. In many of the numerous articles which might be cited, little or no discrimination is made between rules which are of fundamental importance and others which every lawyer, in his serious moments, would admit have never changed the result of a single case. The same men who criticize the rules often tell us not to criticize the judges because to do so will bring the bench into disrepute. They also tell us not to criticize the legislature because it will become difficult to get measures passed. In the course of such a policy of timidity, sight is lost of the fact that even with inadequate rules, strong judges and strong prosecutors enforce the law promptly and vigorously.

[7] See my *Politics and Criminal Prosecution,* 44, 45.

Such stressing of the unsubstantial is not helping the American states to solve the problem of crime. It is drawing an inference which is not justified. It suggests that some of the legal critics are apparently quite willing to offer up the rules of procedure as a scapegoat, while many more fundamental difficulties are overlooked.

IV. *The Study of Procedural Rules*

The legal rules which govern an act of judicial administration are intimately related to the mental bent of the person responsible for the act, and to the customs which tradition has created, and it is often difficult to tell whether the rule or the person or the custom is responsible for the result. Mere statistical enumeration is not sufficient. An intensive examination of a few cases is not convincing. Neither is a purely *a priori* conclusion as to what may happen. Such guesses often fall wide of the mark. If those intent upon a reform of criminal procedure wish to present a convincing case, they ought to devise a way to demonstrate with a reasonable degree of certainty what may be expected from the proposals. That such a formula is yet to be discovered is quite certain, although two or three very interesting attempts are on record which are worth describing here.

It is far more easy to find fault with those who propose procedural reform, on the ground that they have no substantial factual basis for their conclusions, than to devise actual ways of getting at such a fact basis with precision. No statistical method has yet been devised to apply scientific measurements to the operation of rules of procedure. The whole study of procedural matters both civil and criminal is still in the realm of guesswork, and there is not much promise that this generation will get far beyond the stage of rough estimates.[8] Two methods of subjecting criminal justice administration have been used within recent years which throw some light upon the problem, although their specific objectives are not the measurement of the effects of rules of procedure.

---

[8] It is significant and gratifying that the new Institute of Law of The Johns Hopkins University has started an attack upon this problem by a very comprehensive study of civil litigation in Ohio.

The first of these has been in use for years. It is merely an elaboration of methods by which clerks of courts have from time immemorial reported their cases. The first systematic development of this plan, which has been variously named, was in the early reports of the Chicago Crime Commission. Beginning with 1909, this organization tabulated the results of cases tried in the criminal courts of Cook County. As will be shown in a subsequent chapter, the Chicago Crime Commission based its operation upon a card index of these cases, the procedural history of each case being entered upon a card which was filed in the offices of the commission. At the end of the year it was a simple matter to draw from these files the total number of cases disposed of in various ways during the year and to elaborate these into tabulations. In the survey of criminal justice conducted in Cleveland in 1921 the method of the Chicago Crime Commission was adopted, and somewhat more elaborate tabulations were made. These were somewhat aptly called "mortality tables" by Alfred Bettman, one of the staff of the *Cleveland Survey*. The figures which have been used in some of the preceding chapters of this book throw light upon those stages in the criminal process which account for the disposal of large numbers of cases and thus draw attention to certain procedural and administrative steps. Beyond this, however, they do not measure the significance or the effects of rules of procedure. For example, a case may be dismissed on motion of the defendant's counsel because the indictment is faulty or for many other reasons, but in the tabulation the case merely appears as having been dismissed by the court. It is unreasonable to expect this method of itself to clarify procedural reform.

Another type of factual study which throws some light upon the operation of the rules of procedure first appeared in the *Missouri Crime Survey*. Judge Hugo Grimm, in that volume, presents the results of an analysis of the decisions of the Supreme Court of Missouri in criminal cases over a ten-year period. He was able to present the proportions of cases reversed, remanded and affirmed, also the reasons for reversals and the crimes involved. The analysis of the cases provided an interesting picture of the attitudes of the Supreme Court. A similar study by Dean A. J. Harno of the decisions of the Supreme Court of Illinois over ten years appears in the *Illinois Crime Survey*. Another study, by Professor C. G. Vernier and Philip Selig, Jr., was made of reversals of criminal cases in California over a period of seventy-seven years.[9] All of these studies are useful in showing the extent to which courts of appeal reverse cases for various "technical" reasons and the various errors in applying the rules of procedure which are fatal to a case. They do not, however, provide a complete picture of the rules of procedure in action because they deal with only a small proportion of cases. Furthermore, they possess the limitation that studies of opinions always have. The reason selected by the appellate court on the basis of which it grants a new trial or reverses a verdict outright may not be the real reason at all. An appellate court may be denied the right of reviewing the merits of a case, but a reading of the record convinces the judges that substantial injustice has been done. A decision is handed down that looks as if technical considerations are paramount, but really a substantial injustice is being remedied by a technical gesture. It has never been hard for appellate courts to wear the livery of legalism in serving the substantial ends of justice.

The study of procedural rules must, if it is to be helpful, adopt a combination of several techniques. It must content itself with minor and tentative results until a long period of intensive and, it may be added, expensive work has been done. Such research should have several characteristics:

1. It should proceed in the courts of a number of different states which offer contrasting types of procedural rules.
2. It should be done by the close observation of cases proceeding through the trial stage.
3. The observers should be trained, not only in legal technique but in the sort of skill in observation acquired by the best newspaper reporters.
4. The recorded observations of a case should be a complete case history, including not only what was done, but so far as possible an explanation of why it was done.

[9] Published as "The Reversal of Criminal Cases in the Supreme Court of California," 2 *So. Cal. Law Rev.*, 21 (1928).

5. A study of the reports of the field observers should be made as they are turned in, but only tentative conclusions should be made until such study has been under way for several years.
6. Such work should preferably be supported by philanthropic effort. The long, sustained effort it entails would make such non-political support almost a necessity.

V. *The Model Code of the American Law Institute*

In spite of objections to procedural reform which does attempt the revolutionary, there is need for a systematic attempt to simplify the rules now in use. Such a simplification can best be achieved by some national agency which prepares for the various state legislatures a model code, complete in every respect and based upon the broad outlines of the system now generally in use. Fortunately the American Law Institute conceived it to be one of its functions to undertake the preparation of such a code, and in 1925 authorized it. Professors W. E. Mikel and E. R. Keedy of the University of Pennsylvania were selected, and the work has been proceeding with the assistance of an advisory committee of lawyers and law teachers. The result of this labor will be a completely integrated code which has had the consideration of a group thoroughly informed as to the practice and experience of the various states and every section of which has been constructed with due regard to the organic unity of the whole. In a country where the rules of procedure have "just growed," and where changes have been made only through the casual and unenlightened tinkering of a thousand legislative sessions, such a workmanlike model will serve a genuinely useful purpose.

It would be very unwise to draw the inference from this chapter that such a task as the American Law Institute is performing is not of great importance. It is undoubtedly the first step to be taken in the larger task of readjusting the procedural and substantive law to the needs of a changed world. The work of Professors Mikel and Keedy is being carried on with such scrupulous care and with such conscientious consideration at every step, for the legitimate rights of defendants, that the completed code will stand for a long time as a superb expression of the legitimate rights of the individual before the courts. This code will probably be widely adopted and will forestall hasty and unwise changes in the law which various states are bound to attempt in response to waves of public opinion demanding more severity for defendants in criminal cases. It is always to be assumed that a legislature is likely to pass ready-made legislation, especially if it comes to them with the great prestige of such an organization as the American Law Institute. There is no reason to suppose, as some doctrinaire critics of the code assume, that to pass the code in its present form will seriously interfere with a much more radical readjustment of criminal procedure. There is no need for indulging extravagant hopes of a rapid drift among the forty-eight states in the direction of radical change in this dealing with crime. In the generation or two that must elapse before such changes take place, the rights of defendants must be adequately protected, and there is no more practical way to do so than to provide for legislative action a code written with such workmanlike skill as that of the American Law Institute.

CHAPTER VII

THE DECAY OF TRIAL BY JURY

WHILE the point remains unproved and may not be susceptible of proof, there are many symptoms which suggest the decline, if not the utter dissolution, of trial by jury in criminal cases. The flood of current criticism of the jury system is probably an outward sign of a deep underlying distrust. Certainly the tone of the proposals of responsible and thoughtful lawyers and judges, the trend of legislation and the bent of administrative practice, signify a fundamental transition. It may mean that we are witnessing in these days a legal evolution as epochal as that of centuries ago when the ordeal, the trial by fire, or battle, slowly yielded to the jury system. Or it may be the less portentous process of a partial shift of power from jury to judge and prosecutor. In either case, the tendency is marked and quite unmistakable. The more significant factors in this drift are the increasing extent to which criminal cases are terminated by means of some agreement or compromise among the interested parties and agencies, the argument for and the legislative drift toward increasing the power of the judge, and the slowly growing practice of permitting defendants to elect trial by the judge, without a jury.

I. *The Jury Under Fire*

Now that all aspects of the League of Nations have been thoroughly and almost universally debated, those valiant oracles of public sentiment, the high school debating teams, have turned their attention to the jury system. During the past five years this apparently has been discussed more widely than almost any other public question. There are sentimental, legal, statistical, psychological, historical and many other kinds of arguments for its abolition, while, on the other side, those who argue against its abolition find no difficulty in overwhelming their opponents with a demand that something better be substituted. As a subject for a debate, the abolition of the jury is admirable, but as a practical question for the serious consideration of statesmanship and scholarship in this country, it is rather empty. In the first place, no one with any practical sense of reality expects the jury to be legally abolished in this or the next generation, and no one with any sense of critical discrimination will admit that there are any dependable data current in all this discussion which warrant an opinion as to whether the system should be discarded.

Note the naïveté of one exponent of reform:

"In the interest of justice, truth, efficiency and economy, this elimination of the use of the jury should be speeded up until its use is reduced to a minimum, with the definite understanding that it be abandoned entirely as soon as society can be induced to adopt the only intelligent course open to it—that of placing the whole matter of dealing with crime in the hands of persons specially trained to deal with it." [1]

Thus the reader is exhorted to speed up the elimination of the use of the jury and to enter into a "definite understanding" with some unnamed party who, it seems, can abolish the jury, this covenant to be fulfilled when "society" can be induced to adopt an intelligent course. And presumably by that time there will be persons "specially trained" to deal with crime.[2] This simple conception of how suspensory agreements can be made with the forces that change institutions is refreshing but not wholly reassuring.

Like many other brands of dissatisfaction, discontent over the jury system has been intensified by the workings of prohibition. Juries have, in plain disregard of the law and the evidence, brought in verdicts of acquittal not only for violators of the prohibition laws but for those who have killed violators of the prohibition laws. In both cases, the opposition has been loud in its denunciation of the juries and of the system under which they operate. Not only in prohibition cases, but in certain other

[1] Parsons, *Crime and the Criminal* (New York, 1926), 221.
[2] In spite of the apparent doubts of the more enlightened psychiatrists of this generation, see p. 136.

well-advertised criminal prosecutions, have juries brought upon their heads the weight of criticism. In the Sinclair and Fall-Doheny cases, the juries which brought in acquittals were subjected to very widespread censure.

This criticism frequently revolves around the personnel of the jury. It is undeniable that the more fortunate and better educated persons in a community are successful in avoiding jury service. Undoubtedly they are more determined to get off and the state offers them legal loopholes. They are, moreover, in numerous instances, deliberately excluded from personal-injury cases because of their remote or immediate connection with corporations of a capitalistic nature. In a corporate age such as ours, this means that most persons spend much of their period of jury service in idleness, or in lengthy, unpleasant and often impertinent examinations by lawyers.

It may be presumed that this absence of the well-to-do and the well-educated, whether voluntary or compulsory, means that the quality of juries will fall below the level of the average of the community.[3]

In New York, the following exemptions are made by law:

Clergymen, physicians or surgeons, dentists, licensed embalmers, pharmacists, optometrists, veterinary surgeons, undertakers, lawyers, professors and teachers, editors, editorial writers, and reporters, office-holders, foreign consuls, captains, engineers, officers and pilots of vessels making regular trips, railroad superintendents, conductors and engineers (other than street railways), telegraph operators, grand jury or sheriff's jurors, members of the Old Guard or of the National Guard, a general or staff officer, members of National Guard discharged after five years' service, persons honorably discharged from the military forces of the state after seven years' service, all veterans of the Civil War, veteran firemen, persons physically incapacitated, firemen, policemen, and duly licensed engineers of steam boilers.

To remedy this tendency, newspapers, surveys, women's clubs, civic organizations, bar associations, and other well-intentioned community forces have begged the better brethren to show more "civic pride," to become more public-spirited, to respond quickly and ostentatiously to the call of the jury commissioner. It will,

[3] See, for example, *Criminal Justice in Cleveland,* where it is shown that excuses of "illness" or failure to get mail or some other reason were given more frequently by those residing in the "better" residential districts than elsewhere, 340-343.

however, require more than mere unsupported optimism to make a very convincing case as to the likelihood that these appeals to public service will have any noticeable effect upon the personnel of juries.

Moreover, those who lightly assume that the more fortunate classes are the "best" jurors should bear in mind that a great deal of scientific investigation must be done before it can be granted that a jury drawn from a less fortunate economic class, consequently, a class without the advantages of formal education, will reach a fixed standard of justice any less readily than a group drawn from a higher economic scale and with more education, loaded as such groups always are with a heavy burden of irrational prejudice, traditions and selfish interests. And if it is possible to place nice valuations, rates and ratios in balancing tradition against ignorance, what, it may be inquired, should a standard of justice be? Much of the argument on this point seems to assume some undetermined, perhaps indeterminate, standard. The answer to this perennially argued question is still in the lap of the gods—or, perhaps, of the psychologists. It has not yet appeared to ordinary mortal men.

This, however, is not so serious as it seems, because in the last analysis the juries in all the states judge the law and the facts, whether they say so or not. The modification of the present law in several states might lessen the obvious absurdity of the system, but the change would be merely formal. It is not likely that the actual result of such a change would be important. Even judges are sometimes unable to distinguish law from fact; and juries, after in some way reaching the conclusion that a certain end is desirable, will pay little attention to what the judge has said about law and facts. This tendency is well illustrated by the story about the judge who instructed a jury to bring in a verdict of a certain nature, "unless you feel that you know more about the law than I do." The judge was extremely irritated when he found that they had entirely disregarded his legal advice, so he reminded them of his charge, whereupon the foreman of the jury replied, "Well, Jedge, I reckon we considered that point, too."

It is quite probable that in the length and breadth of the

land, juries will continue in spite of any advice to consider all the points, legal and otherwise, which enable them to reach a conclusion agreeable to their sense of what should be done. Yet, in many cases, it is doubtful whether the questions at issue are proper subjects for juries. Matters of fact are often as difficult for an average juryman to grasp as matters of law. What qualifications, for instance, has a second cook, forty-five years old, for judging whether naval officers had reason to suspect trouble with Japan in 1921? And how could a steamfitter's apprentice, twenty-four years old, know whether the exchange of royalty oil for construction work was an improper invasion of the legislative field by the executive; or, a news stand proprietor, who happened to be the foreman of the Fall-Doheny jury, know whether $100,000 sent in cash by Doheny to Fall was a bribe or a loan, and whether in either case it was the consideration of a contract containing a joker clause under which the lease was subsequently granted? These are the kinds of questions upon which equally unqualified persons are passing judgments in court every day. The very fact that they approach such problems without predisposition or previous knowledge raises serious questions. One juror is quoted as having said, "I don't read the newspapers hardly at all. Maybe the comic page once in awhile, or the baseball news or a big accident, but that's all. I don't have the time. I work every day, and at night I'm out having a good time. I never heard of any of those cases. I guess if they had anything to do with this trial they would have told us about them." [4]

Then, too, the sensational cases which have caused much of the recent criticism of the juries have in reality been attempts to establish in a court of law propositions which are almost impossible to prove. The Daugherty and the Sinclair cases involved the crime of conspiracy. To secure conviction for this crime, the prosecution must prove that there has been a plotting or scheming together to accomplish an unlawful purpose or act, and that an act has been done to achieve the purpose of the conspiracy. When a judge charges that all of the points must be proved, the jury, if it is honest, must usually return a verdict to the effect that they have not been proved. The trouble with

[4] "The Sinclair Jury Explains," by Paul Y. Anderson, *The Nation*, May 9, 1928.

enforcing the law against conspiracies is that conspiracy is hard to prove. The jury is not to blame. A frank prosecutor is usually quite willing to admit this. The special assistant attorney-general who tried one of the most sensational conspiracy cases of recent years concludes:

"If we regard the Stoneham, Daugherty and Sinclair cases as illustrative, their careful study will serve to establish, so far as the juries' part in the verdicts is concerned, a high sense of fairness, an almost astonishing ability to comprehend and digest the facts, and a discriminating intelligence of the highest order in applying them to the law as expounded by the court. What is more, it will disclose a sturdy readiness, which is more fundamentally laudable, to resist popular clamor and hue and cry." [5]

There is no disposition here to claim that efforts to improve the administration of the jury system are not wholly commendable. In the face of the almost settled fact that the jury will remain with us permanently as a means of determining certain questions, some improvements are highly desirable. One of the most hopeful attempts at improvement is the "Blue Ribbon" jury provision of the law of New York State. It provides that in each county having a population of one million or over, a special jury panel may be provided. The commissioner of jurors in a county having the required population may "select from the persons qualified to serve as trial jurors in such county such numbers of special jurors as the justices of the Appellate Division of the Supreme Court, or a majority of them . . . from time to time direct." In practice, the commissioner of jurors asks certain substantial citizens on the general jury list to act as special jurors, and these are used in important cases.

When we turn from the uncertainties involved in the arguments against, the criticisms of, and the proposed substitutes for the jury, and direct attention to actual tendencies in law administration, the going is much more certain. Here it is possible to speak of ascertainable facts, and these show such a positive drift toward the decline of the use of the jury that there is little point in either wasting our efforts arguing about the abolition of a thing which is actually abolishing itself, or in proposing sub-

[5] House, Victor, "Are American Juries at Fault?" *Atlantic Monthly,* 142: 227 (Aug., 1928).

stitutes or remedies for an agency which is stricken with a fatal illness. The criminal jury may already be in the twilight of doomed institutions.

A hundred years ago, Lord Brougham made this classic statement:

> "In my mind, he was guilty of no error, he was chargeable with no exaggeration, he was betrayed by his fancy into no metaphor, who once said, that all we see about us, Kings, Lords and Commons, the whole machinery of the State, all the apparatus of the system and its varied workings, end in simply bringing twelve good men into a box."

In the modern American community, however, the work of getting twelve good men into the box is one of the least important things with which the machinery for the administration of criminal justice is concerned. In New York County, for example, in the year 1925 only 455 felony cases reached the end of a jury trial, although 1,932 were actually found guilty; and 19,884 cases were initiated by the police. Thus, all the vast machinery for the consideration of felony cases in New York County, including a district attorney's office with about fifty assistants, approximately twenty magistrates holding preliminary hearings, an army of police, clerks, probation officers, and others—were engaged in the business of enforcing the criminal law with regard to felony cases, but only a handful of the cases actually involved selection of a jury. About the same relative unimportance is attached to practically every jury in the United States. Thus, in the administration of the criminal law, trial by jury is coming to assume an aspect of less and less importance in the determination of criminal cases.[6] Another way in which the jury is declining, and this is significant, is through the use of trial by judge in a number of American jurisdictions, chiefly in misdemeanor cases, and, in several states, in felony cases. Wherever this method has been put into operation, defendants elect, in marked majority, to be tried by the judge rather than by the jury. Thus trial by jury loses favor not only with judges and prosecutors but with defendants and their lawyers as well. Finally, there is a distinct

---

[6] See the chapters entitled "The Vanishing Trial Jury," and "Justice by Compromise" in my *Politics and Criminal Prosecution* for a detailed discussion of this tendency.

tendency in the law to limit the jury's powers in the actual trial of cases, and to give the judge more authority over them and more control over their decisions. Everywhere there is a tendency in the direction of administering criminal justice without the use of juries. In the face of this drift it would seem to be beside the mark to discuss remedies.

Nor is the steady decline in the use of the jury in criminal cases by any means confined to the United States. There is the same tendency in England, where for nearly ten centuries the jury has been a significant institution in the judicial system. The last year for which statistics are available over ten per cent were handled by the court directly without a jury, in 1926.

If we consider further that a considerable proportion of the ten per cent who elect to be tried by jury subsequently plead guilty, it is apparent that only a handful of cases actually reach a jury. An eminent English jurist observes that "the criminal jury is smoldering to extinction without protest and with little debate." [7]

It is idle to speculate upon what may take the place of the jury. The persons who would, in no sense, trust a thing of value to its caprice would probably rise to its support if a serious effort were made to bring about its abolition. A dying monarchy is precious only as an emblem. It would seem that if those who recognize and deplore the shortcomings of the jury trial would turn their attention to the limitation of the jury by placing more authority in the judge and properly supervising administrative activities, such as bargaining for pleas of guilty and other devices, more substantial progress could be made in effecting rational reform in judicial administration. Practically all reforms and methods of control look to the judge as the hope of a more effective enforcement of control. A small residuum of criminal cases will always remain in which jury trials will be necessary and desirable.

[7] Five per cent is the estimate of an American student of the English courts. Pendleton Howard, "Trial by Jury," *Century Magazine*, April, 1929.

II. *The Judge's Control of the Jury*

In the year 1670 two persons, named Penn and Meade, were placed on trial in the Old Bailey Court for the crimes of "tumultuous assembly" which, it appears, consisted, in this case, in Penn's preaching a sermon in Gracechurch Street. According to Stephen the trial was distinguished by the remarkable presence of mind and vigor of expression of the defendants, although, since the trial was reported by the defendants themselves, it may be that much of what they said they said was what they later thought they should have said. The dispute between the court and the defendants waxed so warm, we read, that the Lord Mayor so far forgot his dignity as to tell Meade that "he deserved to have his tongue cut out," and subsequently both defendants were removed to the "Bail Dock," which they describe as a "stinking hole." The jury could find no other verdict than that Meade was not guilty and that Penn was guilty of "speaking in Gracechurch Street." Subsequently, according to Penn, the jury was shamefully reviled and locked up for the night "until 7 the next morning (being the 4th instant, vulgarly called Sunday)." Ultimately the jury returned the verdict of not guilty for both, "though not until the Recorder had expressed his admiration for the Inquisition and the Mayor had said he would cut Bushell's (the foreman's) throat as soon as he could." [8] The members of the jury were fined forty marks apiece and sentenced to prison until payment was made. Bushell and his fellow jurors obtained a writ of *habeas corpus* and the judges who heard the argument on the writ decided that the discretion of the jury to believe the evidence or not could not be questioned and the jury was therefore discharged from custody without paying the fines. This, it appears, was the last instance in which an attempt was made to question the absolute right of a jury to find such a verdict as it thinks is right.[9]

This case, best known as "Bushell's case," which stands in the history of criminal procedure as decisive in regard to the proper

[8] Stephen, *History of Criminal Law of England*, I, 374.
[9] *Ibid.*, I, 375.

function and right of the jury, ended a long struggle between jury and judge in English jurisprudence. In the reign of Edward III, the judge had so far controlled juries that they were occasionally locked up without food or fire to hasten their agreement, and if they took unduly long, they might be placed in a cart, carried to the border of the county, and upset in a ditch. If jurors ignored the orders of a judge and acquitted victims when he had directed that convictions be found, he might fine and imprison them. In 1667, however, Parliament took official notice of this state of affairs and by resolution declared the practice illegal. Since that time the power of the jury to find a decision in accordance with their own view of the evidence has been fairly well established. The English practice, however, has never prevented the judge from freely offering his recommendations to the jury and his opinions concerning the various questions which they were called upon to decide.

Under the rules which, at present, govern most of the state courts in the United States, the judge has numerous, if not important, powers. The famous American judge, Chief Justice Shaw of Massachusetts, says that "it is within the legitimate power, and it is the duty of the court, to superintend the course of the trial; to decide upon the admission and rejection of evidence; to decide upon the use of any books, papers, documents, cases or works of supposed authority, which may be offered on either side; to decide upon the collateral and incidental proceedings; and to confine the parties to the issue." [10] The judge has many powers which are necessary to the order and dignity of the courtroom. He may clear the room of spectators if they become noisy and unduly demonstrative. He may order night sessions where it seems advisable. His permission is necessary if tests or experiments are to be performed in the presence of the jury. The trial judge enjoys a wide discretion in controlling witnesses. He may regulate their conduct on and off the stand, urge them to greater speed and accuracy of statement, prevent verbosity and levity. He may force responses to questions and may, upon the request of the witness, give assistance in interpreting questions. In some states whenever justice requires it, the judge may himself conduct

[10] Commonwealth v. Porter, 10 Metcalf, 263.

an examination of witnesses. He may put questions which are properly intended to elicit information on material points of the case.

Under present practice in most of our state courts, the selection of a jury is largely in the hands of counsel. In England and Canada the judge takes an active part. In this respect the results show a sharp contrast. Notorious examples are on record of the time and expense involved in American practice. In California the selection of a jury once took ninety-one days, and in Chicago 4,821 jurors were examined at a cost to the state of $13,000. In another Chicago case a jury was obtained after exactly one month spent in questioning more than one thousand veniremen.

Canada affords an interesting contrast where Justice Ridell of the Ontario Supreme Court can say, "I have never in my thirty years' experience seen it take more than one-half an hour to get a jury, even in a murder case, and never but once heard a juryman ask a question." He amends this statement, however, by citing a special case in 1927 when it took nearly forty-eight minutes to find a jury, "a record time in my experience." [11]

The English practice is similar:

"The impaneling of an English jury is a dignified and impressive performance. They have already been selected for character and intelligence, like the judges themselves, and their names can be obtained by counsel for a shilling in advance of the trial, if there is any desire to investigate them with a view to a challenge. As a matter of fact, this list is almost never asked for. The clerk, as the representative of the Government, not of the parties, draws and swears them, thus giving them a status independent of the contending parties, like that of the judge on the bench. Freed from the hostile inquisition of the rival lawyers, the jurors undoubtedly approach the case in much more judicial frame of mind than would be possible under the American practice and this clearly manifests itself in a closer cooperation between jury and judge." [12]

It is important to note that the difference between English and American practice is largely due to the personnel of jury panels, not as is commonly understood to the power of the judge.

[11] In a letter to the *New York Times*, November 12, 1927.
[12] Sunderland, E. R., quoted in *N. Y. Crime Comm. Report, 1927,* 54.

In addition to some recommendations that the types of those exempt from jury service should be greatly curtailed, the most common recommendation would place within the power of the judge the determination of whether a prospective juror could render a fair and impartial verdict in spite of having read or heard of the case and in spite of having formed an opinion as to the guilt or innocence of the accused. This, it will be noted, places great power in the hands of the judge, but after all, if power in regard to such a question is to be vested in anyone, it would seem that the judge is the only person fit to exercise it and its abuse can easily be controlled by the Appellate Court.

In the exercise of these powers, however, the judge must with punctilious care avoid conveying any direct or indirect expression as to the defendant's guilt, whether by conduct or by words.[13] The Ohio Supreme Court has gone so far as to say:

"A court in charging a jury should so evenly balance the scales of justice as not to indicate by a wink, look, shake of the head, or peculiar emphasis, as to his notions as to which way the verdict should go. When a case is to be submitted to a jury at all, it should be impartially submitted, and if the court feels that the case is so clear as to require an indication from him, he should direct a verdict, and then his action can be easily reviewed in a higher court; but if he gives a charge which looks fair on paper, but which is in fact distorted by his looks, attitudes, emphasis, winks, and rolling of the eyes, an unjust result is often attained which cannot be corrected in the higher court."[14]

His control over the jury is limited. He may discharge the jury in case it is manifestly unlikely that an impartial verdict will be rendered. He may order a new trial when any juror is known to communicate with improper outside sources. He may recall the jury from its deliberations and give it further instructions in open court. He may even communicate privately with the jury if such communication is not prejudicial to the defendant. He may receive a confidential communication from the jury if he makes no reply to it and takes no action regarding it. He may not, however, threaten to discharge them for the remainder of the term for failing to reach an agreement. He may not threaten to

[13] As to conduct, see People v. Becker, 210 N. Y., 274.
[14] 68 O. S. 614, 622.

hold them without food until they agree. While he may direct an acquittal where the state's case is manifestly weak, he may not, according to the best opinion, direct a verdict of guilty.[15]

The most important power which is specifically denied the judge is that of commenting upon the evidence.

"At present in some forty-two states the trial judge is prohibited by constitution, statute, or controlling decision from commenting upon the weight or credibility of the testimony. . . . In some states he may review the evidence, but he must not indicate his opinion about it; and in none of them can he say a word as to the credibility of a particular witness. In some half dozen states the court has the privilege of comment. . . . In the federal courts the privilege is unimpaired. . . . The prevailing practice is unwise and it should be provided by statute:

"The trial judge may express to the jury, after the close of the evidence and arguments, his opinion as to the weight and credibility of the evidence or any part thereof." [16]

The powers which we have described with reference to judges in state courts are, in reality, an outline of the powers enjoyed by a referee in a game which must be played in accordance with specific rules and in which the entire interest, so far as the court is concerned, is in seeing that the rules are obeyed and that "the best man wins." They do not describe a judge who is in any sense the representative of an all powerful state which is essentially concerned about seeing that justice is done. Justice, in accordance with these rules, consists in protecting the parties in a well-ordered game. The interest of the state in the fundamental question of convicting or acquitting a defendant rests primarily with the jury.

In the English courts and in the federal courts the position of the judge is quite different. It is not clear that the federal courts have exercised this power from the time of their establishment, but it is clear that in the course of a period of Federalist control over the courts in the early years of the nineteenth century, they came to utilize this power and to establish what seems now to be

[15] Lucas v. Commonwealth, 118 Ky., 818. Perkins v. State, 50 Ala., 154. People v. Berridge, 212 Michigan, 577. For a good summary of these powers, see 19 *Michigan Law Review*, 228.
[16] *The Laws of Evidence, Some Proposals for its Reform* (Prof. Morgan's Committee). In 1928 the laws of Louisiana were amended so as to give the power to comment on the evidence to the trial judge.

a permanent right to exercise vastly greater powers than have generally been allowed the state courts. That this power was exercised from the beginning without clear recognition of the fact that although the judge might offer advice, the jury was wholly free to accept or reject it, is shown in a statement made in 1792 by John Jay, the first Chief Justice:[17]

"It may not be amiss here, gentlemen, to remind you of the good old rule that in questions of fact, it is the province of the jury, in questions of law, the province of the judge to decide. But it must be observed that by the same law which recognizes this reasonable distribution of jurisdiction, you have nevertheless a right to take upon yourselves to judge of both, and to determine the law as well as the fact in controversy. On this and every other occasion, however, we have no doubt you will pay that respect which is due to the opinion of the court; for, as on one hand, it is presumed that juries are the best judges of the facts, it is, on the other hand, presumable that the courts are the best judges of the law. But still both objects are within your power of decision. . . . Go, then, gentlemen, from the bar, without any impressions of favor or prejudice for one party or the other; weigh well the merits of the case, and do on this as you ought to do on every occasion, equal and impartial justice."

At the present time a federal judge may comment upon the evidence quite freely if he makes it clear at the time that the jury is entitled to reject his advice. In a case decided in 1920, the Supreme Court upheld, although it condemned as regrettably peremptory, the following statement made to a jury by a federal judge: [18]

"In conclusion, I will say to you that a failure by you to bring in a verdict in this case can arise only from a wilful and flagrant disregard of the evidence and the law as I have given it to you, and a violation of your obligation as jurors. . . . I cannot tell you in so many words to find the defendant guilty, but what I say amounts to that."

There is little question about the effect upon a jury of such comment as a judge may make. His influence is so great that his opinion is, if widely exercised, almost conclusive. A great constitutional lawyer clearly points this out:

[17] Georgia v. Bradsford, 3 Dallas 1.
[18] Horning v. Dist. Col., 254 U. S. 135 (1920).

"A judge who urges his opinion upon the facts to a jury decides the cause while avoiding the responsibility. How often would a jury be found bold enough to declare their opinion in opposition to that of the judge upon the bench, whose words would fall upon their ears with all the weight which experience, learning and commanding position must always carry with them? What lawyer would care to sum up his case if he knew that the judge, whose words would be so much more influential, was to declare in his favor, or would be bold enough to argue the facts to the jury, if he knew the judge was to declare against him?" [19]

The previous chapter has shown that the main theme of much of the recent discussion concerning the revision of criminal procedure has been to propose amendments which have the effect of reducing or limiting the advantages possessed by defendants in criminal trial. It seems to be taken for granted that juries have been altogether too lenient toward defendants and that means ought to be devised to counteract such leniency. One of the suggestions most commonly urged is to restore to the state judge the right possessed by English judges under the common law, and retained by our federal judges, to comment upon the evidence. The late Chief Justice Taft, one of the most outspoken and active exponents of this point of view, made the following statement in 1927:

"This means that the law should not prevent the charge of the court from being enlightening and clarifying. It should obviate the camouflage that is so often created in the courtroom by the skill and histrionic ability of the counsel. We must trust somebody in the supervision of the trial, and that somebody must and should be the judge.

"Neither the English judges nor the judges of the federal court are restricted in the aid which they can give the jury to enable it to understand the real issues and to weigh evidence intelligently. But judges are more restricted in other courts.

"The truth is that the American people in many states have distrusted the judges and preferred to let the juries wander through a wilderness of evidence without judicial suggestion or guide, and often to become subject to an unfair and perverted presentation by counsel of the evidence, leading to a defeat of justice.

"The chance of conviction of innocent persons by a jury of twelve men, of course, by judicial conduct and tyranny must be minimized by fair review on appeal. But the danger is not sufficiently great to require that

[19] Cooley, *Constitutional Limitations*. (Boston, 1868) 147.

the reins should be thrown on the back of the jurors to follow their own sweet will in their conclusions. They constitute the tribunal to pass on the facts, and they are the ultimate judge of the facts.

"But the judge is there, and it should be his sworn duty, with his experience, to help the jury to consider and analyze the evidence and weigh it with common sense." [20]

Advantages other than those presented by Chief Justice Taft, which are claimed for the restoration of the power, are that it would save time and expense by bringing quicker verdicts, would reduce the number of disagreements, and diminish the number of new trials and applications for new trials. It would probably save time by causing attorneys to spend less time in examining prospective jurors with the customary unpleasantness and impertinent objections. It would, moreover, induce the trial judge to pay close attention to the conduct of the trial itself. [21]

The arguments for the restoration of this power, however, have been vigorously contested. For several years there has been before the Senate of the United States the so-called Caraway Bill which would deny to federal judges the power which they now possess to comment upon the evidence. Advocates of this proposed legislation have argued that the federal judges possess altogether too much power, and that they become despotic and intolerant. Such complaints are particularly notable in that section of the press which is opposed to the Eighteenth Amendment. Among the arguments advanced against any change in the law to permit state judges to comment upon the evidence, the most familiar one is that they already possess the power to influence the jury by indirection. This is, of course, true, as is shown by the extent to which the New York Court of Appeals permitted a trial judge to go in charging a jury. [22] The defendant in this case was a man· charged with murdering his wife. The judge, in charging the jury, made the following statement, which the

---

[20] Address by Chief Justice Taft to the National Conference on the Reduction of Crime, Washington, D. C., November 3, 1927. For other discussions of the question, see Root, "Public Service by the Bar," *Proceedings of the American Bar Association*, 1916, 363-364; Muller, "The System of Trial by Jury," 21 *American Law Review*, 859; Sunderland, "An Appraisal of English Procedure," 14 *American Bar Association Journal*, 776; *Illinois Crime Survey*, 167-169.

[21] See Morgan, *The Law of Evidence*, 20-21.

[22] People v. Smith, 180 New York, 125.

court on appeal found to be fair and in no sense commenting upon the facts:

"If you believe from the evidence that masked burglars entered the bedroom occupied by the defendant and his wife, dragged him from his bed into the dining room and allowed him to put on his trousers and his socks because he was cold, sandbagged and pounded him and he made no outcry, compelled him by holding shining revolvers to his head, to disclose where his money was hidden, which they took from under the bureau without disturbing the dust which covered the floor where the cigar box was located, and then bound and gagged him and tied him to the leg of the dining table, upon which there were dishes apparently undisturbed, and then because his wife made an outcry they shot her and then the burglars left the house one or both of them going through the windows upon which there was mosquito netting, without tearing the netting from the window or disturbing the dust on the window sill or the grass under the window, then, gentlemen, it is your duty to acquit him. But if you reach the conclusion that burglars did not enter the house that night and shoot his wife, and that his statements were false, then you may determine from all the facts and circumstances whether of his own accord he put his trousers and socks on, and the purpose of putting them on at that hour of the night."

It is quite doubtful whether such indirection should be encouraged, even though it may occasionally be permissible. Moreover, the judge in the case just cited was taking a long chance in offering such comment and in many states would probably have been reversed. Such instructions, however, are rarely offered.

To the objection that the juries would be indirectly influenced, Professor Morgan has offered the following convincing answer:

"A jury incapable of properly appraising the remarks of an impartial judge, and of exercising its independent judgment in the light of those remarks, is obviously incompetent to determine the credibility of witnesses, to detect the fallacies in the arguments of counsel not unskilled in sophistry, to keep in mind a complicated mass of testimony, distinguishing that actually received from that merely offered, and to analyze the evidence so as to make the truth appear." [23]

Mr. Justice Holmes, moreover, in the Horning case already cited acutely commented that "the jury has the power to bring in

[23] Morgan, op. cit., 18.

a verdict in the teeth of both law and facts, the jury were allowed the technical right, if it can be so called, to decide against the law and facts."

In the English practice, the judiciary has not often over-stepped the bounds of propriety. It is, of course, not altogether common for judges to comment upon the evidence there, but when they do it, it is always in the face of the danger that juries will feel that their rights are being overridden by the judge and unless the judge seems fair and the evidence rather conclusive, the jury is likely to bring in a verdict contrary to the judge's recommendations, if for no other reason than to rebuke the judge who thus attempted to deny the jurymen their apparent rights. Any examination of the practice in English courts shows clearly that the exercise of this power is properly safeguarded by the very fact that juries are not likely to welcome the exercise of unwarranted power by the judge.

The whole question deserves a good deal more research than has been expended upon it. It would be useful to know, for ex-ample, how frequently judges are exercising this power where it is granted to them. It is still more important to know the circumstances under which it is exercised in a series of cases. It is important to know how often juries follow judicial comment. These are questions that remain to be answered and, of course, the fundamental question to be determined is whether such power would attract a better quality of judges to the service of the state. If this could be accomplished as a by-product of such a change, it would unquestionably be worth trying.

III. *The Waiver of Jury Trial*

In the Year of Grace 1743, one John Spurgeon, charged in the Baltimore County Court with selling liquor without a license, "appears and humbly submits himself to the Grace of the Court here, whereupon all and single the premises, &c., considered and by the Court fully understood it appears that there is no cause of presentment against the said John, he is accordingly discharged." Without any formal pleas, issues, juries and verdicts, this case, a misdemeanor, was disposed of by the judge acting alone. This disposition, "upon submission," was common in the province of Maryland, and probably in various other places throughout the American continent.[24]

After many years during which apparently no jury was ever used in a misdemeanor trial, an act was passed in Maryland in 1809 providing that the courts of criminal jurisdiction should "determine on the whole merits of the case which may be to the said courts respectively submitted." For some time, this act of 1809 appears to have been used only for minor cases, but in 1823, James A. Buchanan and James W. McCulloch, indicted for conspiracy to defraud a branch of the Bank of the United States, appeared, pleaded not guilty, and "put themselves on the court for trial instead of the jury," under the act of 1809. Thereafter the act was invoked very frequently in major offenses, there being some difference of opinion as to its use in such cases. In 1852, the legislature enlarged the method of waiving jury trial and finally, in 1860, adopted a measure which provided that,

"Any persons presented or indicted may instead of traversing the same before a jury, traverse the same before the court, who shall thereupon try the law and the facts."

In 1864, the constitution was amended to provide that,

"The parties to any cause may submit the same to the court for determination without the aid of a jury."

Whether this constitutional provision applies to criminal cases seems doubtful, but it has not been necessary to raise the question, because apparently various clauses in the constitution of Maryland providing for trial by jury have never been held to prevent the waiving of a jury trial, if the defendant so desired.[25]

A simple provision for waiver of this kind is the Michigan statute enacted in 1927 which provides that "in all criminal cases arising in the courts of this state, whether cognizable by justices of the peace or otherwise, the defendant shall have the right to

[24] Particularly in Massachusetts; cf. *Massachusetts Law Quarterly*, August, 1923, 7.

[25] These statements of fact are based upon a pamphlet, *The Maryland Practice of Trying Criminal Cases at the Election of the Accused by Judges Alone without Juries*, by Judge Carroll T. Bond, Chief Judge of the Court of Appeals of Maryland. See also an article by Judge Bond in *American Bar Association Journal*, II, 699.

waive a determination of the facts by a jury, and may, if he so elects, be tried before the court without a jury."

The Washington statute expressly excludes capital cases and the New Jersey act does not apply to indictments for murder. In Indiana and Washington the consent of both the prosecuting attorney and the judge must supplement that of the defendant in all cases. In New Jersey it is within the court's discretion to grant or deny the prisoner's request to be tried without a jury. In Maryland, Connecticut, Wisconsin and Michigan, however, only the consent of the accused is required.[26]

All of the states above mentioned have adopted this change recently except Maryland. The Baltimore Criminal Justice Commission claims that ninety-three per cent of the criminal cases in Maryland were tried by judges in 1925, a very considerable increase over ten or twelve years earlier, when about seventy per cent were so tried. In Connecticut it has been reported that about seventy per cent of all criminal cases are tried before judges without juries. In Milwaukee in 1926, there were eighty-six felony trials by jury and 428 by judge. In the trials by jury fifty-six per cent were convicted, in those before a judge the percentage of convictions was about ninety. In Washington, however, it appears that waiver is not common.[27]

The legislature of Michigan in 1927 adopted a provision which provided for the waiver of jury trial "in all criminal trials." An interesting statistical study of the results of this system during the first year of its operation in the Recorder's Court of Detroit has been made by the Sociology Department of the University of Michigan.[28] In this study it was found that, of all criminal cases which reached the trial stage and in which a plea of not guilty was entered, 952 waived jury trial and 634 did not. Thus, approximately three-fifths of the criminal cases which came to trial were tried by the judge alone. This is somewhat less than Milwaukee, Baltimore or Connecticut. This may be because the sys-

[26] For complete list see Code of Criminal Procedure of American Law Institute, Draft No. 2, 250.
[27] *Illinois Crime Survey*, 43.
[28] A preliminary report of this study is embodied in an article, "Waiver of Jury in Felony Trials," by W. Abraham Goldberg, 28 *Mich. L. Rev.*, 163 (1929). The study was made under the direction of Professor Arthur E. Wood.

tem is new. Of those cases in which juries were waived, 59 per cent resulted in convictions; while in those cases which were tried by juries 58 per cent resulted in convictions. The data concerning the type of sentences given in the two classes of cases show clearly that waiver of jury trials resulted for the most part in lighter sentences. This can probably be interpreted largely as a disposition on the part of the judge to be somewhat lenient in cases where the defendant has thrown himself directly upon the mercy of the court. There are complicating factors, however, which should be considered. It is shown in the study that for the most part it was a tendency on the part of defendants who were charged with very serious crimes not to elect to be tried by the judge but rather to go to a jury, and this would necessarily affect the result. It is rather disconcerting for those who argue that trial by the judge is a much more expeditious proceeding to know that it is shown that trial by judge required only a day and a half less than trial by jury. The exact median time intervals for the two methods was slightly less than 32 days in cases where juries were waived, and slightly more than 33 days in cases where juries were not waived.

The rapid growth of the practice of waiving trial by jury in the United States is in accordance with recent English tradition where the extension of "summary" jurisdiction has been very rapid and apparently has been growing in popularity. It should be noted, however, that summary jurisdiction as practiced there permits serious indictable cases to be tried by minor magistrates. The Criminal Justice Act of 1925 further enlarged the schedule of indictable offenses triable summarily. This criminal Justice Act undoubtedly resulted from a recognition of the efficient manner in which the courts of summary justice discharged their functions during the war period. Under the Canadian practice it is possible in most indictable offenses for a defendant to "elect" to be tried by the judge alone.[29] This Canadian legislation has been in operation about twenty years.[30]

The experience of England, Canada and of those American

---

[29] See Crankshaw's *Criminal Code of Canada*, Sec. 771-799.
[30] For a discussion of the Canadian practice and certain reliable opinions concerning it, see report of the *Crime Commission of New York State*, 1927, 88.

states which have adopted this system has been so uniformly satisfactory that it is likely that the practice will extend to other states. The advantages to the prosecution include celerity of trial, saving of expense, a reduction in the number of appeals and reversals. There are advantages for the defendant also, particularly in cases where possible prejudice is likely to be created against the defendant, because of the nature of the crime, the race or color of the defendant, and the extent to which newspapers have exploited the case.[31]

A consideration of such inadequate facts as are now available concerning the work of this system leads to a very important possibility. As has been indicated,[32] there has been a tremendous increase in the number of defendants pleading guilty on arraignment and it is seen that this practice is due to the ease with which defendants, their lawyers, prosecuting officials and judges are able to make adjustments of criminal cases prior to trial. Is it not quite reasonable to suppose if the law be amended to enable a defendant to be tried directly by the judge that he will be more likely to plead not guilty and elect to be tried without a jury, thus placing the entire disposition of his case in the hands of the judge? Some slight evidence points out that subsequent to the adoption of the waiver in Connecticut such a reduction of pleas of guilty took place.[33] One of the most important reasons why a person pleads guilty is because he is able by that means to show the judge that he is willing to trust his fate to him and that through such an expression of confidence, the judge may be inclined to deal with him leniently. This expression of confidence will be just as potent if, under a system of waiver, he elects to be tried by the judge alone. The advantage of a plea of not guilty followed by the waiver of a jury as against the present practice of bargaining for pleas of guilty is very great. The considerations that enter into the final determination of the case are placed in the record. They are subjected to systematic and legally sound rules of evidence. They are submitted to an impartial judge rather than to a prosecutor who is desirous

<hr />

[31] For a further discussion of trial without jury see Maltbie, "Criminal Trials without a Jury in Connecticut," 17, *J. Cr. L.*, 335.

[32] See page 113.

[33] See my *Politics and Criminal Prosecution*, 163.

of reducing the cases which he must try to a jury. In every way a trial by a judge is superior to the bargaining that now takes place. This, it would seem, is the most significant reason for favoring this system.

Thus, from the loss of the jury's prestige and power, the judge emerges as a greatly enhanced figure. Curiously enough this has happened in spite of the fact that there are no signs that the state bench is receiving or is entitled to receive more respect than a generation ago. It is probable that judges are now drawn from a relatively less expert stratum of the bar than they were a half century ago. Certainly there is no marked improvement sufficient to justify turning to the present-day judge to lead the criminal trial out of the wilderness. The present disposition to grant him increased power probably rises partly from a conclusion that the judge with all of his shortcomings is preferable to the jury, partly because a judge, even if far short of the ideal, can perform certain acts better than the best of juries and largely because there is a widespread faith that one way to make the bench better is to give it more power. And such a transition is by no means revolutionary. It is, as Dicey has shown, a return to first principles:

"Trial by jury is open to much criticism; a distinguished French thinker may be right in holding that the habit of submitting difficult problems of fact to the decision of twelve men of not more than average education and intelligence will in the near future be considered an absurdity as patent as ordeal by battle. Its success in England is wholly due to, and is the most extraordinary sign of popular confidence in the judicial bench. A judge is the colleague and the readily accepted guide of the jurors."

CHAPTER VIII

THE RIDDLE OF INSANITY

THE analysis of legal insanity presented in this chapter can
lead to only one conclusion: that the problem of legal insanity, and the related problem of responsibility, must be considered in connection with a much more fundamental question
which goes to the basis of the whole legal theory of crime, and
its punishment. The hopeless confusion of lawyers with regard
to the meaning of insanity, and the growing belief on the part
of psychiatrists that there is no specific insanity and no specific
feeble-mindedness, make it clear that the only sound way to view
the problems occasioned by the commission of an anti-social
act is to consider the extension of some kind of control over the
offender in order that the act may not be repeated. Nothing is
gained by those who argue the value of deterrents. Supervision
and control are needed—needed so much that the specific question of the rightness or wrongness of a given act ought to be
and must be subordinated. The whole drift of this discussion of
the law of insanity is in exactly the same direction as most of
the other subjects considered in this book. They point to the need
for less definiteness and determinateness in fixing responsibility
for crime and more means by which society may supervise the
conduct of those who have committed acts of which society does
not approve.

There are four aspects of criminal justice upon which the
question of mental capacity has a bearing:

1. When a defendant appears before a court, the question
may be raised as to his capacity to be tried at all. His fitness
to plead or to stand trial is usually settled by the presiding judge,
who, ordinarily, is permitted by law to call to his assistance expert
opinion—either that of a commission or of individual physicians
—although in some instances a jury is used for this purpose.

Obviously, the question of a person's capacity to be tried is a good deal easier to settle than that of his responsibility for the crime with which he is charged. The present method of determining this question seems to work in a fairly satisfactory way, although such questions can be met much more readily if there is a clinic within the court itself.

2. Perhaps the most baffling problem facing criminal justice is the determination of the defendant's mental responsibility for the crime with which he is charged. This involves two aspects, both of which have been subject to wide discussion, first, what the legal tests of insanity should be, and second, how the tests are to be applied in the actual trial of cases. In this chapter, these two questions are separately treated under the sub-titles, "The Tests," and "The Expert."

3. In the disposition of cases, psychiatry ought to loom very large. The mental condition of the convicted criminal ought to be considered with regard to whether probation should or should not be granted, with regard to the kind of prison to which he is to be committed, and in connection with the term of imprisonment. Such service can most adequately be provided through a court clinic.

4. Perhaps the most important function which psychiatry can perform with relation to crime is to discover means for the prevention of crime. This involves the much discussed topic of how far mental defectiveness is responsible for certain crimes, the answer to which raises the whole subject of the character, methods and claims of psychiatry itself. It also raises the question of how psychiatry can best be applied in schools and in other institutions in which the child can be studied and guided before criminal tendencies develop.

I. *Changing Conceptions of Insanity*

Maitland's classical dictum, "We study the day before yesterday, in order that yesterday may not paralyze today, and today may not paralyze tomorrow," deserves to be taken seriously by those seeking to reconcile what seem to be hopeless differences between the law and medical science. As Europe emerged from the Middle Ages, ideas about insanity covered a vast range. Great numbers of people regarded it as the mark of an evil visitation. If in an individual case this happened to be the conclusion of authority as well, the unfortunate might be chained in a dungeon, the straw on the floor raked out, as from an animal's cage, and his food thrown in to him. He was sometimes whipped. Sightseers came to gaze upon him. He was in all respects treated as a wild beast. Many insane persons were executed as criminals. In a measure this was a reflection from certain theological doctrines of the period, with belief in a carnal, corrupt body and a detached mind, or soul; leaving no room for the idea of a derangement which might have its root in some disordered bodily function. Madness was a state of wickedness, descending upon the ungodly, and meriting punishment accordingly.[1]

But ample historical evidence attests that this attitude was by no means universal. Among the Greeks, Hippocrates condemned the excessive use of bodily restraint and advised kindly treatment and pleasant work. The insane, so one reads, were cared for in the temple of Æsculapius, the god of medicine. In the temple at Epidaurus a well-known spring provided the means for hydropathic treatment. The Jews, too, made humane provision for the insane, not only in the practice of religion but in the law. The Romans likewise, while seemingly less considerate of the insane, provided, through law, for their rights.

Nor did the recognition of the insane as persons deserving the solicitude of society disappear during the Middle Ages. In many countries monastic charity cared for the mentally deranged with kindness and intelligence. In the very heart of the "Dark Ages" a cleric author gives remedies for melancholia, hallucinations, mental vacancy, dementia, and folly. It is not strange, therefore, that Shakespeare, in this as in many other ways the mirror of the most enlightened thought of his time, should, throughout his plays, manifest a deep and accurate knowledge of the nature, causes and treatment of mental disorder. This is particularly true in *King Lear,* when the doctor explains Lear's

---

[1] Cf. Maudsley, *Responsibility in Mental Disease* (New York, 1896); Jacobi, *The Unsound Mind and the Law* (New York, 1918).

madness and suggests treatment almost wholly in harmony with
the best psychiatry of our day. Such understanding could not
arise from sheer genius. It shows how a great artist gleaned
the most searching ideas about insanity which existed, but were
not current, in a somewhat barbarous age.

Yet the attitude of public authority and of law by no means
reflected this enlightenment. Nearly two centuries after Shakespeare the morbid throngs of London visited Bedlam Hospital [2]
to observe the antics of the insane patients, and it seems that in
a single year more than a hundred thousand persons paid a
penny each for this form of entertainment. In the administration
of the criminal law the insane were often punished for no offense
other than their oddness, which was held to be evidence of being
bewitched. It is difficult to believe that in 1870 an English Lord
Chancellor could be quoted as having declared, so late as 1862,
that "the introduction of medical opinions and medical theories
into the subject has proceeded upon the vicious principle of considering insanity as a disease." [3]

The survival of this mass of superstition until the very middle
of the nineteenth century indicates how difficult it has been to
secure adequate recognition of the rôle of mental disorder in
the causation of crime. If it took so long to learn that insanity
itself is not a crime, it is not strange that even now scant recognition is given to the idea that many crimes are due to insanity. It
is true, as will presently be shown, that as far back as Bracton,
insanity was offered as a defense for crime; but it was recognized
as a valid defense only when the insanity was stark and obvious.
Lesser degrees were not until recently regarded as either explaining or excusing illegal conduct. The scientific exploration of the
border area between what is generally accepted as normal and
that which is obviously psychopathic has not only thrown light
upon criminal behavior but has raised knotty questions as to
the legal term "responsibility."

The psychiatrist's concern is not limited to those whose conduct sharply marks them as distinct from their fellows. He

[2] An abbreviation of Bethlehem (in Hebrew, "house of bread"). This hospital
dated back to the fourteenth century. As early as the beginning of the sixteenth century,
Tyndal used the word "Bedlam" to mean madman.
[3] Doe, J., in State v. Pike, 49 N. H., 399, quoting Hansard, CLXV, 1297.

is concerned with all manner of subtle and almost unseen symptoms. Viewed thus, the term insanity is shorn of its earlier exactness and in the vocabulary of the psychiatrist has ceased to have meaning or standing, although in popular and legal thought it still is the emblem of an indefinite meaning. This development has greatly increased the attention given to mental disease and disorder in the study of crime. Crimes due to mental disorder include many more than the long recognized "madman's" crimes. They include the occasional offense of the emotionally unstable "psychopathic personality," a form of pathological behavior well recognized by science but not by law. Forms of mental disorder have been discovered which explain various sorts of violations of the criminal code, while psychological repressions are recognized as causes of a vast range of juvenile delinquency. This rationalistic mode of accounting for many crimes greatly simplifies the problem of treatment and prevention. It dissipates, in the practice of social welfare and of mental therapy, even if not in law and in the popular mind, the hopelessly irrational notion of free will as applying to all forms of misconduct except that of the "maniac." [4]

This broad view of the nature and possible regulation of human conduct opens the way to a decidedly useful service for the psychiatrist. As Dr. Bernard Glueck, one of the most intelligent of the profession, points out:

"It is still necessary to indicate that this branch of medicine as practiced to-day does not limit its scope to the mere determination of whether a man is defective or insane, or to what degree he may be responsible for a criminal act. It takes hold of the pertinent facts of the various sciences which in one way or another have to do with man as a biologic and social unit and endeavors to determine the relation which these facts may have

[4] An interesting commentary on mental disorder and crime causation was found in the *Missouri Crime Survey* but was omitted from the final report. Experts sent by the National Committee for Mental Hygiene found that Dunklin County, in the extreme southeastern corner of the state, had a very considerable number of "feeble-minded" children. They examined 258 public school children and found fifty-two "feeble-minded" and eighteen of border-line intelligence. Thus more than twenty-seven per cent were defective. In the Survey of Criminal Justice in Missouri conducted soon thereafter, it was found that a greater proportion of murders had been committed in this county than in any other county in the state. The coroner's records indicated twelve homicides in a single year. An examination of all the prosecutions conducted in that county indicated a larger proportion of offenses against the person than were found elsewhere.

to the particular behavior tendencies of an individual. It studies the individual from the point of view of his hereditary background, his physical makeup, the organization of his energies, the intellectual equipment which he has at his disposal in his endeavor to adapt himself to the demands of life. It aims to discover what modification in the innate equipment of a given individual has been brought about by deliberate training and education, good or bad, and by the various life experiences with which he came in contact.

"It aims, furthermore, to discover what purposes have been cultivated by a given individual and what means he has found attractive for the realization of his purposes. It endeavors to discover the handicaps, physical, mental, or moral, permanent or remediable, which might stand in the way of an individual's adequate adaptation to the demands of life. It also seeks to evaluate correctly the various personal assets which an individual may call upon to assist him in a better adjustment to life. In its search for facts which will enable it to understand the entire individual as a concrete, functioning social being, psychiatry aims at the same time to give the individual a better understanding of himself and of his relation to the world about him, and thus make it possible for him to manage himself more efficiently." [5]

But the extreme position of some impetuous friends of psychiatry, who are ready to ascribe practically all crime to mental defectiveness and who propose to substitute mental therapy under the direction of psychiatrists for the present processes of law, makes it difficult, particularly for the psychiatrists themselves.

In the face of such confidence, leaders of the medical profession beg to be rescued from their friends. Dean William Darrach of the College of Physicians and Surgeons recently sounded a significant warning:

"The tremendous growth of the mental hygiene movement is most hopeful. Unfortunately, though, it seems that the early history of the X-ray is being repeated in this field. Methods of investigation and treatment are being used recklessly before their dangers are comprehended and understood.

"During the past twenty-five years, progress in the field of psychiatry has perhaps been more marked than in almost any other period. A quarter century ago there were two problems: first, to decide whether an individual was insane or not; and secondly, if so, to provide a place where he could be protected from society and society protected from him and his acts.

[5] "The New Approach to the Offender," in the *World Tomorrow*, 8, 236-7 (1922).

"Today, although this second problem is even greater than ever, because of the numbers of these pathetic people, the main problem is to recognize the early symptoms of mental disorder, to ascertain the causes, and to re-establish normal adjustments.

"Psychiatry is leaving its former isolated position and infiltrating all other branches of medicine. It is being welcomed with open arms by practitioners in those other fields who have recognized that their patients are only too often mentally as well as physically ill and require treatment for both conditions." [6]

To thrust upon the profession of psychiatry a task regarded by the law and public opinion as essentially a proper subject for the action of statecraft and jurisprudence would unduly burden and confuse the profession itself in the most critical moment of its evolution to truly scientific proportions. A great psychiatrist wrote, in 1927:

"For more than twenty-five years I have been studying motives of conduct, thought and feeling, with the enormous advantage of witnessing the cruel experiments which nature performs in the production of mental development and distortions of mental life, yet tomorrow, if I were appointed a judge in a trial court in New York State by some misguided governor, my fear of inadequacy would not deal nearly so much with my almost complete ignorance of law but with the great defects remaining in my knowledge of human behavior. I should not say, 'Who am I to attempt to administer justice when I know nothing of the Law?' What I would say is, 'Who am I to administer justice when I have an incomplete knowledge of the deep springs of conduct and the motives of human beings?' " [7]

Psychiatry is encountering the perils that lie in the path of every science during its adolescent stage. The unreasoning public invests it with mysterious, occult powers. It asks for miracles, sudden cures, unerring diagnosis. Such responses cannot come from an evolving science, which is always the slow and pains-taking articulation of many known—yes, commonplace—factors. Mental diagnosis and therapy are simply the painstaking adjust-ment of many bits of knowledge assembled from the experience

---

[6] Quoted in the New York *World*, February 16, 1930. See also the temperate view of Dr. Herman Adler in *Criminal Justice in Cleveland*, 439-485.

[7] Dr. Thomas W. Salmon who, as Brigadier-General, was the head of the neuro-psychiatric service of the American military forces abroad, as quoted by Professor Felix Frankfurter in an address for the National League of Women Voters, April 16, 1929.

of men and applied to human situations. The psychiatrist is first a medical man. He knows, as a layman cannot, conduct-determining physical factors, many of which are outside of the nervous system itself, such as various intoxications and auto-intoxications, the effect of digestive disturbances, and of the thyroid and sex glands. He has added to his equipment the discoveries and hypotheses of modern psychology. Finally, he acquires expertness in human, social relationships. The mingling of these scientifically acquired disciplines, and the determination from this co-ordination of a course of diagnosis and treatment, is more in the nature of a great art than of a science. Nor is this use of the term intended to disparage either art or psychiatry. It is simply the designation of what is, in the last analysis, the genesis of every scientific discipline. As Spencer has profoundly suggested, all science finds its genesis in art.[8]

In prevention and treatment, and in the deepening of our understanding of conduct, the psychiatrist has offered an immense contribution to the attempt of the state and of society to suppress crime. But to leave to him the entire determination of what should be done about crime is to overlook several important factors.

In the first place, it is wholly absurd to speak, as we commonly do, of "crime" as a single unified species of conduct.

"One reason why so many unwise things are said and written about crime these days is our habit of considering the word crime as a concept possessing unity of meaning. It does not have that unity in fact, except in one respect—that it is an offense against an established law. Beyond this single point of similarity the term comes to mean many widely distinct and different things. There is really no such thing as crime. There are, instead, crimes, in infinite variety and immeasurable significance.

"It is convenient to recognize in what is known as the field of crime a broad distinction between two quite different sorts of persons and two quite different problems. The first is commonly called 'professional' crime, and involves a variety of offenses, practically all of which concern the taking of property. Such crimes actually provide a means of livelihood for these persons, who continue the business of committing them year after year with only occasional interruptions. They become the basis of a quite

---

[8] The Genesis of Science included in Essays, Scientific, Political and Speculative, II, 1 (New York and London, 1916). The essay was first published in 1854.

distinct profession, with specialized methodology, traditions and a code of ethics.

"Lying outside of this group of crimes are hundreds of others involving all sorts of offenses. Perhaps the most significant group within this area is that which includes the so-called crimes against the person, which frequently are the result of defective mentality, drunken brawls and overcharged emotional personalities. In addition, there are those committed casually and in many instances without much moral condemnation by the community—violations of traffic ordinances, of the customs laws, and the occasional crime of the person who has lived a lifetime of lawfulness and then is sorely tempted and steals from his employer. Many of these are crimes that occur only once in the lifetime of the offender or under very unusual circumstances." [9]

With certain minor reservations it may be asserted that organized crime in American cities is a problem not for the psychiatrist but for the social philosopher and statesman. It has been demonstrated, repeatedly and conclusively, that organized crime does exist, that those who carry it on apparently possess all the mental qualities which distinguish the most "normal" individual, and that there is an organized group composed of those who have accepted certain standards and are prepared to carry on their activities within the state but mostly in opposition to it. Organized crime in Chicago, for example, is a society within a society, a government within a government, a state within a state.[10] There is nothing mysterious about this. Those who profit from organized crime have constructed a code of their own which they obey in preference to that enacted by the state. Whenever a professional criminal has a choice between obeying the code of his group and complying with the law of the state he will accept the former and will wage vehement war upon the one who does not. This acceptance of a code which in many respects runs contrary to that of the entire community is one of the oldest characteristics of social life. A loyal political partisan does essentially the same thing when he refuses to recognize lawlessness and anti-social activity on the part of another partisan. A most

[9] "Crime as a Profession," by Raymond Moley, *Current History*, XXX, 6 (September, 1929), 999.

[10] See the remarkable study by John Landesco, *Organized Crime in Chicago*, published as a section of the *Illinois Crime Survey*, op. cit., 1055-1057.

interesting example of this divergence between the code of a group and the law of the state is presented in a thought-provoking play, *The Criminal Code,* recently presented on the American stage. In this play, the code held by the inmates of a prison conflicts with the enacted law of the state, and it is demonstrated that whenever a choice is offered between the code of a convict and that of the law books the convict accepts the former and in his heart feels that he is doing what is "right." Thus, an attack upon organized crime must be made through a consideration of this primary divergence in loyalties. It cannot be reached on the basis of personal mental defect. If it could, there would be reason to use psychiatry to attack most social problems, including business ethics, political party practices, and, to some extent, religious loyalties. To attempt to define crime upon any other basis is to become entangled in vastly confusing issues.

Another problem, related to this, is pertinent. To ask the psychiatrist to assume society's burden of defining and treating crime is like leaving to the medical expert the question of defining the limits of prohibition. The legislature may ask the physician what effect a given percentage of alcoholic content will have upon an average person, and receive a fairly definite estimate; but to ask him to express this effect in terms of such a generalized concept as intoxication has quite properly elicited the answer that it is for the statesman to determine what he wants to prohibit in the way of intoxication. To ask the psychiatrist either to define crime or to provide means for its definition is to invite an answer from him in these terms. "What kind of behavior do you want to prohibit or punish? What extent of deviation from the normal do you expect to tolerate?" If the state continues, as it undoubtedly will, to reply that it expects to use the term "crime" to mean deviations from certain norms of business practice, or the expression of ideas not held by the majority, or social habits not approved by current standards or by religious authority, the determination of the exact nature of such conduct will have to rest with the recognized authority of the state, and the enforcement of such prohibition must remain within the power of the political agents of the state. That such agents may in the course of time use the profoundly important counsel of the experts to an increasingly greater degree is inevitable.

II. *The Tests*

We shall attempt only a brief discussion of the vastly complicated "tests" of insanity as they are applied to the determination of guilt in a criminal trial. The problem is largely one of substantive law while this book concerns the administration of law. It will suffice to show that the evolution of scientific knowledge of human motives and of the nature of the psychological processes is apparently driving us toward a method of meeting the issue by ignoring the present basis of substantive law entirely and seeking to apply the most practical method of treating the accused and thus protecting society without settling the question of responsibility at all. This drift is of great significance to the administration of justice and is in clear harmony with the tendencies noted with respect to other aspects of modern judicial administration. If this can be made clear, the infinitely detailed aspects of the legal nature of a crime can be very lightly touched upon here.

The law has long recognized that if a person commits a criminal act while suffering from a lack of capacity due to mental disorder or insanity, an essential element in the making of a crime is lacking, and therefore no crime has been committed. The extent to which this lack of capacity has been recognized, however, has varied greatly, to some degree in accordance with the accepted belief of the judges and of the public concerning the character and effect of mental disease. The determination of exactly what constitutes lack of capacity to commit a crime is commonly called a "test of insanity." The history of the various tests of insanity in Anglo-American jurisprudence partially reflects the slow-moving progress of the law with reference to the conclusions of medical science. It appears that in the Middle Ages a defendant who committed his crime while mad was not entitled to an acquittal but to a special verdict that he committed the offense when mad. This gave him the right to a pardon.[11]

[11] Stephen, *History of the Criminal Law of England*, II, 151. See also Pollock and Maitland, *History of English Law*, I, 478.

From the time of Bracton in the thirteenth century until well along in the eighteenth century, the test seems, in the main, to have been the one finally enunciated, in 1724, in what is known as Arnold's case,[12] and called the "wild beast test." This famous case evolved the proposition that to be exempted from punishment the offender "must be a man that is totally deprived of his understanding and memory and doth not know what he is doing, no more than an infant, than a brute, or a wild beast." Hale seems to have introduced into the law the theory of partial insanity, a notion which was later discussed by Erskine in 1800 in Hadfield's case.[13]

It seems that James Hadfield placed himself in Drury Lane Theatre and when King George III entered, fired two shots in his direction, neither taking effect. After his arrest it was ascertained that he had been a private in a dragoon regiment and had received several saber wounds on the head. He had been discharged from the army because of insanity and had suffered from attacks of maniacal frenzy. Prior to the trial he said that he was tired of life and that he had made the attempt on the life of the king to bring about his own death. The presiding judge, in summing up, is reported to have said that the sanity of the defendant "must be made out to the satisfaction of a moral man meeting the case with a fortitude of mind knowing that he has an arduous duty to discharge; yet, if the scales hang anything like even, throwing in a certain amount of mercy to the party." [14] Hadfield was "insane" at the time he committed the act, although the evidence showed that he knew he was firing a loaded pistol in the direction of the king, and that such an act was punishable by law. Thus it was established that there was no responsibility in a case in which such a delusion existed as to overpower the reason completely and that such delusion should be associated with the act in question. This test has come to be known as the delusion test.

Earlier than this, a number of cases had established a test based upon the ability of the defendant at the time of the commission of the act to distinguish between good and evil. Per-

---

[12] 16, St. Tr., 695, 764.   [14] Hansard, LXVII, 719.
[13] 27, St. Tr., 1282.

haps the best known statement of this test is to be found in Ferrer's case, decided in 1760.[15]

As a result of conflicting and varied decisions, and a steady increase in the understanding of insanity, the law became greatly confused. Finally an attempt at restatement was made in the case which is the basis of our present tests. M'Naghten's case, which was decided in 1843,[16] possessed an interesting background. It seems that M'Naghten had, for more than two years, been suffering from what the psychologists call a "persecution delusion," and that on many occasions he had complained to his father of being followed by spies day and night. He said that they did not speak to him, but that when he turned around, they frequently looked into his face, shook their heads at him, raised their arms, shook their fists in his face, and made gestures at him with sticks. He also told of a man who carried straws in his hand, that he shook, and which meant that M'Naghten was to be reduced to a state of beggary. He left Glasgow to avoid this imaginary persecution, went to England and subsequently to France, but the delusion followed him. Finally he decided to kill the Prime Minister, Sir Robert Peel, watched his house for that purpose, and, seeing the Prime Minister's private secretary, Mr. Drummond, leave the house, shot the latter, under the impression that he was the Prime Minister. In the trial, evidence was clearly presented by competent testimony to the effect that the defendant was a man suffering from partial insanity, and that when the crime was committed the mind of the defendant was so absorbed in the contemplation of his fancied persecutions that he did not distinguish between right and wrong. The chief justice, in summing up, is reported to have said that "the point . . . will be whether . . . you are satisfied that at the time the act was committed he had not that competent use of his understanding as to know what he was doing with respect to the act itself, a wicked and wrong thing, and whether he knew that it was a wicked and wrong thing that he was doing,

[15] 19, St. Tr., 886. See also Reg. v. Oxford (1840), 9 C. & P., 533; and Parke's Case. Bowler's Case (1812), Bellingham's Case (1812), Collinson on Lunacy, 477, 673, 636, respectively.

[16] 10 Cl. & F., 198, 8 Eng. Rep. R., 718. For a very intelligent discussion of this case, see Glueck, op. cit., Chapter 6.

or that he was not sensible at the time he committed the act that it was contrary to the laws of God and man." The jury returned a verdict of insanity, and shortly after that a discussion arose in Parliament as a result of which the House of Lords decided to put certain questions to the judges. These questions and the answers given to them constitute the so-called "M'-Naghten tests of insanity." [17]

The answers established as the test the defendant's capacity to distinguish between right and wrong, with relation to the particular act. In the words of the justice, "to establish a defense on the ground of insanity, it must be clearly proved that, at the time of the committing of the act, the party accused was laboring under such a defect of reason, from disease of the mind, as not to know the nature and quality of the act he was doing; or, if he did know it, that he did not know he was doing what was wrong"—the question for the jury being, "whether the party accused had a sufficient degree of reason to know that he was doing an act that was wrong."

The justices also expressed the opinion that in the case of "delusion in respect of one or more particular subjects or persons," assuming the person is not in other respects insane, "he is nevertheless punishable according to the nature of the crime committed, if he knew at the time of committing such crime that he was acting contrary to law." Where he is under "an insane delusion as to existing facts," "he must be considered in the same situation as to responsibility as if the facts with respect to which the delusion exists were real."

The views enunciated in this famous case are usually cited as the authority for the "knowledge of right and wrong" test. These views have been subjected to no inconsiderable scrutiny and criticism by many learned legal and medical experts. The gist of such criticism may be summed up as follows:

(1) It was not a judgment on definite facts before the judges.

(2) The answers given were not intended to be exhaustive. They look to the knowledge element only, and omit the volitional element, or any consideration of the effect of insanity on the emotions and will. Responsibility in law presupposes voluntary

[17] Hansard, LXVII, 724. The questions and answers are in the appendix, p. 259.

action, which requires both the elements of knowledge and power of self-control. Moreover, modern medical evidence tends to show that most insane persons have knowledge of right and wrong; the question is their capacity of self-control.

(3) The judges' remarks on delusion show that they were considering the case of a person laboring under a mistake of fact in certain particulars but in all other respects sane; whereas delusion is simply one symptom of a disease reaching to the whole mind, and it is impossible to say that the act, however seemingly remote, is not directly derived from the delusion, or the delusion does not show the existence of a disease which prevents knowledge that the act is wrong.[18]

(4) Finally, as Glueck points out, the questions referred to one type of mental disorder while the answers were in subsequent cases held to apply to all types of mental disorder.[19]

The English courts have been vexed by grave difficulties in applying the M'Naghten rules but on account of the procedure in that country in cases where the jury is convinced that "responsibility" was not present the practical results have been much better than in the United States. A workable system has been developed, because the English law provides that if the jury believes the act was really committed by the defendant, but that he was insane at the time, a verdict must be returned which is in substance "guilty but insane." [20] If such a verdict is found, the court orders the accused to be kept in custody as a criminal lunatic during "the King's Pleasure," which in effect is the Home Office. Thus a perfectly rational practice is in operation which protects the public in any case either by imprisoning a guilty person in a prison or a dangerous lunatic in a proper institution.[21] This queer contradiction in terms in the English verdict is due to an interesting incident. Various attempts had been made upon the life of Queen Victoria, and finally, in 1882, an attempt was made by a person named McLane. No one was injured, but

---

[18] Stephen, J., *History of Criminal Law*, II. Parsons v. State (1887), 81 Ala., 577. Keedy, 30 H. L. R., 546 (1917).
[19] Glueck, *Mental Disorder and the Criminal Law*, 426.
[20] The law actually provides for this verdict in the following words: "The jury shall return a special verdict that the accused guilty of the charge was insane." Trial of Lunatics Act, Section 2.
[21] Harris, *Principles and Practices of Criminal Law* (London, 1926, 14th Ed.), 14-17.

McLane was tried for "high treason" and was found not guilty, upon the ground of insanity. The form of the verdict displeased the queen, because she felt that "the man was guilty because she saw him do the act." Overlooking the fact that crime comprises both an unlawful act and an unlawful intent, "she maintained that, whether the man was guilty of high treason or not, he was guilty of firing a pistol at her." [22]

While the queen's constitutional advisers did not agree with her view, they could not persuade her to accept theirs, and her attorney-general rationalized his explanation to Parliament. The act was passed without controversy, but it has always been subjected to criticism by the English Bar. In 1922, a committee was constituted by the Lord Chancellor "to consider what changes, if any, are desirable in the existing law, practice and procedure relating to criminal trials in which the plea of insanity as a defense is raised, and whether any and if so what changes should be made in the existing law and practice in respect of cases falling within the provisions of the Criminal Lunatics Act, 1884." A committee of the British Medico-Psychological Association appointed a committee of experts who forwarded to the official committee the following recommendations:

"(1) The criteria of responsibility expressed in the rules in the McNaghten case should be left as a question of fact to be abrogated, and the responsibility should be left as a question of fact to be determined by the jury. (2) In every trial in which the prisoner's mental condition is at issue, the judge should direct the jury to answer the questions (a) Did the prisoner commit the act alleged? (b) If he did, was he at the time insane? (c) If he was insane, has it been proved that his crime was unrelated to his mental disorder? (3) When a prisoner is found unfit to plead, the trial, on the facts, should be allowed to proceed. (4) The verdict 'guilty but insane' should rank as a conviction for purposes of appeal. (5) A panel of experts should be appointed, any of whom can be called to give evidence when insanity is raised as a defense."

The committee rejected these proposals, and in its report in 1923 recommended that the M'Naghten rules be retained, with a change in the wording of the verdict to be returned when the person was found irresponsible on the ground of insanity.

[22] Cf. *The Law Relating to Lunacy*, by H. S. Theobald, London, 1924.

The English practice, however, provides that when a verdict of "guilty but insane" is brought, the defendant is immediately placed under the control of the Home Secretary, to be confined as a criminal lunatic "during his Majesty's pleasure," although provision is made for an appeal in such a case. The effect is to prevent such a state of affairs as often arises in this country when, after one has made a plea of insanity, he is found not guilty but is not placed in the custody of the state as an insane person. It is provided, in English law, that when the defense of insanity is raised in a criminal trial, the existence of mental disease is established by the evidence of competent medical experts, the verdict of the jury is made in accord with such evidence, and the offender is consigned to the institution best adapted to his needs. Ten American states make provision for the automatic custody as a lunatic of persons acquitted on the ground of insanity. In Ohio the proceedings of such a trial are automatically certified to the probate court which is required to regard the verdict at the trial as prima facie evidence of insanity. Most of the states however make insanity proceedings a matter of discretion.

American courts have fallen into boundless confusion in attempting to apply the M'Naghten rules or in seeking to improvise substitutes. It is unnecessary here to elaborate the confusion which has resulted. A general criticism of the various rules of the states points out that:

"All these tests, without a sufficient background upon which they may be projected, are too artificial, requiring certain symptoms to be present before they will exempt from responsibility; they overlook the fact that the symptoms are but manifestations of a generally disordered mentality, ignore the fact of the essential unity of mental process, and disregard the fact that no disorder of mental activity can exist without affecting the efficient operation of the mind as a whole." [23]

As a result of this generally uncertain state of the law, juries frequently break through all restraining influences and bring in decisions based upon a rough, extemporized conception of what they believe to be the best immediate policy. Two very significant examples of this tendency are in point.

[23] Glueck, *Insanity and the Criminal Law*, 440.

The case of George Remus has probably given more occasion for public discussion of the question of insanity in the criminal law than any other in recent years. Remus was a resident of Cincinnati who seems to have owned a number of distilleries and to have been in the business of manufacturing and selling liquor for medicinal purposes. In 1922, he was convicted in a federal court and subsequently served a term at the federal penitentiary at Atlanta. After his release from prison, he killed his wife, asserting that he did so for "society's sake," and that his act was a legal crime and not a moral wrong. He is said to have told the alienist employed by the state that he did not set up the defense of insanity because he was not insane, but subsequently he found that it would be necessary to plead insanity, and he did so, serving as his own attorney. He alleged a type of insanity which has no standing among scientific men: "transitory maniacal insanity," and attempted to prove a diseased state of mind for the two years preceding the crime. The trial was very confused, and extremely sensational. Remus raved and shrieked in court, told of persecutions, and used violent and profane language. The jury brought in a verdict of acquittal on the ground of insanity. One of the jurors stated that the vote had been unanimous, and that if it had been possible Remus would have been released without any suggestion of insanity. "We decided that the man had been persecuted long enough." Under the laws of Ohio the verdict placed Remus in the hands of the probate court for a lunacy hearing, which resulted in his being committed to the state hospital for the criminal insane. He immediately applied for a writ of habeas corpus, and after hearings by the Court of Appeals, and subsequently by the Supreme Court of Ohio, he was released.

The absurdity of this case is accentuated by the fact that while Remus could with slight justification claim that he was insane at the time of the killing but sane at the time of the trial, later, at the time of the habeas corpus proceeding, the state was compelled to contest it on the ground that Remus was insane then but sane at the time of the trial, because the trial had been held after the state had established, to the satisfaction of the court, "that Remus was sane, and, therefore, could be subject to trial."

This utter lack of well-defined principle on the part of the courts of another state is well illustrated by a recent study made of capital punishment in North Carolina.[24] In the course of this study, twenty-six persons whom the courts of the state had sentenced to death for capital offenses were carefully examined by competent persons, under the direction of the State Board of Charities and Public Welfare, and the results of their examinations were set forth. Of the twenty-six, fourteen rated below ten years of intelligence according to the Binet-Simon scale. Eight more were rated between ten and thirteen years, while four were classified as suffering from some constitutional mental disease. It was probably chiefly because of these mental defects that the governor issued twenty-one commutations of sentence. Five of the offenders were, however, executed, and of this group one was a paranoia dementia præcox, another had a mental age of four years "with psychopathic tendencies," a third was classified as feeble-minded, a fourth had a mental age of five, "with psychopathic tendencies," while apparently the most intelligent and sound member of the group was a negro whose intelligence test indicated eight years.

Assuming the competence of the examiners, it is very easy to draw a number of inferences from this study. It shows that in most of these instances the courts were proceeding without any regard to whether the defendants were actually represented by lawyers who were able to offer a defense of insanity. It is probable that the defense of insanity was made in only a very small number of these cases, if in any. It is clear, moreover, that in many instances the courts proceeded with the cases and permitted the defendants to be convicted, with a definite expectation that the governor would make the necessary adjustment in the light of what he found to be their mental condition. In other words, the judicial side of government begged the question of insanity entirely and permitted the executive to make the "test." It is likewise clear, from a general consideration of what happens in certain states, that for the most part those convictions were

[24] *Capital Punishment in North Carolina.* Special Bulletin No. 10, published by the North Carolina Board of Charities and Public Welfare, Raleigh, 1929. For a summary of this report see my review in the *Survey*, entitled "The Convicts They Kill," September 1, 1929.

arrived at in pursuance of a public policy which assumes that the conviction and the execution of persons for crime have a deterrent effect upon vast numbers of inferior people belonging to a practically subject race, and that such deterrence can be effected as easily through the execution of a defective as of anyone else.

While this is no place to raise the question of the soundness of such a public policy, it shows how completely the courts of this state are following a practice which has no relation to finespun tests of insanity. It is quite likely that many, if not the majority, of states are equally inchoate with respect to mental responsibility. In Texas, for example, a recent trial of a person charged with murder revealed clearly that he was a most unfortunate mental defective. The arguments of the defendant's counsel proceeded entirely on the basis of the injustice of subjecting such a helpless person to the treatment of ordinary prison guards. The jury, however, found him guilty and he was sent to the penitentiary, not, as one of the jurymen explained, "because we thought he was sane, but because we had only the option of turning him loose or sending him to the penitentiary, and bad as the penitentiary is, it at least provided for some kind of control over the poor man's actions." Thus do fine-spun rules of law come to grief in the face of concrete instances.

In an attempt to escape the confusion attendant upon the attempts of American courts to apply the M'Naghten rules, the New Hampshire courts have boldly broken through all pretense and have held "that the presence or absence of knowledge of right and wrong, or irresistible impulse, or delusion, or any other of the conceptions and symptoms of mental disease which elsewhere have individually or in various combinations been raised to the dignity of rigid tests, constitutes a question of fact determinable by the jury." [25] This doctrine at least has the value of perfect frankness and honesty. It is thus commended by Glueck:

"From the point of view of the fundamental principle of the criminal law—the requirement of a *mens rea* in a mentally sound offender as a *sine qua non* to guilt—we found that the New Hampshire practice is the most consistent. For it proceeds upon the assumption that there are no tests

[25] Glueck, 254, commenting upon State v. Jones, 50 N. H., 369 (1871) and State v. Pike, 49 N. H., 399 (1870).

of irresponsibility, but that the existence, and presence in the accused, of delusions, capacity to know the nature and quality of his act, capacity to inhibit his impulses to illegal behavior—in a word, the existence of a *mens rea* in the accused at the time of the offense—is a question of fact for the jury. We pointed out that the New Hampshire rule proceeds upon the recognition of the fact that, *in actual practice,* the jury is not governed as much by the formal tests as expounded by the trial judges in their charges, as the elaborate treatises and judicial opinions on the subject of the tests would imply. For it must always be remembered that the state can not appeal from a verdict of acquittal on the ground of insanity (and irresponsibility); hence, it is difficult to check up on the motives which prompted the jury to acquit a defendant, in any particular case. Moreover, the strict separation between *insanity* and *irresponsibility,* or, in other words, between *some evidence of mental disorder,* and conclusive proof of lack of knowledge of right and wrong, is frequently not maintained in American courts; and the judicial decisions themselves frequently confuse insanity and irresponsibility."

This New Hampshire solution seems to represent the drift of the best opinion. Another expression of a similar sort was in a prepared bill presented in 1915 by a Committee of the American Institute of Criminal Law and Criminology, of which the chairman was Professor E. R. Keedy.[26] In substance, it provided that the jury decide whether defendant was at the time of the act charged "suffering from mental disease and by reason of such mental disease did not have the particular state of mind that must accompany such an act in order to constitute the crime charged."

This form of test eliminates from the law entirely medical tests and permits courts to instruct juries to construct their ideas of mental disease in accordance with the medical knowledge presented to them in the trial or by the courts' instructions. It permits these ideas to be reconstructed from time to time in accordance with the changing medical science of succeeding generations. It does away with legal definitions of insanity. The mental condition of the defendant at the time of the offense would be determined by medical experts and on the basis of such evidence the jury would determine the question of responsibility—as a question of fact. This provision retains for the jury its legal

[26] It was a joint committee of doctors and lawyers. See Professor Keedy's discussion of it in 30 Harv. L. R., 535, 724 (1917).

function, that of passing on the question of responsibility, and so does not violate constitutional provisions, as the more radical reform of complete abolition of the defense of insanity was held to do.

The much more radical recommendation has been made that the question of responsibility be removed from the jury entirely, it being left to that body to determine only that the offense was committed by the defendant, disposition of the offender being based upon a study of him by qualified and impartial experts coöperating with the courts. Thus, if the protection of society be considered the aim of an effective administration of the criminal law, the commission of a dangerous act by the insane as well as the sane should be amenable to the criminal law. The one is no less a source of danger to the community than the other. As Dr. White points out, "It is no more pleasant to have one's throat cut by a lunatic than by a criminal. The act is just as destructive in its social tendencies in the one case as in the other." The conclusion is inescapable that "however legally right under existing legal conceptions, it is really wrong, sociologically wrong, to find a man not guilty on the ground of insanity.[27] . . . From this method of approach the individual who committed an antisocial act would by that fact alone move under the control of the state and that control would not be relinquished until there was evidence that he could live a reasonably useful life as a free citizen." [28]

The State of Washington passed a statute providing that:

"It shall be no defense to a person charged with the commission of a crime, that, at the time of its commission, he was unable by reason of his insanity, idiocy or imbecility to comprehend the nature and quality of the act committed, or to understand that it was wrong; or that he was afflicted with a morbid propensity to commit prohibited acts; nor shall any testimony or other proof thereof be admitted in evidence."

The statute further provided that whenever in the judgment of the court an offender was insane at the time of the offense or

---

[27] Report of the Special Committee on the Commitment and Discharge of the Criminal Insane, N. Y. *State Bar Association Report*, XXXIII (1910), 391-403.
[28] White, *Insanity and the Criminal Law*, 167-8.

at the time of trial, he shall be committed to an insane asylum "until such person shall have recovered his sanity." In determining the question of sanity or insanity, "the court may take counsel with one or more experts in the diagnosis and treatment of insanity, idiocy and imbecility, and make such personal or other examination of the defendant as in his judgment may be necessary to aid in its determination."

In 1910 this statute was held unconstitutional by the Washington Supreme Court. The decision was rested mainly on the ground that by denying to the defendant the privilege of placing before the jury the very important substantive fact of state of mind the statute violated that provision of the constitution guaranteeing trial by jury.[29]

III. *The Expert*[30]

When we leave the question of legal doctrine and rules and come to the more important matter of mechanical methods of applying those rules, we find conditions still more unsatisfactory. Usually the issue of insanity is raised by some sort of modification of plea. Ordinarily a plea of not guilty is entered and the defendant attempts to show that he is not guilty because of insanity. The question of responsibility is then argued through the presentation of evidence as to the defendant's mental state at the time when the crime was committed. Expert testimony is offered by both sides and all the problems involved in expert testimony generally are raised. Testimony is offered in reply to hypothetical questions phrased in accordance with legal tradition. In general the questions are not of the kind which a psychiatrist is able to attack. He finds himself in the position of Dr. William A. White, who says, "If I were called to the stand I would be asked questions formulated one hundred years ago."

Under the present legal system each party to the litigation hires its own experts, who, like any other witnesses, are subject

---

[29] Strasburg v. State, 60 Wash., 106 (1910). In 1929 the Supreme Court of Louisiana declared a similar statute unconstitutional. State v. Lange (not reported).

[30] For a summary of this whole subject see Glueck, S. S., "State Legislation Providing for the Mental Examination of Persons Accused of Crime," published in *Mental Hygiene*, VIII, 1, 1.

to cross-examination in open court. The result is that both their honesty and their qualifications are likely to be questioned. Since the witness is hired and paid by the lawyers on one side, he is consciously or unconsciously influenced toward establishing the end they seek to maintain. He is supplied with his facts from the one side only, and these may be broken down in court through the unexpected development of contrary evidence brought out in examination of witnesses, thus lending the appearance of partiality or concealment. Like the judge, jury and all others connected with the trial, he is subject to ordinary human prejudices, which may be influenced by the heinous nature of the crime or the repulsiveness of the criminal. He is, besides, in the anomalous position—unlike any other of the participants—of acting in the capacity of both adviser and witness. Under circumstances which almost prohibit giving impartial testimony, the expert witness is expected to exhibit a degree of impartiality not compatible with human nature.

There are, in addition, cases in which the witness is hired solely because his opinion, whether honest or not, is expected to further the purpose of the party hiring him. As the judicial rebuke has it, "the particular kind of opinion desired by any party to the investigation can be readily procured by paying the market price therefor." [31]

The problem of the qualifications of the expert likewise presents difficulties. In the first place, there is no standard for determining who is a capable expert in the subject, and there have been instances of frauds or quacks delivering wholly incompetent opinions. In the process of cross-examination, the witness is often subjected to unnecessary hectoring in the effort of counsel to discredit his qualifications. Frequently his opinion must be given in answer to a hypothetical question, rather than as a conclusion based on investigation of actual facts. The question is prepared by lawyers on supposed facts not necessarily substantiated by the evidence and is lengthy and artificial. Yet the expert answers with the circumstances of the particular defendant in mind. This tends to produce a seeming conflict of opinion

[31] 8 *Amer. Bar Assoc. Jour.*, 171, 5, citing Roberts v. N. Y. Central R.R. Co., 128 N. Y., 455.

between opposing experts, and, consequently, confusion in the minds of the jury. Hence the opinion of the experts is often repudiated by the court, and the judge or jury come to a decision without regard to it. The trial has been unnecessarily prolonged, at increased expense, and the public afforded a spectacle upon which to vent destructive criticism.

To remedy the evils involved in the employment of expert witnesses, a number of suggestions have been made, aimed chiefly at the application of impartial psychiatric opinion to the trial of cases. Usually, each of the parties concerned appoints experts who examine the defendant and report their opinion to the court. A typical proposal was made by the Crime Commission of New York State in 1929 and was repeated in 1930.[32] The proposal was that whenever the defendant pleads insanity the court should suspend the trial until the question of sanity has been settled. The procedure for the determination of the mental status of the defendant should be as follows: The defendant and the district attorney should each select not more than two, and the court one, certified psychiatrist. These psychiatrists should, at a time and place fixed by the court, examine the defendant and report their findings to the court. The significant provision is the requirement that the examination be made in the presence of all the examiners, the purpose being to bring the experts together, to reduce their conclusions to a written report, and to attempt to secure unanimity of opinion. The psychiatrist making the report should, of course, be subject to examination in the trial by the attorneys for both sides or by the court. The function of the report in the trial should be to provide "conclusive evidence of the mental condition of the defendant as to his sanity at the time of such examination or at the time of the commission of the crime." The submission of the report would automatically exclude all other witnesses as to the mental status of the defendant.

Such provisions as these fall far short of the Massachusetts system. There would necessarily be great difficulty in bringing about agreement among those selected to make the examinations,

[32] See *Report of the Crime Commission of New York City for 1929*, 179 to 193. See also the provisions in the Code of the American Law Institute.

and the procedure would be put into operation only in case a plea of insanity were offered.

Numerous bills of this general character have been proposed from time to time to regulate the use of expert testimony, but few have been passed. A feature of most of them is that the judge be given power to appoint one or more, but not exceeding three, impartial qualified experts, to testify as experts whenever required, their fees to be fixed by the court and paid by the county. The right of cross-examination—a powerful weapon for testing qualification—is retained by counsel for both parties, who may, in addition, call in their own experts. The objective of such legislation is to minimize the element of partiality. It has been made law in but few instances.[33]

These remedies do not operate as a matter of routine, but are put into operation only when the issue of insanity is raised. It would seem that there should be some way of making the determination of mental capacity a matter of routine, not dependent upon the initiative of those in charge of the accused, for they are usually non-expert and prejudiced.[34]

The best example of such legislation is the Massachusetts law of 1921, which provides for the examination, *as a matter of routine,* of all offenders of a certain class—namely, those indicted for a capital offense, or known to have been indicted for any other offense more than once, or to have been previously convicted of a felony—with a view to determining their mental condition and the existence of any mental disease or defect which would impair their criminal responsibility. This legislation differs from that in other jurisdictions in that the examination is compulsory for all alleged offenders of the specified class instead of being left to the initiative or discretion of some prescribed official or of "any person" having reasonable grounds for believing that the accused is insane. What is more, the examination in Massachusetts is not left to the judge or a jury or a commission, but is in the hands of scientific experts appointed by the department of

[33] Rhode Island, 1896, 1909; Michigan, declared unconstitutional; New York, 1915; California, 1925. The California statute was amended in 1929.

[34] See *Mass. Acts 1921,* Chapter 415, amended by *Acts of 1928,* Chapter 333, and for the nature of these changes, and for a general discussion of the whole operation of this law see Glueck, *Mental Disorder and the Criminal Law,* pages 58-72.

mental diseases. The provisions and operation of this law are not perfect. For instance, the class of persons thus compulsorily examined is specifically limited, especially in the "third group"—those known to have previously been convicted of a felony. This stipulation is based on the distinction between felony and misdemeanor, artificial for any purpose, and especially from the psychiatric point of view. Besides, there is nothing to compel the court or the prosecution or the defense to follow the recommendations of the experts; and it appears that a number of offenders have escaped examination because they were out on bail and could not be found. But its decided advantages are well emphasized by Dr. Glueck. The examinations are made before trial, and therefore before it is decided whether or not to resort to the defense of insanity. There is no technicality ridden procedure. The mentally unsound are spared the ordeal of trial, while the state is saved the expense of prosecuting those who ought not to be tried, in those cases where all parties concerned accept the conclusions of the unbiased experts that the case be disposed of without trial. The accumulation of valuable scientific data should result. The hope is also expressed that better treatment of the semi-responsible will result from the psychiatric point of view impressed upon the judges and district attorneys by the reports of the experts.

The steps thus briefly outlined show a definite trend toward the elimination of much of the public wrangling of expert witnesses. Legislation like that referred to looks to the determination of cases involving insanity by the utilization of unbiased medical testimony, rendered entirely outside the partisan atmosphere of the trial.

IV. *The Clinic*

The frequency with which mental disorder is found among those charged with crime suggests the necessity for providing for psychiatric examinations somewhere within the court organization or very close to it. It has been clearly established that the probation department can make little headway without the constant use of psychiatric examinations. A psychiatric clinic can provide for the probation department a psychiatric analysis of the cases and suggestions as to treatment.

Psychiatric services within probation departments have long been recognized in juvenile court work. In 1909, the Chicago Juvenile Court employed Dr. William Healy as a court psychiatrist. His activity came to be know as a "court clinic." Similar clinics were established in juvenile courts in many other cities. In a few cities adult criminal courts established them too, beginning with the Boston Criminal Court in 1913. In 1928, 110 out of 1,168 courts (including juvenile courts) reported that they were served regularly by a psychiatrist. A psychologist was reported by seventy. In more than half of the courts reporting them, those services had been instituted after 1921—showing that this type of court service is a fairly recent development.[35]

Psychiatric clinics in a court are used to examine convicted persons and to advise the judge in fixing sentence. The fact that such a vast number of persons plead guilty, and that the plea of guilty is taken in connection with negotiations in which the district attorney and the judge, and sometimes the probation department, participate, indicates the extent to which psychiatry can be used in making broad decisions as to the disposition of cases. Psychiatry has come to be the guiding force in the individualized treatment of offenders by many of the most modern and effective courts in the United States.

[35] Dr. Winfred Overholser of the Massachusetts Department of Mental Diseases has performed a distinct service in publishing a number of articles dealing with the extent to which psychiatry can be used in the administration of criminal justice. The most significant of these are: "The Rôle of Psychiatry in the Administration of Criminal Justice," 93 *Journal of the American Medical Association,* 830-834; "The Place of Psychiatry in the Administration of Criminal Law," 201 *New England Journal of Medicine,* 479-484; *Use of Psychiatric Facilities in Criminal Courts in the United States,* published by the National Committee for Mental Hygiene, 1929.

CHAPTER IX

THE ART OF HUMAN RELATIONS

THE most important reason for considering probation in this book is not that commonly urged in its favor. The subject is included here because probation service has come to mean much more than a method of supervising persons who are offered an alternative to imprisonment. Its more significant function is to provide for many courts a species of intelligence service. It studies the prisoner at the bar, interviews him, defines his characteristics, discovers his problems, weighs his possibilities, and, when the court finds it necessary to pass judgment upon him, is able to provide intelligent information and advice upon which to base the decision. With the other and more commonly known function of supervising those on probation, the treatment here is indirect and incidental.

Similarly in the case of parole, the chief interest here is not its function of substituting some sort of organized supervision for confinement in a prison. The most significant aspect of parole in connection with a study of the courts is this: the extent to which parole power is expanded is the measure of the denial to the court of its power to fix punishment for crime. Carrying the principle of parole to its logical extreme would deny a judge the right to fix sentence at all. It would leave to the court a single question: Did the accused commit the crime? The question of what the punishment should be would rest with some other authority. The judge would assist in determining guilt but would have no authority to determine punishment. Another agency would fix the term of the defendant's imprisonment on the basis of its own study of his case. Perhaps such an agency of treatment would be a parole board. The function of supervising the person who is permitted a limited amount of freedom is, in connection with parole as well as probation, a question with which this discussion is not primarily concerned.

But there is something common to both probation and parole which is very pertinent to our present interest. What are the methods used to measure a personality through study by a social agency? This process of individualized study is of enormous importance not only to penology but to judicial administration. It cannot be pointed out too often that there are essential differences between the objectives and the approach of the modern sociologist and psychiatrist to a criminal act and that of the traditional law. In the one, interest attaches to the person charged with the act; in the other, to the act itself. The first is concerned with the personal characteristics and needs of the convicted person, and the other is based upon a theory which has dictated the particular law which applies to the act committed. It is the application of the point of view of the first, through the forms of the second, that distinguishes those few courts which are showing the way and are performing the necessary experimentation for a revised criminal jurisprudence.

I. *Probation*

To write or speak of the growth of probation without sentiment is almost impossible. The theory of mercy which is so large a part of its fundamental basis, its wide use in dealings with delinquent children, and its frequent associations with religious ideals, all lend to it a highly emotional coloring.

Its origin in America was romantic, too. As the story goes, John Augustus, a Boston cobbler, who apparently possessed deep humanitarian impulses, appeared before a judge in that city one day in 1849, and asked that a youth who was charged with drunkenness be released on bail, with the understanding that for a short time he should be subject to the unofficial guardianship and direction of the cobbler. This was permitted, and, according to the diary of John Augustus, the first probationer was not only saved from the evils of imprisonment but improved in his habits. "At the expiration of his period of probation, I accompanied him to the courtroom. His whole appearance was changed and no one, even the scrutinizing officer, could believe that he was the same person who less than a month before had stood trembling on the prisoners' stand. The boy continued industrious and sober and without doubt has been from this treatment saved from a drunkard's death." [1] So encouraged was John Augustus by this success that he began to apply his philosophy in other cases. In six months he had bailed seventeen persons and taken them under his care. During the next fifteen years, hundreds of men and boys and women and girls were watched over and assisted by him. In a rough, primitive way, John Augustus seems to have attempted to apply the essential principles of the modern probation officer. Before he accepted responsibility for a case, he made an investigation, in order, as he wrote in his diary, that "he might be assured of the merits of the case and the character of the individual." He justified his theory that the reform of an offender could be achieved without imprisonment in the following intelligent terms:

"Individuals and communities are prone to infer evil if they occasionally observe it in an individual. If one person fails who has received leniency in the court, there are always those who are ready to predict that all others will conduct themselves in a similar manner. This they persist in believing although instances are very frequent when such people become good citizens and regain their former station and relationship with society. I shall leave this matter for others to discuss and decide. I am content, knowing as I do, that by such humane treatment hundreds of fallen have been raised even by so humble a person as myself."

Probation in some form has long been a feature of juvenile court procedure. As early as 1861 the Mayor of Chicago was given power to appoint a commissioner by whom boys could be placed under supervision. Other states followed in applying this method of treating child offenders.[2] By an act of the legislature in 1869, Massachusetts created a state visiting agency, empowered to accept the custody of juvenile offenders and to place them in private families. In 1869-1870 about twenty-three per cent of the juvenile offenders convicted in Boston courts were so dealt with. It was in the same state, by a law limited to

[1] *Probation,* the official organ of the National Probation Association, VIII, No. 4. December, 1929.

[2] For these and many other historical facts concerning probation see Sutherland, Criminology, Chapter 23.

Boston, that the first probation system without restriction as to age was legally established. That was in 1878. In 1880 this was given state-wide application and in 1891 the appointments of probation officers were made mandatory and were transferred from the local authorities to the courts.[3] Until 1899 Massachusetts was the only state with an authorized probation system, but by 1918 every state in the Union except Wyoming had provided legislation for juvenile probation. Of these, forty-five per cent had regular probation service, but in only eight states was there a recognized probation officer for each court.[4]

The principle of probation is common in some other countries. The State Children's Act of South Australia, passed in 1895, provided for probation and the separate hearings of charges against children under eighteen years of age. Two-thirds of the European countries have probation systems (sometimes called conditional sentence or suspension of execution of punishment), most of which apply to both juvenile and adult offenders. In Belgium, France, Germany and Poland, however, probation is definitely confined to minors.[5]

As compared with the forty-seven states which have adopted juvenile probation legislation, only thirty-six and the District of Columbia have provided for adult probation. Nineteen of the thirty-six have adult probation officers, and in eleven we find provision for some supervision or control of the work. Only nine can be said to have state-wide systems of administration. In all of these states except Massachusetts, limitations, either with regard to previous conviction or the seriousness of the offense, have been placed upon probation. In 1926 alone this state collected two million dollars—a sum fully five times the cost of the service—from probationers, for the benefit of their families, for restitution, and for fines. Progress in the use of probation methods is illustrated in New York, where the number of adults on probation grew more than five hundred per cent in sixteen years.

In 1925 a federal probation law was passed providing for the

[3] Lou, *Juvenile Courts in the U. S.* (Chapel Hill, 1926), 17.
[4] Belden, *Courts in the U. S. Hearing Children's Cases* (U. S. Children's Bureau, 1920), 10-15.
[5] Trought, *Probation in Europe* (London, 1927), 186.

application of suspended sentences and probation for offenses not punishable by death or by life imprisonment. Federal judges may appoint volunteer probation officers and each judge one salaried officer. By January, 1930, apparently only eight of the ninety-one federal districts had appointed salaried officers. The law allows each of the 144 judges to appoint one. Congress appropriated for this purpose only $25,000. There is now before Congress a Bill which provides that each Federal Judge may appoint as many salaried full-time probation officers as he deems necessary to carry out efficiently the tasks of probation investigation and supervision within his district. These appointments are to be subject to the approval of the Department of Justice, which has the power to fix salaries. The Bill provides that the administration of probation in all United States courts shall be under the general supervision of the Attorney-General, or his authorized agent.

The friends of probation have frequently made too much of the extent to which the system has been authorized by law while the real test of its effectiveness lies in the kind of provision made for its proper administration. Here the picture is not so hopeful to those who believe in the new order. Many states permit probation but have no probation supervision. Many others provide officers who, frequently, are wholly incompetent political henchmen. Only a few well organized and properly manned adult probation departments exist anywhere. Of these the New York Court of General Sessions, the Detroit Recorder's Court, and the Newark County Court are probably the best. They set a standard which may not be approximated by any appreciable number of American cities for many years.[6]

While probation began primarily as a means for the control of delinquents who had been found guilty and who were permitted to remain at large in lieu of imprisonment, in the most effective courts probation has come to mean a sort of intelligence bureau to aid the court in dealing with defendants. A probation department frequently makes a report on practically all the defenders tried. It submits to the sentencing judge the result of its study. It makes recommendations which the judge almost in-

[6] For a very informing account of the work in New York see Edwin J. Cooley's *Probation and Delinquency* (New York, 1927).

variably follows in granting probation. In only one case out of five has it recommended probation when guilt has been established. In that way the judges are able to have at hand expert advice with regard to every case. This, it would seem, is the most important contribution which probation has made to the administration of justice.

A survey of the present state of probation and parole leads irresistibly to a single conclusion, the statement of which may perhaps be considered by the more passionate friends of these devices as a most unfortunate expression of an unfriendly attitude toward them. Essentially, probation and parole supervision must be done by extraordinary people, in order to be measurably effective. It is possible that for the most part these methods can never command the service of persons sufficiently extraordinary to make them in the highest degree workable. Certainly, as the prestige value of these positions is now rated, they cannot command the type of persons who are needed. With a few illuminating exceptions in the adult probation field probation is being pretty badly served. A work which ought to call to its service inspired men and women is often being performed by routineers, political misfits, untrained though well intentioned nobodies. Even with civil service standing guard this tendency is likely to be present, because the recruiting of probation officers cannot rise much higher than the persons who are available. At the end of an examination of more than fifty candidates for jobs as probation officers in a city where the salary is not at all inadequate, the examiners turned to each other with the question: "Where are the persons to be secured for these positions? Surely these candidates are not the kind that we need." The successful prosecution of probation work requires a combination of personal qualities of a very high order. To establish a personality in the ways of right living, to bring back self-respect, to temper the embitterment that sometimes leads to crime, to fire with new and more constructive ambition, to win the confidence of the suspicious and warped mind—these are difficult. To do them well requires the devotion and capacity of men and women possessed with both intelligence and spiritual integrity of a high order.

To get laymen with these extraordinary qualities will be impossible if judges are not themselves aware of the character of the problem with which they are dealing. In the last analysis, the quality of probation officers will depend on the quality of the judges served. Thus, we are brought to the essential need for a stronger, more intelligent and more humanly educated judiciary.

In addition to the difficulties in getting proper personnel under present political conditions is the problem of scientific progress. Heroic efforts remain to be made to determine to what extent certain types of offenders may be identified. In addition, there should be developed, if it be possible, more scientific methods by which treatment may be planned which meets the individual needs of these types. The extent to which this can be done will finally depend upon the extent to which "human relations" can be subjected to scientific analysis.

II. *Parole*

In the United States, parole has been a development of the past fifty years, although as early as 1776 philanthropic societies had undertaken the task of aiding ex-prisoners. Prior to 1875 the release of prisoners before the expiration of their fixed term was limited to two sorts of action: the first, the exercise of the pardoning power by the governor; the second, the "good time laws" which permitted prisoners to be released because of good behavior during their term of imprisonment. This, however, did not constitute parole in the true sense of the term. There was little supervision or assistance for those who were thus released, although some states released prisoners by indenturing them to employers. But here and there inspectors began to appear who were vested with the responsibility of seeing that released prisoners were not exploited by their employers. In 1845 Massachusetts appointed a state agent to aid released prisoners, allowing him the use of state funds for such work. During the past fifty years a new period has begun with the establishment of the Elmira Reformatory in New York, and the creation by law of a system of parole for that reformatory. Following this there spread over a great part of the United States a tendency toward indeterminate sentences and parole laws, which took a wide variety of forms.[7] By 1930, forty-six states had adopted parole laws.[8]

Space does not permit a detailed consideration of parole in all of its multitude of aspects. A student of parole in the United States is struck by the complicated character of the material with which he is dealing. If he seeks to measure parole in terms of success or failure, he must take into consideration first the various meanings given to these terms by different students of the subject. He must, then, make due allowance for the failure of all who have attempted to measure the success of parole to reach a final exact conclusion as to the conduct of all the persons who are placed on parole—in other words, the failure to follow up such cases. He should note that much of what is called parole is really a way of terminating a first sentence. Again, he must make allowance for the difference in laws governing release from prison.

Even so, an examination of the fairly extensive material on parole [9] justifies certain definite conclusions as to its operation in the United States, which may be summarized as follows:

1. Parole boards have been created with casual indifference as to the great importance of the work they should perform. They are chiefly *ex-officio* with an occasional member appointed by the governor, usually on a small salary, to act with the *ex-officio* members. Almost invariably parole-board membership is part-time. Such jobs are looked upon as unimportant bits of patronage thrown to persons of a semi-political character who wish to "uplift" convicts. As recently as twenty years ago members of the New York State Parole Board had to pay their own expenses in visiting prisons, and, of course, received no salary at all. The official members of these boards range from the governor down, frequently including the superintendent of prisons or the

---

[7] Ohio extended parole to state prisoners in 1884. A federal parole law was passed in 1910 for prisoners serving more than one year. The facts in the foregoing paragraph are from Sutherland, Criminology, pp. 524-525.

[8] See Bramer, *Parole* (New York, 1926), 34-42, for a chronological list of these enactments.

[9] See A. F. Kuhlman, *Guide to Material on Crime and Criminal Justice* (New York, 1929), 569-577.

person occupying a similar position, wardens of prisons, and occasionally the attorney-general. A state usually has several parole boards acting for its various institutions. No state has a genuinely centralized parole system for all of its penal and correctional institutions, although Massachusetts, New Jersey and Illinois are attempting to do it.

There is no real supervision, so far as can be determined, in any of the states. While competent case-workers testify that the number of persons which a single official can supervise properly ranges from forty to seventy [10] and that no competent estimate places the number of parolees per parole officer at more than seventy-five, even the best parole systems range very much higher, while in some states a single parole officer attempts to exercise supervision over hundreds of released convicts. It follows that there is practically no supervision. A casual system of reporting is provided which places upon the released convict, himself, the responsibility of calling at intervals at the office of the parole board or mailing a report on his activities.

Few genuinely free decisions are made by parole boards. The entire system is so involved in legal technicalities that a parole board generally finds itself passing in a most perfunctory fashion upon claims for parole which it would be difficult to refuse either because of the commitments of the recommending officers or on account of the generally accepted standards which have been put into operation by almost unanimous consent. The 1924 Report of the New York Board of Parole shows clearly how little independent judgment is permitted.

"When a man receives an indeterminate sentence he is usually advised that with good conduct he will doubtless receive parole at the expiration of the minimum term. In fact, our contact with the courts infers that it is the intention of the court that the man shall be released at the expiration of the minimum terms if he complies with the prison rules, etc. It would certainly destroy the spirit and any good results should he be kept without there appearing to him any good and sufficient reason therefor; so that if we are to have the indeterminate sentence and the Parole System, it is of the utmost importance that we retain the respect and confidence of the prisoner.

[10] On this point, see George Alger's report of *Board of Parole and Parole System of the State of New York* (Albany, 1926), 17.

"Is it not true that he must be released at some time? And this being so, is it not the psychological moment with him to release him at the time he expects to go and when he feels that he has earned his parole? And would it not be quibbling to contend, in arguing, one person with another, as to whether the man should be kept a few months longer? The great objective should be to give him a chance, then, if he does not avail himself of the opportunity, return him for further correction."

As a result of this theory of parole, approximately ninety per cent of all cases have been paroled in New York on the expiration of their minimum sentences. Obviously, the decisions of such parole boards are made upon a wholly formal basis.

No scientific method of guidance has yet been used by parole boards. A parole board may decide to place emphasis upon certain factors, and at the very next meeting to disregard these factors in individual cases. It changes its policies as the political winds change. It leads prisoners to expect certain criteria as measurements, and before the cases of these prisoners come up for consideration their determining factors are changed. Little more than the blind enactment of a warden's recommendation characterizes the actions of any of the parole boards of the United States.

Enough has been said to indicate that parole systems in general have been established on such haphazard and limited bases that it is impossible to form a judgment as to the ways in which parole could actually operate if it were given a chance. Consequently, we have legislative timidity manifested over and over again through a process of passing parole laws which are not adequate to provide a real test of the system, and then when the inadequate system fails, matters are made worse by the further limitation of parole. Apparently no state has yet recognized the necessity for a real test of parole. It would seem that the wisest legislative policy would be to recognize the fact that the remedy for the evils which spring out of the present inadequate parole systems may be to provide more adequately for parole. But it seems impossible for legislatures to meet the situation in any such fashion. Meanwhile, the tiresome round proceeds.

One of the most distressing facts which emerges from any consideration of present-day policies of dealing with crime is capriciousness in administration, particularly as manifested in parole. A study in practically any state of the exercise of parole power over a period of years would probably show violent fluctuations in the proportion of persons released on parole. The reason for this is the effect upon parole policy of certain external forces which influence those responsible for parole. For example, there is a wave of public hysteria concerning crime. Magazine articles appear denouncing the sentimentality with which criminals are treated. Politicians cry out for more severity in dealing with criminals. Thereupon, the public officials responsible for parole administration decide that more severity is required, with the result that a wholly irrational tightening of parole is effected. This continues over a period during which congestion becomes more pronounced in prisons, and, after the temporary hysteria has passed, the prisons are emptied by indiscriminate and just as irrational liberality. Such policies evoke nothing but discontent and bitterness. It is very significant that prison riots in New York followed rather closely upon a public demand for a period of great severity toward prisoners.

Politics in the administration of parole can be taken for granted. A very interesting series of letters illustrating this was recently copied from the files of certain parole authorities. They concern a man who had been sent to a reformatory upon conviction of first-degree robbery. His sentence was for five years, and at the time when his political friends were able to secure his release he had served only seven months. Almost immediately after his conviction, a state senator wrote to the superintendent of the reformatory, saying that the sister of the convict had been his secretary for some time and that he was interested in the boy and considered that his part in the crime had been brought about by his association with bad companions. The senator promised that if paroled to him he would secure employment for the man. Six months later, the governor of the state wrote to the superintendent, stating that the senator was interested in the particular convict, adding that he "would be glad if you could let him have an opinion as to the merits of the case." The superintendent replied to the governor, "I am not very favorable to special parole but have a good deal of faith that one would not be

misplaced in this case." The next day, the superintendent wrote
to the senator that "while it had been the rule of the prison board
to require the recommendation of the trial judge and prosecuting
attorney for special paroles, if the governor wishes to put the case
up to the prison board without such recommendation, I would be
glad to approve the application you have sent me." The senator
then replied to the superintendent that "if the board desires to
parole A. on his record, I will be perfectly willing to sign the
papers if there are any papers to come to me." The superintendent then formally approved the application for parole and
forwarded it to the proper person. The record indicates that the
convict was released on a Christmas furlough, and there is no
further evidence that he returned to the institution. In fact, four
days after Christmas the superintendent wrote to the convict as
follows: "This is to advise you that the prison board has not yet
taken definite action on your parole, but you may continue to
remain home on your Christmas furlough until disposed of
within a short time." The story ends the following month, when
the parole was approved. It is instances like this, which undoubtedly occur very frequently, that have given so much trouble to
those who believe that parole ought to be given a fair trial.

If parole is to succeed, it must be established upon a basis
quite different from that which now exists in any of the states
where it is operating. A number of fundamental conditions are
necessary to its success, most of which are lacking in all the states
where it is recognized in law. The six principles which follow
were formulated by and are stated in a report of a committee
appointed in 1930 by Governor Franklin D. Roosevelt, to plan a
parole system for the State of New York.[11]

1. It is important that the state itself recognize that parole
is a state function, and that the responsibility for its maintenance
rests upon the state. In many instances, supervision of paroled
prisoners is assumed by private agencies or individuals. This has

[11] The report of this committee, while its application is limited to the conditions
of a single state, expresses the condition which friends of parole recognize as necessary
to its success. The membership of the committee was Sam A. Lewisohn, Chairman,
George W. Alger, Edwin J. Cooley, Jane M. Hoey, John S. Kennedy, Raymond Moley.
The recommendations of this committee were embodied in a bill and passed by the 1930
Legislature. Senator Baumes and Assemblyman Esmond were largely instrumental in
securing its passage.

been the system in operation in New York State. The difficulties of supervising the agencies are frequently very great, and the irregularities resulting from supervision by the agencies themselves are also frequently great.

2. The parole function, both in the determination of the persons who should be paroled and in their supervision, should not be exercised by the prison authorities themselves, as is the case under most parole systems at the present time. While there should be close coöperation between parole agencies and the prisons, the custody and control of those who are on parole should be taken from the prison itself. This suggestion is a decided break from most parole systems, in which parole officers are attached to prisons, and the persons on parole are in the legal custody of the wardens after parole.

3. The body charged with the duty of carrying on the parole work must have broad powers in law, high prestige and a definite procedure in the release and after-care of prisoners.

4. The prisons and reformatories themselves must be reorganized to such an extent that they will truly become schools of industry and training in the responsibilities of right living. Such preparation in the prisons is a necessary factor, if parole itself is to succeed. It is wrong to expect that parole can succeed, if some preparation for parole is not provided in the prisons themselves.

5. A parole board must be provided which has prestige, tenure and salary equal to or greater than that of the judiciary. If such qualities are proper to be invested in judges, whose functions and jurisdiction are rather strictly limited by law, surely those who exercise the power of release in the way a parole board should, ought to be equally endowed. The relative importance of parole and the judiciary has never been recognized in law or in the budgets providing for parole boards. At this point it is proper to say that there is no justification for the frequent assertion that parole boards ought to be composed of psychiatrists, physicians or other specialists. Neither is it necessary that these boards include members of the legal profession. Such boards are supposed to exercise broad discretion in a field in which technique is as yet only a subordinate consideration. They are judges and users of the technique of others, and within their staff they

should have psychiatric, legal and other technical services to provide material on which judgments may be made. The judgments themselves are of necessity lay judgments, unfettered by dogmatic professional rules.

6. The state should make adequate provision for an organization and staff of sufficiently high-grade individuals to assure that parole supervision and selection will be exercised intelligently and effectively. It should be noted that two groups of individuals will be subject to the interest of a parole system. The first will be those prisoners who are prospective candidates for parole from the time of their commitment. The work with this group is in the nature of investigation and study, and a sufficient number of trained investigators and case workers should be provided to enable this staff to function properly. The other group consists of those who are on parole, and they, of course, should be supervised by a staff that is able to provide constant and effective control and guidance. Those who have had the greatest experience say that each worker should have a case load of not more than forty persons. In addition, there should, of course, be general services—such as an employment bureau, a psychiatric clinic, and other necessary adjuncts to the work of the staff itself. In states like New York, Pennsylvania and Illinois, such a staff would cost not less than a·million dollars. The nearest approach to such an outlay was made by Illinois, whose expenditure over a period of three years has averaged between five and six hundred thousand dollars. The State of New York spends less than one hundred thousand·dollars. Such expenditure is an economy over prison care, which has proved quite unable to deal with prisoners effectively. The average cost of maintaining a prisoner in the state prisons and reformatories of New York was $1.29 a day for the fiscal year 1928-1929. *The unit cost of parole supervision under a quite adequate parole system would be less than thirty cents a day.* Modern prisons are becoming more and more costly. A new state prison now under construction at Attica, New York, will cost more than twelve million dollars. The wall alone will cost a million dollars, and each cell between six and eight thousand dollars.

III. *Human Relations, an Art Trying to Become a Science*

The so-called case records of a first-class social agency indicate the thoroughness with which every individual who has committed an offense against the criminal law should be examined and the variety and scope of the information which a genuinely efficient agency in either parole or probation work should furnish for the guidance of the judge or the parole board or the governor who is exercising the power of pardon.

The development of such case studies has been the contribution of social and psychiatric work during the past generation. Starting in a period when a person making a decision as to a dependent or a delinquent had nothing more to guide him than a look and a few casual questions, the social work of the time has proceeded in the direction of a genuinely scientific method. Naturally this method cannot yet claim the accuracy of an exact science. Generations of experience will have to be carried on before exactness can be attained.

Human factors cannot be measured and tested in the way that engineering problems can be analyzed. Social work is still an art rather than a science; but an art which is acquiring the intellectual attitude of science and is already using some of its technique. Under the best modern systems of social and personal diagnosis the facts bearing upon the conduct of a criminal are gathered with the same care and that same devotion to scientific accuracy evolved by the science of medicine. True, many of the factors upon which final judgment must rest are indeterminate, but that is partly true of medical diagnosis also. The diagnosis of a single case should be so detailed and carefully conducted that an officer making such studies should be assigned not more than twelve investigations a month. The standard information sheet of the Court of General Sessions includes scores of items. The diagnostic procedure is outlined as follows:

I. LEGAL HISTORY

> Previous Court Record—(Offense, Disposition)
> Abstract of Indictment—(Details of Charge)
> Offense

Complainant
Mitigating and Aggravating Circumstances
Attitude of Complainant

II. ANALYSIS OF ENVIRONMENT

Personal History—(Age, Racial Origin, Time in U. S. and in City, Citizenship, Marital Status)

Education and Early Life—(School Progress, Mentality, Psychopathic Traits, Amusements, Early Associates, Habits, Religious Training, Age First Delinquent, Home Life and Relation to Adult Career)

Family and Neighborhood—(Family History, if Broken, Reared by, Circumstances, Living Conditions, Moral Conditions, Reputation, Present and Previous Addresses)

Industrial History—(Occupation or Trade, Length of Time Employed, Wages, Reliability, Skill; if Unemployed, Dates and Causes, and Means of Subsistence; Industrial Ambition, Vocational Maladjustment, Influence of Daily Work, Thrift, Army-Navy Service)

III. ANALYSIS OF PERSONALITY

Physical and Mental—(Normality, Heredity, Alcoholism, Drug Addiction, Glandular Disturbances, Tuberculosis, Social Disease; Capacity, Traits, Interests; Mental Conflicts, Psychoses, Examinations, Institutional Commitments—Intelligence Quotient)

Character and Conduct—(Characteristics, Temperament, Attitude toward Authority, Sociality, Aptitudes and Interests; Temperance, Sense of Responsibility, Conduct in Relation to Home, School, Work, Community, Impulses; Urges, Philosophy, Stability, Introvert, Extravert, Attitude toward Life—Offenses, etc., Recreation, Habits, Associates, Religious Observance, Manner and Appearance)

Etiology—(Of the Maladjustment—Subjectively, Constitutional Conditions, Internal Factors, and, Objectively—Environmental Conditions, External Factors

Decisions made on this basis must of necessity be unrestricted by too many predetermined rules of criminal law. The criminal law is, after all, a rather crude affair. It picks certain well-identified types of conduct and fixes a penalty. Then, through certain rules, it attempts to determine the conditions under which these acts, if committed, will be considered crimes. Beyond that, legislation is powerless. However, if the limitations of legislation were frankly recognized and sufficient discretion given to someone to insure that the infinitely varied human types of conduct which fall within the broad confines of the criminal law would be subjected to a more equal determination, justice in its most enlightened sense could be more definitely achieved. A grant of such discretion to the court or to a parole board should be accompanied by facilities for making the kind of determination required. In a court such facilities are provided by a well-organized probation department; and in a parole board by a staff of the proper size and competence. The necessary corollary to a grant of discretion is provision for the wise exercise of such discretion.

There must, however, be much scientific study before decisions as to parole and probation can get far beyond the stage of guessing. Extensive and thorough studies of the effects of probation and parole must be made, and such studies will of necessity have to build up their own technique. One of the most interesting and significant studies of this nature has been made by Dr. Sheldon Glueck in collaboration with Eleanor T. Glueck.[12] A detailed investigation was made of all former inmates of the Massachusetts Reformatory whose parole periods expired during the years 1921-1922. These comprise 510 cases. The distinctive feature of the study was the extent to which these former inmates of the Reformatory were followed up and the ingenious statistical methods by which various factors in their histories were considered and measured. Translated into terms of the success or failure of those who were thus released, the study shows that a very large percentage failed to adjust themselves to society. Therefore, measured in terms of the success or failure of parole, the study has been somewhat disillusioning to those who claimed complete success for the system. It is, however, just as severe an indictment of the prison system which preceded parole.

Another significant study of parole and parole failure was made by Professors E. W. Burgess, A. A. Bruce, and A. J. Harno, in Illinois.[13] The net effect of these studies is not to discredit parole as a principle but to indicate means by which parole can

[12] Published as 500 Criminal Careers (New York, 1930).
[13] Illinois Crime Survey, 427-579.

be made more effective. The continuation of such studies is the only possible means by which administrative discretion vested in the courts and parole boards can secure the necessary intelligent direction to justify itself. As Dean Pound says in commenting upon the Glueck study:

"At the moment, reaction from administrative justice, the chief agency of individualization, and from the modes of thought and procedures which it involves, is to be seen in every field of the law. Everywhere we are seeking a real certainty as distinguished from the illusory certainty of the nineteenth century. In juristic thinking there is the revived analytical jurisprudence which starting from fixed assumptions is to proceed with mathematical assurance. In Continental Europe there is the 'pure science of law' which seeks to give 'clarity and rigor' to the phenomena of the legal order by excluding all interpretation and application. In criminal law there is the positivist movement with its reliance upon research and observation and scientific formulation. Bergson taught us the relation of 'instinct' to administrative action. He showed us that there are things which can be done only through the trained habits of experienced administrators. Yet their instinct may be guided toward more assured results by formulas scientifically worked out on the basis of exact observation. As the emphasis yesterday was upon this trained instinct, the emphasis today is upon the means of guiding it and upon research as a forerunner thereof. . . . Study of the means of insuring that the results of probation and kindred devices of individualized penal treatment may be made reasonably predictable is not merely in the right line of thought of today, it is needed to save for us one of the really epoch-making discoveries of American legal history. Let it once be made clear that probation laws may be administered with a reasonable assurance of distinguishing between the sheep and the goats, let it be shown that the illusory certainty of the old system may be replaced by a régime of reasonably predictable results as compared with one of merely predictable sentence, and the paths of a modern penal treatment will be made straight." [14]

IV. *Prophecy vs. Experience*

In 1927, during his final term in public service and after twenty-five years of intimate knowledge of penal problems, Governor Alfred E. Smith of New York made a bold proposal which did more to focus public attention upon fundamentals in criminal justice than all the philosophers and reformers have done in a generation. He proposed to cut through all of the

[14] 42 *Harvard L. R.*, 298-299 (1929).

musty tradition and pettifogging compromise and confusion in present penal law and take the power of fixing sentence away from the judge entirely, leaving to him and to the court only the determination of the single question of guilt. Punishment and reformation were to be vested elsewhere. The proposal can best be described in the Governor's own forceful words:

"In the first place, I believe that the power of sentence ought to be taken away from judges entirely, and I further believe that fixed and definite sentences should be made dependent upon the finding of a commission. . . . The jury ought to determine guilt or innocence without anything in their minds except did he commit this crime or did he not, and as soon as the verdict is rendered and he is found guilty, he ought to be turned over to the State of New York for such disposition as would be determined by a board of the highest salaried men that we probably have in our community. I do not think it would be a mistake for the State of New York to set up a board properly constituted of psychiatrists, alienists, lawyers and students. It would not be any mistake if we paid $25,000 a year; and let them make the final disposition of that man in the best interest of the state and the best interest of the man himself, and thereafter the control and disposition would remain with that body with the power to recommend parole or transfer probably to a state institution for the care of the feeble-minded or the insane. . . . A clearing house (after conviction and before sentence) ought to be provided where these men could be under close observation for a period that a psychiatrist suggests as necessary to make some diagnosis of his case so as to determine all the factors. . . . After sentence a good many things are found out about a man that the judge does not have in mind when he is sentencing him. . . . There are no two criminals alike. There are no two crimes exactly alike. There is a different set of facts and circumstances that lead up to them all. A great many of them are accidental, and if you can have a board to study this thing, spend money for it, it is worth while spending it." [15]

Governor Smith's proposal was not new. It was not the first time he himself had proposed it. He had advocated practically the same thing in 1920.[16] Coming as it did, however, in 1927,

[15] Sentencing Criminals by Tribunal Separate from Trial Court. Remarks by Governor Smith at conference with Crime Commission of New York State at Albany, December 7, 1927. Published by the Crime Commission.

[16] Governor Smith was probably guided somewhat by a system in operation for less serious offenses in New York City. The law provides that all sentences for certain crimes which are punishable by imprisonment in the district penitentiary are for an indeterminate period, with a maximum of two years. A district parole board is created which has the power to fix sentence. Thus, the magistrates and the Court of

at a time when his political fortunes were so well known to the people of the United States, the fundamental proposal to separate the trial function from that of sentencing received wide publicity and discussion. There is little doubt that Governor Smith's proposal represented a compromise with what he actually thought should be adopted. He undoubtedly felt that in view of the existing state of public sentiment, which was at that time highly charged with an emotional reaction against humanitarianism in dealing with criminals, the recommendation of a clear-cut indeterminate sentence system, with a board of experts to administer parole, would gain no overwhelming public support. Consequently he proposed a system which, though it fell short of the idea of a true indeterminate system, made provision for a sentencing authority that would not only be superior to the judge of any single court in breadth of view concerning the criminal's needs and in facilities for gathering knowledge about him, but would prevent the fixing of sentence in the frequently overcharged atmosphere in which trials are held. It would provide a means for arriving at a sentence at a place other than that of the trial, and at another time.

The great value of Governor Smith's proposal lies in the emphasis which it places upon the proper function of the judge. It makes clear that to impose upon a judge the duty of fixing sentence is to require something wholly inconsistent with his ability, and inconsistent with any proper understanding of the judicial function as well. The weakness of Governor Smith's proposal is that it still calls for prophecy with regard to a subject concerning which prophecies are futile. It provides the kind of commission which ought to be vested with the power to determine sentence, but it requires that this commission perform its function before instead of after the period of imprisonment.

"Indeterminate sentence" is the name commonly applied to a system by which the period of sentence is fixed by some authority other than the court, or by the specific terms of the law. In substance, it means that the law provides that for certain

Special Sessions, and in some instances the county courts, merely determine the guilt or innocence of the accused, and the parole board, after investigation, fixes a definite sentence within the range provided by law. Their sentence, however, needs the approval of the sentencing judge, which in most cases is given as a matter of course.

crimes or for certain types of criminal the period of imprisonment shall be indefinite and that release shall be decided upon
by a board (usually a parole board) or some other administrative or judicial authority.[17]

The complete and unrestricted indeterminate sentence is practically never found. Some maximum or minimum, or both, are
almost always provided. The principle of indefiniteness in sentence is, however, well defined. It means that the punishment
should not be fixed in accordance with the crime, but should
be measured with some reference to the criminal. And such measuring should take place after a period of imprisonment, when,
presumably, there is available a body of knowledge concerning
the individual to guide the determination of release. Indeterminate
sentences are usually related to some sort of parole supervision
subsequent to release, but this is not always required.

The extent to which a person believes in the indeterminate
sentence is the measure of his belief in the theory that the
criminal's treatment should be determined individually and not
generally. It does not necessarily follow that to believe in the
indeterminate sentence is to believe in reform rather than in
punishment. Neither does it follow that the indeterminate system would be more lenient. Rational discussion of the subject
will be greatly promoted if it is placed squarely upon the basis
of when and by whom a criminal's sentence shall be decided
by the exact terms of law, by the judgment of the judge or jury,
or by some authority acting after imprisonment has begun.

A review of some of the controversial points in connection
with this system will clarify its characteristics and possibilities.

Much discussion has been devoted to the question of whether
indeterminate sentences are shorter than fixed sentences. The
classical school says that it results in shorter sentences. The positivists retort that sentences are longer. The figures seem to support the positivists. But it seems that there are grave difficulties
in such "proof." It may be shown that on the average the sentences are longer under an indeterminate system and such figures

---

[17] It is not necessary for the purposes of this chapter to set forth the great variety
of such laws among the American states. Some of their details are in Robinson,
Penology in the United States (Philadelphia, 1921), XI; Sutherland, *Criminology*, XXI;
and Bramer, *Parole*, II.

may be reduced to the specific crimes involved. The terms of sentence which are compared are, however, of different persons, which introduces an element of doubt. And no one can tell what effect either system has upon the judges, juries, lawyers, prosecutors, and the accused themselves, in the process of determining guilt. Many people believe, without much proof, to be sure, that juries are more likely to find a verdict of guilty when the sentence is to be indeterminate. They can pass the weight of responsibility on to the parole board. Apparently the statistical data compiled on this point have been prepared more for purposes of controversy than to aid in ascertaining the truth. When those who believe, with most modern criminologists, that our prisons do their inmates more harm than good, strongly support the indeterminate sentence and offer as an argument carefully compiled statistics to show that their plan results in longer sentences, they are, to say the least, illogical!

Happily, the point does not need to be proved. It is not at all pertinent to the basic question.

Another objection is urged by those who still firmly believe in conspicuous punishment as a deterrent to potential criminals. The argument of this group is that the publication of the news that a person has been found guilty and sentenced to a definite term of, say, twenty years, causes the assumed potential criminal to conjure up in his mind a vision of what twenty years of imprisonment would mean to him and that this mental picture would be so unlovely as to deter him from crime. While competent psychologists have already thrown grave doubt upon the reality of such deterrence, we may, for the argument's sake, assume that it can exist. Perhaps it would satisfy the believers in deterrence to publish under an indeterminate-sentence system the news, not of the conviction and sentence, but of the release from prison. An ironical view might conceive such an account as this:

Today there was released from the state's prison John Ward. He was convicted twenty years ago. He is now forty-six. The prison psychiatrist says he has developed a very serious neurosis which, as long as he lives, will torture his mind with illusory fears. The physician says he has, because of the conditions of prison life, developed a serious organic disease which will reduce his earning capacity to even less than when he was convicted. The warden says his parents died ten years ago. His brothers and sisters have either died or have moved to other parts. His friends have disappeared or have forgotten him. He is returning to the city where he lived with a total capital of ten dollars given to him by the state. He will probably be discriminated against in every relationship of life. The police will often question him with regard to new offenses. When the time came to leave the prison he was scarcely able to prepare himself for the journey. He had to be helped to dress. He was even unable to put on his collar and necktie. Take note, ye potential criminals.

This would at least be less of a burden to the imagination of the potential criminal. The believer in deterrence might compare this with the present laconic, "John Ward was today sentenced to twenty years in state's prison for robbery."

The other points of controversy relate to the competence of a parole board and its ability to resist improper influences. Parole boards, they say, are political, weak, sometimes venal, always casual; it is better to do injustice in individual cases by fixing sentence by law than to run the risk of wholesale incompetence and political partiality. Many answers are pertinently made to this contention. Parole boards, as we have already insisted, should have status, tenure and salary commensurate with their duties. They do work more important than that of trial judges, but have not the same standing. No state has ever had a properly constituted parole board; so the system has never been properly tried. Concentration of power in one body should provide a corrective to the evil of hidden influences. Political pressure has always preferred a decentralized system such as is provided by the scattering of sentencing power among many county and district judges. A parole board may act slowly and deliberately, with proper attention to publicity for sponsors of applicants. The trial judge, as we have repeatedly pointed out, should be made as free of political entanglements as is possible. Hence, to subtract from his burdens the annoyance of political interference in sentence fixing would be to grant him a distinct measure of freedom.

In the last analysis the indeterminate sentence stands upon a principle which is unanswerable. Whether one believes in punishment or in the personal rehabilitation of the criminal, it is essential that a decision be made after a period of imprisonment rather than before. A single year of imprisonment may be a more serious punishment to a sensitive person than ten years would be to a hardened, dull-witted one. The possession of these qualities can best be determined after observation of the manner in which a prisoner reacts to prison life. Likewise, the extent to which a person has equipped himself for a successful return to society can best be known only after the corrective influence has been administered. The indeterminate sentence prefers established fact to theory, experience to prophecy.

PART III

THE PUBLIC'S INTERESTS *VS.* THE PUBLIC INTEREST

CHAPTER X

TRIAL BY THE CITY DESK

IT is unnecessary to discuss here the psychological factors which make crime a primary focus of human interest. From the fourth chapter of the Book of Genesis to *The Greene Murder Case,* the written chronicles of the human race have heavily featured the infraction of social rules and the punishment meted out therefor. The world's literature is deeply colored with crime, punishment and retribution. In one of the great plays Shakespeare captures and fixes the reader's attention with a fratricidal murder and then forces him to hear profound reflection upon human destiny. The greatest of novels portrays a series of deep human experiences, almost unrelated, within the unity of the shadow of a crime, the consequences of which Hugo dramatizes as a great indictment of the inflexible and inhuman criminal law and its faulty enforcement. The crime motif remains a permanent and possibly a growing factor in human concerns.

This vast public interest in crime, exploited as it is by modern methods of publicity, creates new influences which bear upon the administration of criminal justice. This book is not concerned with most of these. It does not consider whether crime news causes crime, whether newspaper accounts of crime prevent the apprehension of criminals, whether crime news is a proper index to the amount of crime, or whether circulation wars are related to organized crime. It is partially concerned with the extent to which the desire for newspaper publicity guides the activities of officials. It is, however, primarily concerned with what has come to be called "trial by newspaper," which means the extent to which newspaper enterprise of certain kinds actually interferes with the fair and impartial trial of those charged with crime.

I. *News, Public Opinion and Trial by Jury*

Maurine Watkins, who created the deservedly successful play *Chicago,* must have been agreeably surprised by the readiness with which the public accepted her satirical humor. The acclaim of critics was to be expected, because most critics are reporters before they attain the heights, and they well know the eternal truth of the playwright's accurate digs at the press. But the enjoyment of the public could hardly have been entirely due to the hilarious burlesque. It was probably due to the fact that the mass of intelligent people was becoming aware of what close observers have known for a long time, namely, that newspaper enterprise under modern conditions exercises a vital and all-pervasive influence upon criminal justice. There is not only trial by the press, but detection, arrest, prosecution, defense and, what is still more significant, extra-legal punishment, governed by the exigencies of news-gathering.[1]

Chicago, however, as Mr. Nathan points out in the introduction, is not merely "a caricature of the Illinois frontier town that hides behind a mask of metropolitan civilization." True, Miss Watkins spent her apprenticeship in Chicago, and during the winter of the play's run in New York it was popular to identify that city with crime. But the play might as appropriately have been given the name of any of a score of other American cities, including New York. It depicts the murder, in the course of a drunken brawl over money, of a clandestine visitor, by a wife of easy virtue. There follow, in picturesque succession, the entry of the police and the representative of the particular newspaper favored by the police through a previously arranged agreement; the stupid preliminary gestures of the police sergeant; the working up of the case for the state by an assistant state's attorney with an eye to publicity values and the possibility that the case may lift him out of his despised three thousand dollar job ("justice and society") and into the ranks of successful defense counsel ("humanity and mercy"); and the inevitable flashlights of the attractive killer. The defendant's subsequent stay in the wretched

[1] The play, with an introduction by George Jean Nathan, was published by Knopf, 1927.

and graft-ridden county jail is largely taken up with interviews with the "sob-sister" engaged in writing the life history
of the prostitute, who has now become the "Beautiful Jazz
Slayer." [2]

Allowing for pardonable dramatic exaggeration, Miss Watkins' play is a most moving and accurate portrayal of "trial by
the press." Its value as a portrayal of life lies in the fact that it
presents through the medium of an imaginary situation the motives, methods and attitudes of a certain type of newspaper enterprise. It would be an unusual newspaper man, if his experience
had extended to any section of the yellow press, who would deny
the accuracy of Miss Watkins' indictment.

The law well recognizes that the public opinion which sur-
rounds a criminal trial is an important factor in determining its
outcome. If the emotional life of a community be surcharged
with prejudice for or against a defendant, the outcome of the
trial is likely to be influenced by this bias. This is true even when
a jury is selected with scrupulous regard for the impartiality
of its individual membership. It is true even when the jury is
carefully protected, during the trial, from the world outside.
It is true even when the judge is strong and fair. Hence legal
tradition has set up safeguards through which changes of venue
and other devices are adopted to protect trials from public opinion.
That such protection is wise, is attested by instances which are
common. The James boys were popular and therefore safe in
counties where they committed countless crimes. Industrial warfare has with impunity tainted the fountain of justice in many
counties. Waves of popular prejudice have carried to conviction
defendants whose guilt, viewed in retrospect, was very imperfectly established. It is commonly said that Washington is so
full of prejudice against "the government" that convictions for
offenses against the state are hard to get. The problem of public
opinion is, therefore, distinctly involved in the enforcement of
criminal law.

In these days of journalistic mass production, in a society so

[2] Her "diary," featured as "The Little Book to Which She Told Her Secrets,"
elicits from her the question, "Say, who do you suppose wrote that stuff?" and a
fellow female prisoner comments, "No sense of honor. They broke into my apartment
the night I left and stole a whole suitcase of letters."

largely literate, the press becomes so important a factor in the formation of opinion that we have coined a phrase to describe its influence in the administration of justice—"trial by newspaper."[3]

It is not the amount of space given to crime that affects public opinion, but the method of presentation. Long accounts of criminal trials are not new in American journalism. In 1833, the Reverend Mr. Avery was tried for murder in Newport. The author of "Thanatopsis," then editor of the *New York Evening Post,* gave the entire front page to an account of the proceedings.[4] But such accounts of criminal actions, although very detailed, were not biased. Then, in the late nineties, when "yellow" came to be associated with certain kinds of newspapers, instrumentalities of emphasis came to be used, such as the enlarged headline, numerous pictures, feature stories, Sunday magazines, "sob stories," and reporter detectives out for exclusive news. The newspaper man became a good psychologist. He secured his emphasis by appealing to elemental emotions. He realized that a witness is not genuinely interested in a conflict unless he can take sides. He learned to know the types of "human interest" material—sex, mystery, uncertainty, the supernatural. The true dramatist provides this interest by creating a lovable protagonist and a hateful antagonist. He never, if he wants to be popular, fails to identify, unmistakably, the hero and the villain. Only in plays and fiction intended for the intelligent does this identification remain indefinite. And so, as the press came to appeal to a tremendously wider audience and its masters came to know the rules of "human interest," trials were dramatized; there was a side which the newspaper took and a side which it opposed. From the moment the press discovered this simple human preference (known to the dramatist from *Everyman* to *The Birth of a Nation*) the mischief which we know as "trial by the press" came into being.

There is no clear evidence to show how a newspaper reaches a decision as to whether it will favor the state or the defense.

[3] "Trial by Fury," as a very acute observer, James M. Kirby, calls it in *Criminal Justice* (New York, 1926). See Alger, Moral Overstrain (New York, 1906), Chapter 2.

[4] See "Trial by Tabloid," by Edmund Pearson in *Vanity Fair,* October, 1927, for an account of the attention given by the nineteenth century press to *causes célèbres.*

Probably such an actual decision is not made at any definite time. The representatives of the newspaper may merely discover that the defendant is interesting—has the possibilities of providing good copy. These possibilities may be poverty, beauty, youth, courage, or some other outstanding feature. Bias may be a matter of growth as the trial progresses. On the other hand, bias may result from the actual belief of the management that a defendant is innocent or guilty. There is no reason to assume that the motive is always selfishly in the interest of the newspaper. The bias may be inspired by the highest considerations of public interest. But however the decision may be made, and whatever the motive, certain newspapers sometimes seem to precede the jury in arriving at a decision as to guilt or innocence.

Methods are so crude and absurd that it is often difficult to contemplate them without losing sight of the serious public problem involved. One is likely to see only farce-comedy of the most hilarious kind. Most of those who enjoyed the play *Chicago* probably missed the satire and saw only comedy.

Irvin Cobb makes trial by newspaper the subject of a genuinely funny story.[5] This story, the fruit of the imagination of a thoroughly sophisticated newspaperman and humorist, tells of an enterprising metropolitan city editor who decides to play the side of Ina Fey, a "beautiful killer." During the trial, her "father" is produced by the city editor, and he stays near her during her "ordeal." The "sob-sister" of the newspaper thereupon writes devotedly of the defendant's father as that "fine, dignified old Confederate veteran . . . that tall old pine from Down-in-Dixie, so sound at the core, so frosted on top." (The author of the story comments that it made no difference to the reporter that Southern pines do not frost readily on top or elsewhere.) The defendant is a "crushed and blemished but still fragrant jessamine bloom of the Sunny Southland." The old man stays on, and "while he stayed the story 'stood up'." Finally, while the jury is deliberating, the editor has newsboys shout under the open window of the jury room, "Extra!—all about Ina Fey's ole mudder dyin'." This is too much for a jury quick with human compassion, and

[5] One of the incidents in a series published as "Alias Ben Alibi" (New York, 1923).

the verdict is "not guilty." The editor, commenting in private later, says, "She was guilty as the devil, but I have helped to convict many a slayer. Why not help one go free? What's a loose murderer, more or less, between friends? . . . And she had an ideal name for headline purposes."

Recognizing the seriousness of the problem involved in the publication of news in such manner as to influence the public to take sides the Crime Commission of New York State in its 1927 report [6] makes the following statement:

"It is a hopeful sign that there are many indications in present day journalism of a more objective way of writing news. Certain papers have made great progress in this direction by following as a definite policy the practice of limiting, so far as possible, the imagination of reporters in writing up news stories. However, the 'warm, personal' contact which some of the more sensational papers seem to want to establish between their news columns and the general public have prevented their columns from serving as an impartial vehicle for the dissemination of facts. The examples are already present in the best newspapers, and it is to be hoped that objectivity such as we have described may spread to other papers. The public should demand the news columns to carry not opinion and comment, but facts simply stated, and if a wider public constantly demands this, we may expect compliance from newspapers. Such a transformation, however, is not to be expected soon, and meanwhile it will be important to protect trial by jury from such extraneous influences. It will help considerably if courts seek to protect juries from contacts with the outside world through newspapers during a trial."

Moreover the extent to which some newspapers exploit sensational trials and crime news gives an altogether erroneous impression of the amount of crime. We think we are having a wave of crime when in reality we may be having only a wave of crime news.

We should realize that the "crime wave," so-called, is largely the result of the exigencies of the newspaper business. The demand for news varies greatly from time to time. A political campaign ends and many columns of news space are suddenly available. Crime news is always to be had. With minor fluctuations it is a constant and usable space filler. Hence we may expect it to expand when it becomes necessary to fill otherwise unused

[6] P. 303.

space. Perhaps the supposed rise in crime which sociologists used to associate with the coming of cold weather in November and December was actually only a rise in crime news, caused by the end of political campaigns and the editors' need for filling space. Such an interpretation, be it said, is conjecture only. It has never been adequately proved, but it is susceptible to proof. The general thesis that there may be a correlation between "crime waves" and crime news waves is reasonable and should be tested by future research.[7]

A small test of this sort was made in the Cleveland Crime Survey, from which the following is quoted:

"Let us compare the actual number of felonies for a given period with the newspaper prominence crime news was given in that period. Let us take the month of January, 1919, in which, according to the newspapers, a 'crime wave' got under way. The following table shows the number of felonies by weeks, exclusive of automobiles driven away, and the number of inches of news space given the administration of justice, including crime news, by the three dailies.

"It will be seen that while the amount of space given the accounts of crime and news of the administration of justice responded to an increase in the amount of crime, yet the response was out of all proportion to the actual increase in crime. Whereas 345 felonies were reported the first two weeks and 363 the last two weeks of the month, the amount of space given the administration of justice, including crime news, the first half of the month was 925 inches and the second half 6,642 inches. The first half of the month the newspapers were saying nothing about a 'crime wave,' the second half the readers were vehemently told that a crime wave was sweeping the city.

NUMBER OF FELONIES, BY WEEKS, COMPARED TO NEWS SPACE

		Inches of News Space		
		News and		Plain Dealer
Week beginning	Felonies	News-Leader	Press	Daily and Sunday
January 1	153	59	51	107
January 8	192	200	236	272
January 15	203	1304	1123	1451
January 22	160	765	813	1098

(Space occupied by headlines is not included in the figures.)

"Space devoted to news of actual crimes did not, of course, increase to so great an extent. A count of the inches devoted to crime news in one of

[7] This was made during the Cleveland Crime Survey in 1921. The account is quoted from "Criminal Justice in Cleveland," Part VII; "Newspapers and Criminal Justice," by M. K. Wisehart, pp. 544-546.

the dailies for January gives the following figures: Week of January 1, 49 inches; week of January 8, 144 inches; week of January 15, 246 inches; week of January 22, 196 inches. Incidentally, the paper publishing the most news of the 'crime wave' gave, in the week of January 15, 26 per cent of its news space to news of crime and the administration of justice."

That newspaper accounts which are biased actually influence readers scarcely needs demonstration. It can be shown, however, by gathering the opinions of newspaper readers in almost every important trial. Research has shown that readers of objective accounts remain in doubt. This is not only an indication of the extent to which the public mind may be influenced but it shows the gratifying fact that certain newspapers present the news in such an unbiased way as to leave the public mind in doubt— exactly as it should remain during a trial.[8]

A number of good examples drawn from well-known cases tried in the past few years are cited by Henry W. Taft in an informing address on "The Press and the Courts." [9]

"The press agitation which followed the recent death of Mrs. Gertie Emily Webb affords a striking illustration. It started with a strong suggestion that Mrs. Webb had been poisoned by her husband, based chiefly on conjectural statements said to have been made by a physician and interested relatives. The trend of the headlines and the text of the news articles were calculated to create an atmosphere of guilt, though evidence, legal or otherwise, was absent. Many intelligent readers were led to entertain a strong suspicion that Webb was guilty, and with many the suspicion has undoubtedly survived his exoneration. . . .

"Another case where the press created before the trial an impression of guilt of the accused was the Ward case. Under a heading on June 1, 1922, 'Tardy Action Started', the *American* said:

"'. . . The tardy move was made by the authorities fifteen days after Peters' bullet-pierced body was found near the Kensico reservoir. . . . It was a search that would have been made immediately after he surrendered if the slayer were the man without financial, social or political standing.'

". . . Throughout the trial Ward was referred to as a rich man. He was described as 'The Tanned Sphinx'. 'Great Ward Killing Mystery', as

---

[8] See the Report of the Crime Commission of New York State for 1927, 318-320.
[9] Mr. Taft's address was delivered before the Association of the Bar in the City of New York on May 24, 1924. It is printed in the *American Law Review* for July-August, 1924, and also in Mr. Taft's volume *Law Reform*, New York, 1927.

a headline, was alternately used with 'Wife Weeps in Court'. Other head-lines were 'Shot Unarmed Man and Lied About the Gun', 'To Let Slayer Keep Secret of Blackmail', 'State Is Sure Ward Owned Both Pistols', 'Confident Testimony Will Prove Contention', 'Ward Calmly Confronts Kin of His Victim', 'To Hear of "Love Nest!"' 'The Great Ward Killing Mystery will only be solved when the debonair Walter S. Ward arises in a courtroom and says, "I killed Clarence Peters."' It was stated that Ward produced his wife at the trial, making her undergo a terrific ordeal, while he blithely played cards with his jailer. The trial resulted in Ward's acquittal on September 28, 1923. . . ."

When the attitude created by the newspaper accounts is hostile to the defendant, the tendency is to destroy the practical value of the presumption of innocence, if not before the court at least before the public whose attitude will have a very important relationship to the subsequent life of the defendant whether he is acquitted or not. Because of the twisted information gained from the newspaper accounts of some cases, thousands of persons probably still believe in the guilt of the defendants. Popular confidence in the courts is not such as to make an acquittal a mitigating influence upon the popular prejudices. This public attitude can go far to visit upon an acquitted defendant a punishment which is almost as severe as the penalty of the law. This danger is one of the most serious consequences in the democratic administration of criminal justice. The initiated know, of course, that an indictment is often a purely technical act not necessarily based on adequate evidence and that it should not be taken as a reflection upon the integrity of the person indicted; yet to say, in later life, that a certain person has been indicted is to throw a serious mantle of suspicion about him.[10]

Moreover, the defenders of these newspaper accounts are not at all convincing in their claim that the jury is protected from newspaper influence. The portrayal of the case in biased terms may begin when an accusation is first made and by the time the trial date is reached the public may be influenced. This makes it difficult to get a jury, and when one is finally secured there is no good reason to suppose that its members have not been saturated with biased newspaper observations on the case. Fur-

[10] See *The Molineux Case* (New York, 1929).

thermore, even during the progress of the trial, newspaper accounts directly or indirectly may reach the judge and the jury.

In the address to which we have already referred, Mr. Taft makes the pertinent comment, "Judge, juries, witnesses, court attendants and hangers-on live in the atmosphere thus created. The customary admonition to jurors not to read the newspapers is based upon an assumption that human nature cannot resist the impression created by press accounts. But in spite of such warnings, what the newspapers say does leak to the judge and jury, and, in proportion as a case excites public interest, it affects their deliberations."

But let us assume that the public and the jury are actually kept apart during the progress of a trial and that the jurymen have neither seen a newspaper account of the case nor talked with anyone who has. Then, if the opinions of the persons who have written biased accounts of the trial are contrary to the judgment of the jury in its decision upon the case as it has been presented to them, there will be a widespread opinion that the outcome does not represent substantial justice. This shakes the confidence of the public in the courts. The average person does not stop to think that the judge and the jury who have reached a conclusion contrary to popular opinion may have been in a better position to know the facts. This would be expecting too much of a public which is sure of the accuracy of its own prejudices.[11]

The influence of the press upon the jury is only one aspect of the damage done by biased newspaper accounts. The jury is not the most important factor in the administration of criminal justice; most of the decisions are made by administrative discretion on the part of the prosecutor or the judge, or both. These persons, whose discretion is so liberally used in the acceptance of pleas, are politically selected and are, therefore, highly sensitive to the drift of public opinion. Their decisions are quite likely to be colored by what they think the public has been led to believe through newspaper accounts. A distinguished lawyer portrays the

[11] "Important as it was that people should get justice, it was even more important that they should be made to feel and see that they were getting it." Alay, *Victorian Chancellors*, II, 465.

effect of this desire on the part of public officials who conform to public preferences created by newspaper enterprise: [12]

"The atmosphere and sentiment thus created around a case are bound to, and do, affect not only the jury, but the court as well. A man does not lose his ambitions or human nature by climbing from the bar onto the bench. Most of our public men are known to us only as they are pictured by the newspapers, which make and unmake men. It is well-nigh impossible to exclude entirely the subconscious influence of press comments on the judge as reflecting the views of the community in which he lives, be he ever so upright. He would rather go with the tide than against it, and he, too, is not infrequently already impregnated with the atmosphere of the community gathered from the press. The prosecutor, who should be impartial, seeking only the truth and not bent upon conviction unless the facts satisfy him beyond a reasonable doubt, is put to a test that few men in public office are able to resist. Imagine such a prosecutor, in a case that has attracted general attention due to its sensational features and the efforts of the press to exploit and magnify them, rising in open court at the close of such a case and recommending to the court to acquit the defendant, as it is the duty of a prosecutor to do if he believes that a conviction would be unjust. It is done every day in the criminal courts in cases with which the newspapers do not concern themselves, but it would take a brave man to do so in what is known in the parlance of the criminal courts, as 'star' cases.

"The abuses that have arisen under this head have become well-nigh intolerable. Prosecuting officers, who are ambitious for further honors, maintain elaborate press bureaus for the distribution of news concerning their offices. The reporters who want to stand well with the prosecuting officer, and get all the news that is to be had, fall into the habit of taking the prosecutor's version. Of late years nothing is sacred. A witness is called before the grand jury, and the testimony given there in important cases manages 'to leak out' day by day. The secrecy of the grand jury room is a thing of the past. The law against disclosing occurrences there is a dead letter. The prosecuting attorney is generally the chief offender and frequently the only one. The main concern of a modern prosecutor in one of the great cities of this country seems to have become to keep himself before the public, which he does by seeing to it that the public is informed of everything that happens in his office from his own point of view. I do not mean to assert that this shocking condition is universal, but it is not uncommon and is growing more frequent." [13]

[12] Samuel Untermyer, "Evils and Remedies in the Administration of Criminal Law," *Annals of the American Academy of Political and Social Science*, 1910.
[13] For an extended discussion concerning the effect of publicity methods upon prosecution, see my *Politics and Criminal Prosecution*, 74-94.

II. *A Review of Remedies*

In viewing the possibilities of remedying this condition, one is struck by the inadequacy of legal methods to achieve any genuine control over the practices of newspapers. Among the present powers of the state to regulate undesirable forms of newspaper publicity, the most important is the power of the court to commit for contempt. The extent to which this can be exercised in the United States is indicated in Mr. Taft's address, with some very wholesome comments upon the use of the power:

"But its free exercise would keep American courts too busy if all improper publications were taken note of. The press would protest against the threatened invasions of its constitutional rights; and it would be difficult to withstand the effect of the newspaper agitation which would be thus aroused. In the end the evil would probably not be checked; for most judges are reluctant to resort to the remedy of commitment for contempt, and not infrequently because of the fear that it might be charged by the press that their action was caused by offense to their personal dignity rather than by solicitude to maintain the dignity of the court. This is in spite of the fact that the spirit of the law is clear and the principle on which it is based sound. As the Supreme Court of Massachusetts said:

" 'It is the inevitable perversion of the proper administration of justice to attempt to influence the judge or jury, in the administration of a case pending before them, by statements outside the courtroom and not in the presence of the parties, which may be false and even if they are true and in law not admissible as evidence.' (Telegram Newspaper Co. v. Commonwealth, 172 Mass., 294, 300.)

"In Minnesota the law has been embodied in a statute which prohibits 'false or grossly inaccurate' reports of court proceedings. In Toledo Newspaper Co. v. U. S., 247 U. S., 402, and Patterson v. Colorado, 205 U. S., 454, the Supreme Court sustained the power to commit for contempt. In the Toledo Paper case there were exaggerated, prejudiced and vociferous statements made in published articles, and the judgment for contempt by the lower court for their publication was sustained, because (1) the effect of the articles was to cause the court to believe that it could decide only one way without causing the public to suspect its integrity and fairness, (2) they had the effect of creating in the public mind the idea that if the court acted according to its convictions it would be subject to odium and hatred, (3) the tendency of the articles was to make the court shrink from the performance of its duties because of the public excitement that would be caused, and (4) the tendency was to create in the popular mind a condition which would give rise to a purpose in practice to refuse to respect any order which the court might render if it conflicted with the supposed rights of the city which were being maintained by the newspaper.

"In the Patterson case a punishment for contempt was upheld for publishing articles and a cartoon reflecting upon the motives and conduct of the court in pending cases. In that case the Supreme Court said:

"'A publication likely to reach the eyes of a jury, declaring a witness in a pending cause a perjurer, would be none the less a contempt that it was true. It would tend to obstruct the administration of justice, because even a correct conclusion is not to be reached or helped in that way, if our system of trials is to be maintained. The theory of our system is that the conclusions to be reached in a case will be induced only by evidence and argument in open court, and not by any outside influence, whether of private talk or public print.

"'What is true with reference to a jury is true also with reference to a court. Cases like the present are more likely to arise, no doubt, when there is a jury and the publication may affect their judgment. Judges generally, perhaps, are less apprehensive that publications impugning their own reasoning or motives will interfere with their administration of the law. But if a court regards, as it may, a publication concerning a matter of law pending before it as tending toward such an interference, it may punish it as in the instance put. When a case is finished, courts are subject to the same criticism as other people, but the propriety and necessity of preventing interference with the course of justice by premature statement, argument or intimidation hardly can be denied. . . . It is objected that the judges were sitting in their own case. But the grounds upon which contempts are punished are impersonal. . . .'"

It is unlikely, however, under present conditions that judges will exercise the contempt power to remedy these evils. Indeed, the tendency seems to be in the opposite direction, although alterations in the rules of procedure might start the pendulum swinging the other way. Many instances in which such power has been exercised do not reflect credit upon either press or courts. There are two sides to this matter. It is as imperative to guard against abuse of power by irresponsible or hot-headed judges as it is to guard against the sinister influence of the sensational press. The majority of publishers and judges take their jobs seriously and wield their power with dignity and discretion. It is the exception that creates the problem.

The editor questions, and with reason, the right of a judge

to try a case in which he himself is involved. This puts the magistrate in the position of prosecutor, jury and judge; and in a case in which he himself is likely to have a strong personal bias. Senator Arthur H. Vandenburg of Michigan has introduced a bill into the United States Senate to make mandatory a change of judges in federal courts in contempt cases involving the press. Such a change would remove much of the opposition of the press to the application of the contempt power. Another current criticism against the existing contempt procedure is that a person under a contempt charge is not permitted the right of a trial by jury. Congressman LaGuardia, of New York, has introduced a bill into the House of Representatives to require a jury in federal contempt cases. The Supreme Court, it might be mentioned, has upheld the provisions of the Clayton Act, authorizing trial by jury for violation of injunctions, punishable under the contempt power.[14] The question is, however, whether jury trial would do more than add another element of confusion to an already highly involved situation. It seems that protection afforded by the possibility of some sort of appeal would be better.[15]

Mr. Untermyer [16] would invoke new legislative power to meet the problem. He suggests the enactment of laws "prohibiting a newspaper from publishing anything concerning a case that is in the courts other than a verbatim report of the proceedings in open court"; also "prohibiting any newspaper from commenting, either at the trial or otherwise, upon evidence in judicial proceedings until after final judgment" and "prohibiting any prosecuting officer from expressing or suggesting for publication an opinion as to the guilt or innocence of the persons accused or from disclosing any of the proceedings of the grand jury or from publishing or being privy to the publication of any evidence in his possession bearing on any case in his control."

[14] Michaelson v. U. S., 266 U. S., 42.
[15] The whole question of contempt by publication in the Federal courts is discussed in "Contempt by Publication in the United States," by Nelles and King, 28 Col. L. Rev., 401, 525, 1928. See also Frankfurter and Landis, "Power of Congress over Procedure in Criminal Contempts in 'Inferior' Federal Courts," 37 Harv. L. Rev., 1010 (1924). The best historical treatment of the whole subject is Fox, The History of Contempt of Court (1927).
[16] Supra, 156.

In this connection a lesson might be drawn trom the comments of Chief Justice Kenyon upon the practice in England:

> "It is the pride of the Constitution of this country that all cases should be decided by jurors who are chosen in a manner that excludes all possibility of bias and by ballot in order to prevent any possibility of their being tampered with, but if an individual can break down any of those safeguards which the Constitution has so wisely and so cautiously erected by poisoning the minds of the jury at a time when they are called to decide, he will be stabbing the administration of justice in one of its most vital spots."

Whether legal methods of protecting the integrity of criminal trials can be achieved or not, there is unquestionably a need for serious attempts by responsible members of the press to bring about improvements on their own account. One of the most important steps would be to develop more objective methods of reporting. It might be suggested that the straightforward account of a criminal trial is usually sufficiently interesting to attract readers and that newspapers should be content to offer this inducement without summoning their public to participate in a crusade. Moreover, it would be of great assistance if newspapers could be induced to employ specialists to report all matters affecting the administration of justice. As Mr. Henry Taft says, newspapers do not employ tyros to criticize music, the drama, literature or baseball. In all of these fields technical skill is invariably regarded as necessary. But police court reporting of criminal trials is considered a type of writing which any reporter is competent to do. It was once a quite common rule for every reporter to start in the police court, presumably because most of the stories which are available there possess that broad human interest so basic to all newspaper enterprise. The practice of employing luminaries, drawn from other fields of literary activity, suggests the attitude of the newspapers concerning court proceedings.

Any attempt to subject newspaper enterprise to further legislative regulation will, naturally, be met by bitter opposition and with scathing denunciations of "censorship" or "repression." There has been altogether too much argument of the proposition in general terms and not enough serious consideration of what can actually be done in the direction of legislative and administrative control. Scientific methods should be used to determine whether the glamorous newspaper accounts of criminal acts go farther than mere dramatic appeal to the popular emotions and actually suggest, to the more susceptible part of the population, imitative crimes. If it is found that such accounts have a traceable pernicious influence, it would seem that legislation is as much in order here as it has been shown to be in other fields of governmental activity. It should not be lightly assumed, merely because newspapers have in the past been the means through which great reform movements have made progress among the rank and file of people, that they should be immune from public regulation in regard to a question which ordinarily has no relation to civil liberties. If freedom of the press is to be absolute, we should remove all restrictions such as are implicit in regulations concerning libel and obscenity. If we admit that these are proper subjects for restrictions we shall be compelled to admit, too, that there is a kind of presentation which is as dangerous to public security as obscenity can be, and that with a sound basis of scientific knowledge concerning the effects of these presentations, distinctions can be made which will not seriously interfere with the necessary political freedom of the press.[17]

Moreover, a continuation of the studies which have been suggested in this chapter should establish quite clearly the danger to the whole system of criminal justice which is contained in trial by the press. Here, again, more knowledge on the subject may suggest legislation that will in no way endanger the deeper values of human liberty. A fruitful source of guidance is undoubtedly a consideration of the methods of control exercised in other countries. This field, except for occasional references to England, has been almost entirely untouched in current literature on the subject. After due allowance is made for cultural factors and political practices, France, Germany and other countries may have much to teach us in meeting this vexing problem. As a mere suggestion of an approach to the study of the question,

[17] For a useful article suggesting means of coöperation between the bar and the press, see Dodd, "The Bar and the Press," *Am. Bar Assn. Jour.*, X, 817-819 (1924).

we are including in this chapter a section concerning the practice of France.

Much of the discussion of measures intended to limit the realm of free publication has been, and is, based upon a fear neurosis which is characteristic alike of the conservatives who attempt to suppress expressions of ideas and the radicals who seek to destroy all methods of regulation. Instead of declaiming resounding generalities as to "freedom of the press" and mouthing ancient platitudes about "great constitutional and political principles," some attempt must be made to determine how various practices actually operate in a living world, and how the regulation of these practices can be developed with adequate safeguards against the dangers involved. Here as elsewhere, preachments are not going to solve a problem which demands social and political engineering. As Justice Holmes has so chastely phrased the essence of common sense, "General propositions do not decide concrete cases."

III. *Crime and the Press in France* [18]

Oliver Madox Hueffer in his unusually discerning studies of "French France" remarks:

"Were you to accompany a Frenchman of Paris or elsewhere to London or New York and ask him the most amazing spectacle they provided for him he would certainly point to that of a whole nation glorying over the disgusting details of sensational murders dished up for them in the pages of even the most respectable daily and weekly newspapers greatly to the benefit (*sic*) of the morals of the coming generation. Anything of the kind is unknown anywhere in France, being forbidden at once by law and by public opinion."

This marked difference between crime in the French press and in the English and American press shows that Americans who desire to meet the problem of "trial by newspaper" may find more helpful suggestions in France than in England. The difference between France and the United States with respect to this subject is apparently not due to any superior morality or

[18] For the data in this section I am indebted to a memorandum prepared by Miss Vera Mikol.

zeal for public service on the part of the owners of newspapers of France but to the necessary economy in the printing of newspapers and the strict provisions of the French law.

In the first place, there are no tabloids in France, as in England and America. The heavy headlines of American papers which are largely intended to provide a means for advertising to the prospective buyer the wares contained within the paper are absent in France. Moreover, the large composite pictures so common in American tabloids are not used on the front pages of French papers. This is probably in part due to the fact that the French papers are folded several times and closely packed away in the news stands. Most papers must be completely unfolded before any portion, except a meaningless portion of the headlines, is visible. Much of the latest news is therefore not printed on the first page. The absence of this glorification of sensational news on the front page is due to two necessary economies. First, the limited space which the dealer has in his kiosk and the great number of different papers which he must carry. There is also the economy of news space itself which the paper must achieve. Headlines would be a great waste of news print and consequently fatal to the French paper that is subject to keen competition.

Another factor which probably reduces the amount of space which French newspapers give to sensational news is the fact that, while the Frenchman of the middle class is tolerant of all sorts of presentations of sensational material, he does not permit this to be brought into his home, and it is probable that a paper which published the news of scandals would not be a welcome visitor. Moreover, the French are able to buy pornographic literature directly and without legal restrictions. It is possible, therefore, to avoid the hypocrisy which characterizes some American newspapers in which materials are set forth on the pretense that they are part of the daily news or that they are serving a moral purpose, when they really constitute attempts to cater to the salacious and scandal-loving. The French, in other words, believe in specialization in the publication of scandal. When they read pornography, they buy pornographic journals; and when they want news, they buy newspapers.

The format and superficial appearance of the great journals, such as *Le Petit Parisien,* with a daily average circulation of 1,700,000—the greatest in the world; *Le Journal,* 1,000,000; *Le Matin,* 800,000; *Le Petit Journal,* 600,000; *L'Intransigeant,* 450,000; *Excelsior,* 250,000—is so much alike that the casual observer would have difficulty in telling them apart without the titles. The front page, adorned with six or seven photographs or drawings, carries a few headlines which run over two columns in width. Not more than two columns of a seven-column page are given to crime news or the reports of sensational trials. It is not rare to find no crime news at all on the front page, if important political events are taking place. On account of the terse and compact nature of French journalism, it is impossible to play up any but the most outstanding of crimes. French *causes célèbres* are usually cases tinged with a political interest, such as the murder of Castan Callume by the wife of Cailloux in 1914, the state trials of Cailloux and Malby for treason after the War, the Alsace-Lorraine libel suits of 1927, and the trial of Schwartzbard for the slaying of Peltieura in 1927. Such cases as these provide exceptions to the general rule as to the limitation of crime news. All the talents of editor, special feature writer, humorist, cartoonist and photographer are brought out, while the American public has been regaled with the revelation of a millionaire's eccentricities or the denouement of a shoddy suburban triangle. While the French press does not hesitate to take sides, it does not engage in the bitter hand-to-hand clashes for or against defendants which are characteristic of American newspaper enterprise. There are usually no sob-sisters and obscure persons caught in the meshes of justice rarely have their emotions and abnormalities exposed to public view.

The French laws governing the press provide a series of disciplinary measures which have a definite effect upon newspaper enterprise. Most of these regulations are in the law of July 29, 1881.[19] Every paper must have a responsible manager against whom action is taken when an offense has been committed. Copies of papers must be deposited with the public prosecutor or his representative. The manager must insert free of charge

---

[19] This law covers 296 pages of the *Code D'Alloz.* A few amendments were added between 1882 and 1925. The references in the text are to the articles of this law.

at the head of the next issue of the journal all corrections addressed to him by any public official with respect to public acts which have been inaccurately reported. The manager must insert the responses of any persons named or designated in the journal or periodical. Such an insertion must be made in the same place and the same type as the offending article. A heavy penalty is provided for the publication or reproduction of false news, when the publication has disturbed public peace or was made with malicious intent. It is forbidden to publish indictments or any other acts of criminal procedure before they have been read in public audience. This includes all preparatory information obtained by the police, all reports of preliminary questioning of witnesses or suspects, evidence presented to the examining official or jury and experts' reports. The report made by the chief of police on a criminal case is only a résumé of data and impressions and may be published. In libel trials, it is forbidden to publish reports. Only the complaint may be published by the plaintiff. In any civil suit, the report of a trial-may be forbidden. Such restrictions do not apply to the judgment, however, which always may be published. Judges may have definite consideration and pronounce the suppression of injurious discourses.

Perhaps the most important section of all is Article 41, which provides that the report of a trial must be faithful. If the exact words are not published, at least the true sense of the proceedings without perversion must be printed. A faithful report must not devote itself exclusively to one side with merely passing reference to the other side, nor can the contention against a party be published by letter addressed to the journal without its printing at the same time an account of the debates relating thereto. Thus, the printing of crime news by the French press is subject to definite restrictions which are intended to protect the integrity of the judicial processes. An honest opinion as to the importance of these restrictions is that they do not involve civil liberties to any serious degree. They are, in fact, regulations not much more serious than any other exercise of the police power.

NOTE

Constructive Services of the American Press

In the enforcement of criminal law, as in other interests in which the public is served by its responsible officials, the best service is assured when public opinion dictates the selection and sustains the actions of honest, intelligent and "socially-minded" officials. This is in fact the ultimate problem. In a democracy we shall have politics, and the best that can be done is to make good public service identical with good political tactics. In bringing this about, the press has potentialities of great importance. The newspapers in the United States which have served as a scourge upon officialdom are innumerable. Throughout the recent political troubles of Chicago, two newspapers, the *Tribune* and the *Daily News,* provided the only effective opposition to the existing political régime. These papers have continued for years a campaign against the alliance between politics and organized crime. Names of accused officials have been used in this campaign with reckless disregard of the consequences of possible libel suits. Charges of protecting crime have been made frequently. The names and addresses of law violators have been published times without number. This warfare finally resulted in an ominous shift of public opinion in the elections of 1928. The murder of Don R. Mellett, a Canton, Ohio, editor, as the result of a criminal conspiracy prompted by his attacks upon corruption, illustrates not only the effectiveness but the danger of such editorial assaults. In many cities of the United States, the only means by which healthy political opposition is maintained is through the press.

In the city of Cleveland, the *Press* has recently provided the materials and the leadership which have completely shifted the balance of power in city government, and have incidentally sent to prison a number of high public officials. This was done in spite of the apparent apathetic conditions existing between the two political parties. Mr. James P. Kirby, a reporter, almost single-handed gathered evidence which made it possible to bring to trial several city officials.

Another aspect of the constructive activity of the press is its service in suggesting and explaining reform measures when political agencies, such as councils and legislatures, are too impoverished intellectually and otherwise to do so. Legislative sterility is due largely to the fact that political exigencies, haste, lack of educational and intellectual equipment make it impossible for legislators to devise constructive measures of their own. The avidity with which the average politician seizes an "issue" shows this. The creation of constructive governmental measures is not an act of Providence, nor usually the result of happy guesses. The materials of statesmanship are born of organized facts, intelligent investigation, and—more important of all—creative intelligence. These things are within the means of a great newspaper, they are not always available to officialdom. Many of the measures recently passed by the New York Legislature which have been directed at shortcomings in the criminal process in New York State were suggested by the New York *Evening World.* A recent campaign to improve the quality of the magistrates has been largely guided by the *Evening Post* of the same city. In a country in which healthy political opposition seems difficult to organize, particularly in local affairs, the constructive services of newspapers are indispensable to a fairly effective and honest administration of criminal justice.

CHAPTER XI

FAITH IN FACTS

THE truism that democracy needs some means by which the demos may measure the efficiency of its servants applies with unusual force to the courts. The very technique of law administration is baffling to a layman. He usually votes for his judge blindly or for wholly irrelevant reasons. And to guide him there is little or no account of stewardship; for none is required of his courts. Judicial administration is largely unrecorded in public reports. It is business without accounting.

I. *Business Without Accounting*

Properly to measure the work of courts, prosecutors, probation officers, and other agencies concerned with that process which begins after arrest and continues until incarceration in a penal institution, there must be more information concerning the hundreds of thousands of criminal prosecutions initiated in the United States every year. The great importance of such data is not difficult to prove. Every year the state legislatures are called upon to enact many amendments to the law of crimes and criminal procedure. They should have adequate statistical information concerning the operation of the rules they propose to amend. Such information a properly organized system of judicial statistics should readily yield. Judicial statistics would also contribute greatly to the efficiency of court organization. They furnish the means of measuring judicial efforts. They show clearly the amount of work being performed by courts and court officers. In the redistribution of judicial personnel from county to county, or from district to district, which is necessary in so many states, properly kept judicial statistics are most desirable.

It goes without saying that scientific study of the process

of law administration can make little progress in the United States so long as the materials are so inaccessible. Wherever serious attempts have been made to study judicial administration, the lack of statistical information has made it necessary to expend a large part of the money and energy available for copying records and assembling statistical data. In fact the sheer labor of such spade work was so great in the Cleveland and Missouri surveys that little time or money was left to interpret the data secured.

So far as they are collected, judicial criminal statistics in the United States comprise certain data transmitted from local to state authorities in accordance with some statutory provisions. When Dr. Robinson wrote,[1] he found some sort of reporting of judicial criminal statistics in twenty-five states. In sixteen the collecting agency was the county or district attorney or solicitor; in the remainder, the clerks. In fifteen of these states, the state agency to which reports were sent was the attorney-general; in the remaining ten they were sent to the secretary of state, a bureau of statistics, the governor, the commissioner of prisons, or the board of public charities. He found that in all but one of these states the reports were published. In eighteen cases the publishing agency was the attorney-general. He found the character of the data published to be very unsatisfactory; in most cases positively worthless and in only a few cases fairly complete.

A review of the state reporting of statistics regarding criminal prosecutions indicates little or no progress since Mr. Robinson wrote. New York district attorneys still report about as they have every year since 1839, except that the law now requires them to report to the commissioner of corrections. The facts reported are substantially the same as they were three-quarters of a century ago. For nearly seventy years these statistics were published in an annual volume, *Report of the Secretary of State on Statistics of Crime.* Since 1919 this volume has been discontinued. A few tables are still included in the annual *Legislative Manual* giving "Convictions of Felony Classified by Crimes," "Convictions of Lesser Offenses by Counties," "Convictions for Murder," "Executions," and "Total Prison Population." These are not judicial statistics. They concern only convictions and what

[1] L. N. Robinson, *Criminal Statistics in the United States* (Boston, 1911).

happens after conviction. The judicial data published up to 1919 are still uncollected, but the returns from the district attorneys gather dust in the office of the secretary of state. They are not even tabulated. We now have less public information concerning criminal prosecutions in New York for 1928 than for 1848.

The status of central collecting in other states is still less hopeful. Biennially California publishes, in the report of the attorney-general, the following data in a single table arranged by counties:

Persons Charged with Felonies	State Prison
Pleaded Guilty	Other Institutions
Convictions	Probations
Acquittals	Fined
Otherwise Disposed of	Otherwise Disposed of After Trial
Pending	Awaiting Sentence
Death	

Minnesota publishes about the same material through its attorney-general; North Dakota, Connecticut, Alabama and Massachusetts publish some judicial data, but most of the remaining states supply little or nothing.

A few of the better organized city courts publish reports containing data on the disposition of criminal cases. Among these the best are issued by the Chicago and Cleveland and Philadelphia municipal courts, the Detroit Recorder's Court, and the New York City Magistrate's Court. An examination of these reports indicates clearly the difficulty of using them as a basis for comparative studies. Their tabulations are of different materials, the basis of compiling totals varies, and, what is more serious, the same words mean different things in different reports. "Convictions," for example, may include both "convictions by a jury" and "convictions on plea," or it may include only the former. For scientific work these reports are almost useless.

A new and promising source of help has developed in the new judicial councils of a number of states. The most important objective of a judicial council as it is developing is to seek the coördination and general improvement of the work of courts through common action, reënforced here and there by a grant of definite authority to the council. Its activities depending so largely upon a quantitative measurement of judicial work, it has in some cases collected and published rather extensive judicial statistics, both criminal and civil. This is especially true of Massachusetts and California. Except for these states, however, the grant of power and the appropriations of funds have been so meager as to make the gathering of extensive statistics practically impossible.

We should add here that certain special research efforts have been directed to the gathering of statistical data in a few places. In Cleveland, Missouri, Georgia, New York, Cincinnati, and more recently in Illinois, the salient facts concerning large numbers of cases were copied and tabulated in order to determine the manner in which courts were disposing of their cases. In these instances a limited number of cases was collected, over a limited period, by means of somewhat detailed card schedules. These surveys show the possibilities of analyzing the judicial process if the data are available.

Another sort of statistical record keeping is illustrated by the permanent crime commissions in Chicago, Cleveland and Baltimore, to which we shall presently refer again. These agencies maintain a card index of criminal cases with provision for entering all steps in their progress. They limit their attention to felonies, however, and in Chicago the record is not kept so completely as it was in the early years of the commission's life.

Beyond these fragments we have few data to serve as a basis for the study of criminal justice in the United States. In individual communities and states we may by dint of heroic efforts and at great expense lift the veil a little, but for the most part we are safe in saying that we know neither the quality nor the quantity of criminal cases passing through our courts; we do not know what happens to them and we have no means other than casual observation and sheer conjecture of determining the quality of service which our codes of procedure and our courts are giving.

In this respect hardly any other civilized country is so badly served. In Canada, for instance, the Dominion Statistician is authorized to collect a wide range of statistical data from those local officials responsible for the keeping of records, including judges, clerks, wardens and sheriffs. The law compels these officers to provide such information as the Statistician may require upon the schedules which he furnishes. The Statistician issues an annual report on Criminal Statistics with the most elaborate data conveniently arranged. In 1924 this report covered 355 pages. In England the Home Office issues annually a report entitled "Criminal Statistics." The Commonwealth of Australia publishes police and judicial statistics in its *Official Year Book*. New Zealand publishes an admirable compilation of "Judicial Statistics," including, of course, data concerning criminal cases. So do the Union of South Africa and other English-speaking colonies. Even the Bombay Presidency publishes a better report than any official judicial agency in the United States.

In determining methods for the improvement of judicial accounting much intelligent preliminary work remains to be done. Some determination must be made of how the published statistics may be used. This is, of course, the most seriously important as well as the most difficult part of the task. It calls for no mere matter of technique, but for an intelligent analysis of the sociological, legal, political and administrative factors which require measurement and comparisons. Some of the groundwork of this kind of analysis has been done in the interpretation of the statistics in various surveys of police and the courts; but none of these has sufficiently analyzed the possibilities of a scientific measurement of the process of law enforcement. There is needed a very carefully considered formulation of the problem of crime and the administration of justice in which exact measurement is possible and at the same time pertinent to an evaluation of proposals for reform. There is also needed a determination of a few minimum standards for the measurement of public office administration, which can be gleaned from ascertainable statistics.

Admittedly no predetermined categories of statistics can satisfy the complex and extensive demands of subsequent research in a field of which so little is known as of crime and criminal justice. There will be tentative and experimental research efforts for which the data may not be gathered by any general scheme for collection. But no small part of the formulation of plans for improving criminal statistics should be a careful consideration from many points of view of the possible uses which may subsequently be made of the data collected. In this way we may not only avoid the accumulation of useless statistics, which has so characterized statistical compilations in the past, but actually and measurably anticipate the exacting demands of research in a field rich in promise and almost wholly unexplored.[2]

A superb piece of constructive work in the field of statistics has just been completed by Mr. C. Bruce Smith for a committee of the International Association of Chiefs of Police. It constitutes a plan for the collecting and reporting of uniform crime statistics by the police departments of the United States. It has already begun to bear fruit and more than 500 cities are making uniform reports. Legislation is pending to attach to the United States Department of Justice a central bureau to which such reports should be made. An extension of this plan to include judicial criminal statistics is urgently needed.[3]

II. *Surveillance*

The permanent crime commissions established in Chicago, Cleveland, Baltimore, and now in Philadelphia, represent an aspect of civic reform quite different from that of the more commonly known survey commissions, different not only in that they are permanent while the survey commissions are presumably temporary, but in that their contribution is not the preparation of a report of facts on a given state or city, but rather the constant surveillance of the administration of criminal justice. Therefore it is appropriate to call them surveillance commissions. In describing the activities of these agencies it will be well to comment on the Chicago Crime Commission, which was the first such commission and was actually and conspicuously the model for the others.

The Chicago Crime Commission was the first crime commission established in the United States. The fundamental idea back of it was probably derived from the experiences of various civic reform agencies which we have had in this country dur-

[2] See Moley, "The Collection of Criminal Statistics in the United States," 27 *Michigan Law Rev.*, 747 (1928).
[3] See *Uniform Crime Reporting* (New York, 1930).

ing the past thirty or forty years. These agencies, such as the Chicago Voters' League, the New York Citizens' Union and others, were established as "outside" associations of private citizens whose efforts should be to maintain a constant and vigilant watch over the agencies of government, and to report to the public instances of failure and instances of commendable efficiency as well. The idea was to urge all public officials to a higher degree of efficiency through making them realize that their deeds were being measured and reported, and if necessary to bring to the bar of public opinion or justice the faithless public servant.

The application of this principle to the administration of justice is significant not only because it embodies this notion of vigilant watchfulness over public agencies, but because in the field of criminal justice administration the commission represents a type of private prosecutor which is necessary because public prosecution is a comparatively recent development. England provided facilities for public prosecution only a few generations ago, but private prosecution is still common. The notion of a public agency which should take the initiative when the criminal law is violated, and bring miscreants to justice, is so new that it is not inappropriate for private initiative to supplement this effort. Consequently the private surveillance agency becomes not only an observer and critic of the public service, but a sort of auxiliary prosecuting body when the need arises. In several instances the Chicago Crime Commission has performed effective service of this kind.

The Chicago Crime Commission was established in 1919, under the auspices and with the support of the Chicago Association of Commerce. Its director was Colonel Henry Barrett Chamberlain, a former newspaper editor of long experience. Colonel Chamberlain created through his own efforts and out of his own experiences the principles and the machinery which characterized its activity. It is important to note this fact, because the most original features of the Crime Commission were largely based upon Colonel Chamberlain's newspaper experience. He knew as few civic reformers have known in the past that the persons who know most about what is going on in the courts are the newspaper men. He knew that the most trustworthy kind of observers were newspaper reporters, and that if in some way there could be enlisted on the side of public reform the skill, the knowledge of the world, the wide acquaintance of persons in and out of the public service, the capacity for shrewd trained inferences, and the ability to put these inferences in writing, an instrument could be created which might serve as a check upon and a valuable critic of public service. This object was accomplished through the creation of the Chicago Crime Commission "observers," one of the most original and important creations of the whole American civic reform movement. The other most important aspect of the Commission's work was the creation of a record system by which the Commission could show the exact status of each criminal case in the courts, also a very significant development in civic work. It may be helpful to discuss in some detail each of these fundamental aspects of the Commission's work.

Most of the observers of the Chicago Crime Commission have been former newspaper men, and whenever possible men were selected who had some knowledge of the law. They constitute a permanent and constant contact between the public and the courts. In a very real sense they are the "eyes" of the community. Their presence in the courts has been valuable for three reasons. In the first place, the very fact of their presence provides a compelling incentive for judges and prosecuting officials to refuse demands made upon them, for bargains with the defense under the pressure of political influence. Second, they have been able to catch and bring to the attention of the Crime Commission, and through it to that of public officials, many instances of undesirable conduct which would never have been detected through a mere examination of the records of the cases. Finally, through their observation it has been possible for the operating department of the Commission to discover relations in certain cases between lawyers, defendants, prosecutors, court clerks and others, which, when intelligently interpreted, constituted a significant indication of tampering with the even course of justice. The very presence of certain individuals in courtrooms at certain times means more to the sophisticated observer than much searching of records and examination of witnesses.

The basic record of the Chicago Crime Commission is a sort of card index of felony cases, kept by the Commission in its own office. From the beginning of its operation it has followed the policy of securing and maintaining the complete docket of every felony case recorded in the city. When the charge becomes a matter of record, clerks of the Commission record the essential facts in a docket which is maintained by the Commission. From that point on the Commission enters everything of importance that takes place with regard to this case, so that at all times the records of the Commission show every important procedural step which has been taken in every case. The records of the Commission become a more complete and centralized record than the court itself maintains, because they constitute a complete record of the procedure of the prosecutor, the court, the police and other agencies. The possession of this record by an unofficial agency constitutes a very significant check upon the public officials who are dealing with criminal cases. When a case lags for any unexplained reason, or is terminated in some way which on the surface appears unsatisfactory, the observer can require the court to explain what has happened.

In the course of years this record becomes the basis and the source for fundamental studies of the whole administration of justice. The ten years' accumulation of records of the Chicago Crime Commission is the most orderly and most complete mine of public information concerning the courts which exists in this country. Some idea of the great value of this basic material can be gained from the fact that the *Illinois Crime Survey,* in so far as it relates to the trial of felony cases in Chicago, is based upon and created from the records of one year's activities of the Chicago Crime Commission—1926. It was possible for the statistical department of the *Survey* to draw its basic information from the offices of the Commission rather than from the courts themselves.

Through these elaborate records the commission is able to maintain a factual control over the public agencies responsible for administration.

Thus the extent of control and surveillance by the commission is twofold: It makes possible a constant watch over the courts through the observers of the activities of the courts themselves, and builds up a cumulative record of prosecutions.

Another aspect of the surveillance commission, perhaps more marked in the Cleveland commission than in the others, is the enlistment of a great many civic agencies behind the commission. Behind the objectives of the work of the commission it is possible through some kind of a federal arrangement which makes it possible for the commission to bring to its support, whenever it is necessary, the strength of many other agencies comprising thousands of individuals interested in civic affairs.

The effectiveness of a commission depends, of course, upon its ability to get its facts before the public. This makes necessary publicity devices of various sorts, occasional reports, bulletins and public letters to officials. A most striking example of this occurred during the 1928 campaign of Robert Crowe for re-election as State's Attorney of Chicago. A long and patient observation of Mr. Crowe's record as State's Attorney convinced the board of directors of the Commission that he was no longer worthy of their support. Consequently they issued a statement condemning his administration and advising his defeat. Experienced observers fully believe that his defeat in this campaign was due to the blast from the Commission.

Another somewhat subtle but significant aspect of such a commission is the extent to which it is able to enlist in its activities the unofficial assistance of men of established position and ability. Perhaps a single example will illustrate this type of civic service. In the city of Cleveland the commission became convinced that the records of the clerk's office in the Municipal Court were unsatisfactory. The clerk, anxious to show his coöperative spirit, met some of the directors of the association and discussed with them the problems involved in his system of judicial bookkeeping. The group of directors included a number of business and professional men of extraordinary ability. These men manifested a genuine enthusiasm in the work of reconstructing the pathetically antiquated methods of the court, and as a result a more or less complete reconstruction was accomplished. Thus, through the mediation of a civic agency, it was possible to bring first-rate ability to pass upon a problem which had always been intrusted to routineers and incompetents. In an age and in a civilization when it is almost impossible to bring able executives into public service, something must be said for a commission which provides a means by which even casual and occasional applications of first-rate ability may be made to public service.

It is important, however, in any consideration of the contributions which a crime commission of this kind can make to the cause of improving criminal justice, to consider a number of problems involved in its practical operation. The most important question that a commission must meet, and it meets it every day in the year, is how much and what kind of coöperation will it seek or accept from public officials? This is a basic question apparently disturbing to the minds of practically every civic and research agency yet created in the field of public service. Many organizations have, in fact, been wrecked by an unwise answer to the question. In the first place, it is obviously advantageous to maintain a friendly relation with the public officials. Coöperation with them means easy access to public records, and friendly and helpful relations of other kinds. It also means that many of the suggestions for change which a commission conceives to be important will be freely and gratefully accepted and adopted by the public officials. There is also the danger, however, that public officials who are desirous of escaping responsibility and particularly grateful to be relieved of work, will gladly "unload" upon the commission work which they should properly do themselves. If it is not wary, a commission may be trapped into a position where it must either refuse to do what a public official asks it to do, or stand responsible before the community for his acts. "It will be damned if it does, and damned if it doesn't." Perhaps the best answer is that no public office should be held by a member of the staff of a civic agency, and that the services which a commission should perform for public officers should never be acts of a routine governmental nature, but only unusual services that require a special technique and that are temporary.

In praising the work of public officials such an agency can praise acts rather than persons. This means that when a public official has performed an act very well he may be commended for the act, but by general praise the private agency puts itself in a dangerous position, because this will be used for political purposes. To praise the official for a certain act leaves the commission free to criticize him for another act later; but to give him a general recommendation is to render subsequent criticism of him ineffective. The best policy of the commission is that which has been developed by the best newspapers: praise for specific acts when such is deserved; attack for specific acts when that is deserved; remain in an independently critical position; accept no office or reward and do not attempt to perform the services which are vested by law in public officials.

Another point, at which there ought to be a specific policy as to the limitation of the commission, concerns the extent to which it will interest itself in individual cases. It becomes very easy for a commission to be prevailed upon by contributors, or prospective contributors, to serve as a prosecuting attorney; in fact, it becomes very difficult to avoid the following of individual cases. Perhaps there is no hard-and-fast rule to govern this, but a commission should interest itself not only in the prosecution of cases in which a wealthy and distinguished person or interest has been injured, but also in cases in which the victim is poor and friendless. Finally, a commission will find that ultimately it will be necessary to extend its interests beyond the improvement of the prosecuting function of criminal justice, and will conceive that it is more important to search the causes of crime, the methods by which public officials are selected, the training of public officials, and to foster the creation of a more enlightened public opinion and interest.

III. Surveys

When he was a young teacher of political science, in 1887, Woodrow Wilson wrote an essay on "The Study of Administration." It proved to be a remarkably prophetic utterance.[4] He said, in substance, that in spite of the voluminous literature on public affairs, nothing had been written concerning the actual administration of government. He challenged the interest of students of public affairs in the actual process by which government proceeds to articulate itself in action, as distinguished from

[4] *Political Science Quarterly*, II, 197-222.

the rules and regulations laid down for its conduct in the law.

"Government," he said, "is so near to us, so much a thing of our daily familiar handling, that we can with difficulty see the need of any philosophical study of it, or the exact point of such study, should it be undertaken. We have been on our feet too long to study now the art of walking. We are a practical people, made so apt, so adept in self-government by centuries of experimental drill that we are scarcely any longer capable of perceiving the awkwardness of the particular system we may be using, just because it is so easy for us to use any system. We do not study the art of governing; we govern. But mere unschooled genius for affairs will not save us from sad blunders in administration. Though democrats by long inheritance and repeated choice, we are still rather crude democrats. Old as democracy is, its organization on a basis of modern ideas and conditions is still an unaccomplished work. The democratic state has yet to be equipped for carrying those enormous burdens of administration which the needs of this industrial and trading age are so fast accumulating. Without comparative studies in government we cannot rid ourselves of the misconception that administration stands upon an essentially different basis in a democratic state from that on which it stands in a non-democratic state."

In spite of this need which Wilson so convincingly explained over forty years ago, very little study of administration was made until the early years of the present century. Students of government then turned their attention to the actual operation of various governmental institutions.

Meanwhile there had been developed, largely by social service agencies, a form of study known as the "Social Survey." This was applied to many aspects of community life in Pittsburgh, and the result was the monumental *Pittsburgh Survey* in the year 1909. This method came to be specialized in definite fields such as education and health. The Cleveland Foundation was created in 1914, and it took as its first task the study of specific aspects of the life of the community. In 1916 it decided that the next important aspect of community life which should be subjected to the survey method was public provision for recreation. In 1919 a plan was formulated for a survey of the administration of criminal justice.[5] A little more than a year after, Dean Roscoe Pound, Professor Felix Frankfurter, and a staff of specialists were engaged to make a survey of the administration of criminal justice in the city of Cleveland, and the survey was published the following year. Thus the idea of a survey came from the fields of education and sociology. The method of procedure had been fairly well worked out there.[6]

The most ambitious criminal justice survey is the *Illinois Crime Survey*. This grew out of the efforts of the State Bar Association of Illinois, under the leadership of certain Chicago lawyers. It will be noted that all of these surveys, with the exception of the one in Minnesota and the very early one in Chicago, were conducted by private agencies. They were likewise supported by private funds. Largely as a result of the widespread interest created by the *Missouri Crime Survey* several states created crime commissions. In 1925 there was organized the National Crime Commission, a private organization with a number of distinguished national figures as directors. This body dedicated itself to the encouragement of efforts for the creation of state crime commissions throughout the United States. It emphasized the need for such commissions to be created by public authority rather than by private enterprise. The New York State Crime Commission has probably contributed more to the literature of criminal justice administration than any of the other publicly supported commissions. While the data are not entirely complete, it is clear that public crime commissions have been established in California, Louisiana, Michigan, New York, Rhode Island, Indiana, Montana, Virginia, Pennsylvania, New Hampshire, Minnesota, Kansas, New Jersey and Nebraska. Private agencies of a somewhat similar nature have been established in Missouri,

[5] This plan was largely formulated by Professor C. E. Gehlke of Western Reserve University. It was not acted upon by the governing board of the Foundation for nearly a year, although it was brought to their attention shortly after it was made.

[6] It ought to be added, however, that certain interesting shorter studies of aspects of criminal justice had been made before, notably *The Report of the City Council Committee on Crime of the City of Chicago*, published in 1915. This Committee served under the chairmanship of Alderman Charles E. Merriam, of Chicago. The next Survey of criminal justice was conducted in Missouri in 1925. It differed from the Cleveland Survey in that it was state-wide. The Department of Public Welfare of Georgia made a survey shortly after, as did the Minnesota Crime Commission.

Illinois, Detroit, Cincinnati, Dallas, Houston, Evanston, Minneapolis, Des Moines, Memphis, Denver and Los Angeles. Many of these have been inactive and some have been discontinued. It is important to note that there has thus been joined in the crime commission movement the idea of a public commission appointed by some official authority for the chief purpose of preparing legislation. It is impossible to speak in general terms of all these agencies, because they differ so much in the extent of their interests and in their methods of operation. But the surveys published, particularly those of the Cleveland, Missouri, and Illinois criminal justice commissions provide the basis for a number of conclusions. These, it should be noted, are in the nature of personal impressions arising from experiences not only in the making of the surveys, but in certain relationships which followed them.[7]

The range of interest of these surveys, as well as the growth of the subject matter covered, is shown in the following presentation of the subjects treated in the most comprehensive of them:

	Cleveland	Missouri	Illinois	New York
POLICE	x	x	x	x
PROSECUTION	x	x	x	x
JUDICIAL ADMINISTRATION	x	x	x	x
PENAL TREATMENT	x			x
PSYCHIATRIC RELATIONS	x	x	x	x
PROBATION & PAROLE		x	x	x
JUVENILE DELINQUENCY			x	x
THE SOCIAL NATURE OF CRIME			x	
CAUSES OF CRIME				x
NEWSPAPER & CRIMINAL JUSTICE	x			x
CRIMINAL LAW				

A survey of criminal justice either by a private agency or by a public commission which makes a study of administrative

[7] The history of the survey movement I have given in much more detail in other places. See particularly a publication of the National Crime Commission, entitled *State Crime Commissions;* see also an article in the *Annals,* CXLV, 68.

practices serves the purpose of arousing public interest with regard to the various questions involved in the enforcement of law. It may be said with certainty that most of the facts published in various criminal justice surveys were well known long before the survey found them out and published them in a new synthesis and with important public sponsorship. These familiar facts became, then, not the mere comment of a newspaper, or the ideas of an individual writer, but rather the reasoned and deliberate assertions of a number of well known citizens acting jointly. The effect of this subsequent public discussion of these facts is, to be sure, difficult to measure. It depends upon the extent to which any public discussion has a "curative" value.

The publication of a survey provides for those interested in reform, a more or less complete perspective of the whole subject. Such a perspective is useful in that it illustrates the many-sided nature of the problem. It helps to prevent easy generalizations as to single causes of very complex public problems.

These surveys provide for the use of public officials many suggestions of new working methods, some of which have been accepted by officials and have become an integral part of the public service. They provide raw material out of which students of the various subjects involved may draw useful data which may have some future scientific importance.

It would be absurd, however, to claim that these surveys do not have decided shortcomings. In the first place, it may be doubted whether the conditions under which they are carried out are such as to provide a completely accurate picture of the whole situation. As in the fable of the blind men and the elephant, the student finds in a social and governmental situation just about what he can recognize. Education, health and criminal justice surveys are statements of a highly complex section of human life, usually expressed from a definite point of view. This is the more likely to be true in such a highly controversial field as criminal justice.[8]

[8] For a discussion of this question of "results" see Moley, "Civic Interest and Crime in Cleveland," *National Municipal Review*, XII, October, 1923, 580.

IV. *Reform, Research, and the Truth*

It is scarcely necessary to add to the foregoing discussion of surveys the observation that the survey method should not be mistaken for a wholly impersonal and impartial search for truth. It is too closely related to and a part of the pursuit of reform. Practical supporters of expensive surveys want to "get something done." They usually have fairly definite ideas as to what they want to do. And they are usually anxious to get it done in a hurry. Their motivating forces are difficult to reconcile with the patient pursuit of an altogether elusive "truth."

The method of conducting a survey should be considered in any attempt to evaluate this means of arriving at the truth. In some surveys a committee was established which was charged with the supervision and control of the final product. In the New York State Crime Commission and in other commissions of an official nature, this function is exercised by the Commission itself. When the "experts" charged with writing a special report submit their completed work, this governing body makes final judgment as to the form and content of the published result. While such control is usually exercised with discretion and fairness, there are many instances of somewhat extensive overhauling of the reports. These liberties were taken, it should be added with every emphasis, without any thought of being unfair and with altogether righteous intentions. Such literary and "scientific" offenses may be shocking to persons with a strong literary or scientific conscience, but they constitute the normal practice in a large part of American life. Practical men who want to get things done feel that they need not hesitate to hack off the "visionary" notions of mere paid grubbers of facts. Nor, if the fundamental objective of a survey be kept in mind, is there any reason to call their action wrong.[9]

This tendency is still more marked when the fact-finding commission is politically created and controlled. The American public is never surprised to find, after a long and expensive "fact-finding" investigation, that the responsible commission is divided on party lines as to the conclusions to be derived from a common

[9] Under the rules of the Cleveland Foundation such changes were not permissible.

body of facts. Such an outcome often prompts the pertinent inquiry that if the conclusions had been made in advance, why the long and involved and expensive inquiry? The world of political strategy has found the survey method useful for gaining time. It makes it possible to defer action and in a world of shifting public interests delay may make it unnecessary even to come to grips with the disagreeable decision. Some of the critics of President Hoover's Law Enforcement Commission have pointed to the difficulties which political strategy has imposed upon the commission. As the cartoonist for the *World* makes the advocates of the status quo in prohibition say to the Commission's chairman, "Now see here, young man, I want a scientific report, reaching my conclusions, and I want it by July 1st."

Nor are the obstacles to the pursuit of truth limited to the method of control of experts by non-experts. The expert investigators themselves often find in their own bias formidable difficulties. When a commission wants to reach a certain conclusion it is not difficult to determine in advance the "expert" who will almost certainly reach the conclusions sought. It would be fairly easy to predict in advance the conclusions that would be reached by certain surveys by merely referring to the prior utterances of the researchers. Instances are plentiful in which contributors to surveys formulate their conclusions quite uninfluenced by their collected data. Authors of reports have a habit of publishing conclusions long since formulated, with the mere addition of scraps of localized supporting data. School surveys have become so standardized that the preparation of a new report consists in little more than altering the name of the city and compiling new tables of statistical data. The pattern remains unchanged.

But these shortcomings of the survey as a means for revealing the truth are not fatal to the real purpose of the survey. Essentially the survey has always been related to some kind of reform. From Booth's survey of London to Mr. Hoover's Law Enforcement Commission, surveys have been chiefly instrumentalities for "getting something done." In Cleveland, Missouri, Illinois, and in many other instances, objectives were quite frankly announced in advance. It was, moreover, frequently emphasized that the survey was a mere first step in a "community campaign." This was not cant or hypocrisy; it was announced as a means of "selling" reform to the community. People are interested in suppressing crime or changing methods of public education or in improving health. They are not, except in unusual instances, interested in the truth, as such. In the last analysis, surveys must be judged on the basis of what they were intended to achieve.

Nor is it entirely fitting for the professedly academic students of social science to ascribe to themselves extraordinary virtues by comparison with the "practical" men whom they often condemn. Much research in the social sciences is not far from special pleading. The calm, undisturbed and impartial mien is not infrequently a shrewdly conceived technique to make more impressive a preordained result after extensive search for facts. The social scientist is often not converted by his discoveries. He is often not educated by them. He is sometimes in the process of building up his case.

The administration of criminal justice is particularly vulnerable to these tendencies. It is full of questions of deep emotional significance, it involves religious and moral differences, and it reaches into disputed professional privileges. But in the face of these almost insuperable difficulties there is need for the collection of new truth. The chapters of this book have with monotonous regularity raised questions only to indicate that they could not be settled on the basis of the information at hand. In spite of a diligent seeking for facts over a space of ten years, the dependable facts are not numerous. This field has need of the same generously supported means for the pursuit of truth that some of the natural sciences have found. Such means must be protected from haste, poverty, special pleading, dogmatism, politics, and, it must be added, the hampering burden of the conservatism of any professional group, acting alone.

In spite of the difficulties that confront the independent and unbiased search for new truth, our faith in facts finds no inconsiderable justification. The contribution of research consists in the facts that are constantly emerging from the field of controversy and doubt and that get themselves permanently and generally believed. To be sure, there are probably just as many beliefs that in the face of the attack fal! from the realm of the generally accepted into that of controversy and doubt. Our faith tells us that the exchange is profitable and our measurements seem to justify our faith.

CHAPTER XII

CAREER MEN

THE problem, as it seems to emerge from the foregoing chapters, is one of personnel, particularly of judicial personnel. After due allowance for the procedural and other mechanical factors in the administration of justice, and after a great deal of allowance for the desirability that justice be equipped with the most recent scientific knowledge and facilities, the persistent conclusion remains that the quality of justice depends upon the quality of those who administer it. General conclusions as to this quality are more difficult to form than most critics of the present bench seem to assume. Little exact and comprehensive information exists. Moreover the measurement of personality is no easy task. The best that can be done is to consider such exact data as there are, review the opinions of a few of the most reliable observers, consider the circumstances under which judges attain and retain office and draw such inferences as may be justified. The most important of these conclusions is expressed in the title of this chapter. The permanent public servant in the administration of justice seems to have arrived, not in the form long advocated by the admirers of European professional competence in public office, but in the shape of lawyers who through necessity, chance or free choice remain in public or political service. Economic, professional and political exigencies seem to require that justice shall be administered by career men. Our judgments as to this state of facts must depend upon our conception of the relative values concerned.

I. *The Magistrates*

In the *Illinois Crime Survey,* I attempted to reduce to general terms the qualifications of the judges of the Chicago Municipal

Court. In doing this I gathered data concerning the 104 judges who had served since the creation of the court in 1906.

In the tabulation, those judges who took office prior to January 1, 1917, and those who have taken office since then are grouped separately. The following table covers the first important item, the ages of the judges.

AGES OF JUDGES

| | BEFORE 1917 | | | 1917 AND AFTER | | |
Age	Number	Per Cent of Total	Age	Number	Per Cent of Total
Under 34	2	3	Under 34	5	12½
35-39	12	19	35-39	10	25
40-44	19	30	40-44	8	20
45-49	15	24	45-49	7	17½
50-54	7	11	50-54	7	17½
55-59	5	8	55-59	2	5
60 and over........	3	5	60 and over........	1	2½
	63	100		40	100

We see that as the newness of the court wore off and able judges who had served during its early years retired to private practice or were promoted to other courts, they were replaced by younger judges. This is probably due to the increase of the number of judges who ascend the bench as a result of holding some minor political position rather than through years of service as practicing attorneys. To be sure, everyone is entitled to his own opinion concerning the value of youth on the bench, but in spite of certain obvious advantages, it means a lack of experience at the bar and probably much less knowledge of law.

Education is another factor in the qualification of judges which can be exactly determined. A majority of the judges who held office in the Municipal Court of Chicago never attended college. In the group before 1917, thirty-two of the sixty-four had attended some college for a time. Of those who attained the bench in 1917 and after, it seems that only fourteen of the forty attended college at all.[1] A great majority, however, attended some law school. In order to indicate clearly the type of legal education enjoyed by the group, we submit the following tabulation

---

[1] Of twenty-four candidates who ran for office at the 1928 election only three are college graduates. See *Bulletin* of the Chicago Bar Association on candidates, September 20, 1928.

showing the law schools which they attended. Most of them were graduated from schools which are not members of the Association of American Law Schools. It should also be noted that attendance does not necessarily mean graduation, and that when one judge attended two law schools, both are included.

LAW SCHOOLS ATTENDED BY JUDGES

BEFORE 1917		1917 AND AFTER	
Chicago College of Law	11	Chicago Kent College of Law	8
Chicago Kent College of Law	11	Northwestern University	8
Union College of Law	10	Chicago College of Law	7
Northwestern Law School	8	Illinois College of Law	5
Lake Forest University	6	John Marshall Law School	3
University of Michigan	6	Hamilton College of Law	2
Columbia Law School	2	University of Chicago	2
Harvard Law School	2	Lake Forest University	1
Bloomington Institute	1	Loyola University	1
Catholic U. of America	1	Notre Dame University	1
Columbia Law College	1	New York University	1
Georgetown Law School	1	Ohio Northern University	1
Illinois College of Law	1	Union College of Law	1
University of Iowa	1	University of Illinois	1
University of Wisconsin	1	University of Michigan	1
Washington University	1	Webster College of Law	1
Yale University	1		

It was impossible to determine the exact number of years of legal practice enjoyed by the judges of the municipal court prior to election; nor was it possible to define the kind of practice. The only guide to this is the median number of years which elapsed between admission to the bar and elevation to the bench, which was about sixteen. This, however, should not be taken seriously, because the records of many of these judges indicate that their activities during those years were in political offices, in many cases assistant state's attorneys or city prosecutors, and such duties involve more politics than law.

All these facts are evidence, but not convincing proof, that the municipal judges of Chicago are incompetent. Incompetence is a relative term and perhaps no final scientific determination of it can ever be made. In conducting the investigation, however, an attempt was made to secure the opinions of those best qualified to judge the ability of the municipal court bench. Advice was sought from many persons, including lawyers who have known most of the judges intimately since the creation of the court. In addition to a general inquiry, cards were prepared for all of the judges who served, with space for confidential ratings of ability.

The following is the tabulated result of these ratings:

Total No. Judges		Legal Ability						Courage, Integrity, Independence					
			High		Medium		Low		High		Medium		Low
	No.	%	No.	%	No.	%	No.	%	No.	%	No.	%	No.	%
1906–17....	64	100	30	46.9	31	48.4	3	4.8	31	48.4	30	46.9	3	4.7
1917.......	40	100	5	12.5	26	65.0	9	22.5	9	22.1	24	40.0	7	17.5

A summary of the study on this subject can best be expressed in the terms of the report to the Illinois Association for Criminal Justice.

"Summing up all we have said concerning the personnel of municipal judges we are forced to the conclusion that we are getting poorer judges from the standpoint of ability, courage and independence. We are getting more political judges and younger judges. We are getting judges whose experience at the bar has covered fewer years."

After the report containing these data appeared in the Chicago newspapers various public comments were made which were without exception confirmations of my conclusions. The editorial comment in the Chicago *Tribune* stated that the "tendency of this judicial branch of which so much was expected years ago has been steadily downward. We are driven to the belief that the direct primary has had one of its worst effects in this particular, and that it is truly responsible for the lowering of the worth, dignity and usefulness of the municipal bench. It has given the courts successful vote getters and political manipulators rather than judges, and the voters have not been able to use any intelligence in keeping unfit men out." The *Daily News,* while it did not agree that the direct primary was the cause, confirmed the judgment, as did the *Herald-Examiner.*

The New York City Magistrates' Court consists of forty-four judges, including the Chief Magistrate. It has jurisdiction in preliminary hearings in felony cases, in violation of city ordinances, and a modified sort of jurisdiction in more serious misdemeanors.

Data concerning approximately one-half of the magistrates show that certain of the tendencies described as characteristic of Chicago are also true of this court, though in a somewhat lesser degree. Approximately one-half of this number had no previous college training. Only one of the group had not held a public office prior to appointment as a magistrate. The others had held an average of three previous public offices. The most common office held prior to appointment was that of assistant district attorney; four had been members of the state legislature; three, members of the Attorney-General's staff; two, members of Congress, and other offices held ranged through a wide variety of the jobs at the disposal of the political organization. The conclusion may fairly be drawn from this information that college education is more frequently found among the New York magistrates than among the judges of the Chicago Municipal Court, and that almost invariably the previous careers of the members of the court included political jobs.

The bench of the Municipal Court of Cleveland was studied in the *Cleveland Crime Survey* of 1921. The conclusions reached were:

"In respect of legal ability the court contains four judges who might be said to measure up to the requirements of the office—one by reason of long experience on the bench; another because of previous experience as a justice of the peace; a third for his long experience at the bar and his previous official connection with the court; and a fourth by reason of years of private practice in a representative Cleveland firm. Two of the others are credited with fair ability, three are mediocre, and one apparently has no qualifications worth mentioning. The list includes two judges characterized as 'playing politics', and two others designated as 'gallery players'.

"On the whole, the personnel of the municipal bench is inferior in quality and ineffectual in character. A close observer of the Cleveland courts for years states that the present Municipal Court judges are not much superior to the old justices of the peace, and that whatever increased dignity they appear to possess arises entirely from the improved physical setting.

"It is the almost universal belief among men whose opinion may be valued that the Municipal Court judges are irreproachable in respect of being influenced by money considerations. The *Survey* did not attempt to follow up such vague and isolated charges as were brought to its attention, for two reasons: In the first place, actual corruption is impossible to prove without the power to compel testimony. Moreover, it is not indicative of the real trouble, since an occasional dishonest judge cannot make a venal bench, nor is an incorruptible bench enough to assure a proper administration of justice." [2]

With the exception of these isolated examples there is little definite and positive information as to the judges of the courts in American cities. Casual observation, coupled with the opinions of qualified persons in a number of other cities, bears out a somewhat similar impression as to judges of inferior courts in St. Louis, San Francisco and a number of smaller cities. Of the Detroit judges mention has been made in another chapter. In Philadelphia the magistrates who conduct preliminary hearings in felony cases are not required to be lawyers and are quite generally known to be of decidedly inferior quality. The magistrates of the cities of the United States generally present a rather sorry picture.

II. *Judges of the Trial Courts*

The administration of criminal justice in America gains a great deal from the fact that its trial judges usually try both civil and criminal cases. Only a very few trial judges are engaged with criminal jurisdiction exclusively.[3] The average criminal trial judge is trying civil cases a large part of the time. Usually he seeks the bench because he is attracted by the civil side of the work, although he is not unfamiliar with criminal procedure, because apprenticeship as a prosecuting attorney is such a familiar step in the political career of a judge. But the attitude of the bar toward criminal practice is so contemptuous that the average judge is much more desirous of succeeding in the field of civil cases. He endures his term on the criminal bench partly because it is diverting, partly because it helps him politically (on account of the superior publicity value of criminal cases), and often because of the human interest involved in criminal cases. For this

[2] *Criminal Justice in Cleveland*, 252-253.
[3] Notably the judges of the New York County Court of General Sessions and the Detroit Recorder's Court.

reason there is probably less to criticize in the trial judges of the United States than in any of the other officials in the entire administration of criminal law.

A determination of the exact quality of the judicial personnel of the trial courts in the United States can be made with little except opinion to provide the basis of judgment. Few factual and scientific data have ever been collected concerning this subject. If half the energy devoted to generalized condemnations of the bench and sweeping denunciation of the effect of popular election upon it went into a careful study of what the personnel really is, we should have the material on which to base a policy of reform. We ought to know, for example, how such qualities as age, education, experience and standing at the bar vary as between state and state, and as between city and country. We ought to know whether we get better judges under a non-partisan elective system than under partisan nomination and election. We ought to know whether a longer term or higher salary makes a distinct difference. We ought to know whether appointment by the mayor of police judges and magistrates yields a different result from election of the same types of magistrates in other cities. We ought to know with more definiteness the history of the personnel of the Federal bench, particularly of the district court. Do the appointments of the past generation differ in any important respect from the appointments of the preceding one? Preliminary to the study of this subject, a standard ought to be determined as to the qualifications desired in a judge.

Perhaps no more carefully considered opinion of the quality of the state judges in the United States has been uttered than that of Lord Bryce. It is, of course, a generalization based upon opinion.

"No one will be surprised at what is, in most states, the combined effect on the quality of the bench of these three factors—low salaries, short terms and election by a popular vote controlled by party managers. The ablest lawyers seldom offer themselves: the men elected owe their election and look for their re-election to persons most of whom neither possess nor deserve the confidence of the better citizens.

"We must, however, discriminate between different sets of states, for the differences are marked. Three classes may be roughly distinguished.

"In some six or seven states, including those in which the governor appoints, the judges of the highest court, and as a rule the judges of the second rank also, are competent lawyers and upright men. Some would do credit to any court in any country.

"In most of the other states (a majority of the total number) the justices of the highest court are tolerably competent, even if inferior in learning and acumen to the ablest of the counsel who practice before them. Almost all are above suspicion of pecuniary corruption, though some are liable to be swayed by personal or political influences, for the judge cannot forget his re-election, and is tempted to be complaisant to those who can affect it. In these states the justices of the lower courts are of only mediocre capacity, but hardly ever venal.

"Of the few remaining states it is hard to speak positively. A general description must needs be vague, because the only persons who have full opportunity for gauging the talents and honesty of the judges are the old practitioners in their courts who see them frequently and get to "know their ins and outs". These practitioners are not always unbiased, nor always willing to tell what they know. All that can safely be said is that in a certain small number of states the bench as a whole is not trusted. In every court, be it of higher or lower rank, there are some good men, probably more good than bad. But no plaintiff or defendant knows what to expect. If he goes before one of the upright judges his case may be tried as fairly as it would be in Massachusetts or in Middlesex. On the other hand, fate may send him to a court where the rill of legal knowledge runs very thin, or to one where the stream of justice is polluted at its source. The use of the mandatory or prohibitory power of courts to issue injunctions, and of the power to commit for some alleged contempt of court, is a fertile source of mischief. Injunctions obtained from a pliable judge are sometimes moves in a stock-gambling or in a political game, especially if the lawsuit has a party color.

"Taking the states as a whole, one may say that in most of them the bench does not enjoy that respect which ought to be felt for the ministers of justice, and that in some few states enough is known to justify distrust. In these the judges of lower rank are not necessarily less scrupulous than are those of the highest courts, but their scanty equipment of legal knowledge means that justice is not only uncertain, but also slow and costly, because the weaker the judge the greater the likelihood of delay and appeals, since American practitioners can always find some technical ground for a postponement or for trying to upset a decision." [4]

Thirty years prior to the publication of this judgment Bryce pronounced substantially the same opinion in his *American Commonwealth:* [5]

[4] *Modern Democracies* (New York, 1921), II, 83-112.
[5] I, 513-516.

"Putting the three sources of mischief together, no one will be surprised to hear that in many of the American states the state judges are men of moderate abilities and scanty learning, inferior, and sometimes vastly inferior, to the best of the advocates who practise before them. It is less easy to express a general opinion as to their character, and particularly as to what is called, even in America, where fur capes are not worn, the 'purity of the judicial ermine'. Pecuniary corruption seems, so far as a stranger can ascertain, to be rare, in most states very rare, but there are other ways in which sinister influences can play on a judge's mind, and impair that confidence in his impartiality which is almost as necessary as impartiality itself. And apart from all questions of dishonesty or unfairness, it is an evil that the bench should not be intellectually and socially at least on a level with the bar."

In the main, Bryce's judgment has been commended by competent American observers. Lord Bryce was a man of long experience in public life, thoroughly familiar with the character of the bench and the bar in his own country. Through his wide contacts with American life during his term as Ambassador and on those earlier occasions when he came to America to study its institutions, he had an unparalleled opportunity to view the American bench from the standpoint of reasoned and detached experience. Moreover, Bryce was no Tory. His opinion would not be that of the average conservative American lawyer who is likely to look upon the present bench, chosen as it is by popular election, as distinctly degenerated since the days when corporations fared more favorably in personal injury suits. He had enough knowledge of human nature and of political affairs to refuse to accept this traditional condemnation of the present bench by the conservative bar. His long experience and observation in the United States was supplemented in his later years by an occasional study of many other self-governing countries and the final results of this life-time of observation of and thought upon democratic practices is published in *Modern Democracies.*[6]

There are those who observe that the quality of our bench, with all its limitations, is probably better than we deserve. There has never been any great amount of willful and deliberate misconduct on the part of state judges. Bribery has been most rare.

[6] H. A. L. Fisher's *Bryce* describes in some detail Mr. Bryce's method of gathering information.

Politically selected judges who had been active in politics and wholly discreet in their political connections prior to their election to trial courts, have, after election, steadily improved in all of the qualifications that mark the good judge. There is much wisdom, and some humor, in the comment of the late Chief Justice White who, in speaking of the American judiciary, said, "As I look at the subject and contemplate the varied methods by which judges have been selected, the frequent shortness of their tenure, the almost usual inadequacy of their compensation . . . the thought cannot be resisted that a result so remarkable has been brought about by the dispensation of a merciful providence." But it is hardly wise to rest securely in the hope of a miraculous intervention, or to fail to accept the pretty certain truth that our judges are likely to be prepared, and their quality likely to be determined, by the system that makes them.

Shortly after Mr. Taft had retired from the Presidency, and at a moment in his life when there seemed to be no possibility that he would ever again participate actively in politics, he uttered this rather pessimistic judgment as to the quality of the state bench:

"It has been my official duty to look into the judiciary of each state in my search for candidates to be appointed to federal judgeships and I affirm without hesitation that in states where many of the elected judges of the past have had high rank, the introduction of nomination by direct primary has distinctly injured the character of the bench for learning, courage and ability." [7]

III. *The Party Tie*

On the day when the state conventions of the two major political parties were held in Springfield, Illinois, a newspaper reporter checked the number of municipal judges who were attending the party conventions. He found that of thirty-three judges, sixteen were absent from the bench, and that thirteen of these sixteen were in attendance at the conventions. Eight of them were Republicans and five Democrats. In his news story he printed the names. Many judges in other cities continue to participate actively in politics in spite of the more or less fixed Ameri-

[7] "The Selection and Tenure of Judges," *Law Notes*, November, 1913, 147-152.

can tradition that a judge who has been elevated to the bench should deny himself active participation in politics. They often retain official positions in political groups and consult with party leaders as to political tactics. They do not, be it said, make political speeches, except in unusual cases, but when one considers what a negligible part political speeches play in modern politics, this omission pales into insignificance.[8]

This party activity is in part the penalty of the elective system. It is not to be expected, however, that an appointive bench would be a non-political one. Many years after the adoption of the American Constitution the appointment of judges in all of the states except in Georgia, was, according to Ostrogorsky, "quite beyond the reach of the fluctuations of the popular vote."[9] Appointments were made by the executive or by the legislature. In 1832, Mississippi inaugurated the system of judges elected for a term of years by the voters. After that the system spread rapidly among the states, and ultimately was adopted by New York in its constitution of 1846. The terms were very frequently short in order to enlarge democratic opportunity. This drawing of the judiciary into the realm of political activity became well established and ultimately every strong political organization assumed control over the selections to the bench. This, of course, means, that when a political organization is governed by a boss the judgeships are determined by him. If it is a political organization of high standards, the judges will be of a better order; but when the political machine is sufficiently entrenched in power, judgeships may be given out with the same disregard of high standards as characterizes the disposition of other offices. That no decisive change has taken place in thirty years is suggested in a statement made by a responsible and honored member of the New York bar, Henry K. Jessup.[10]

"Theoretically they [judges] are elected by the people. As a matter of fact, they are always *selected* by the Boss. Once his decision has been

[8] A very interesting commentary upon the American judiciary by a distinguished foreign jurist is Nerincx, L'Organization Judiciaire des Etats Unis (1909). See particularly Chapter 18.
[9] *Democracy and the Organization of Political Parties* (New York, 1908), II, 91-92.
[10] "The Judicial Office and the Bar's Responsibility," 13 *Amer. Bar Assoc. Journal*, 177, 1927.

reached, the Convention, if there be one, or the Primary, if it takes the place of a Convention, registers for the purposes of the votes of the members of that particular machine, the will and choice of the Boss. Any influence that could effect a change of opinion on his part must have been exerted *before he reached his decision.* Committees on judicial nominees of Bar Associations, commenting upon the qualifications of his candidates after they have been nominated, I venture to assert, never changed one vote. I have seen them published in local newspapers of high respectability but limited circulation, but the voters of the predominant party don't read that report. The members of those committees who are usually equally of two parties have, in very few instances, excoriated any of the individuals selected by the Boss. They use various degrees of 'good' or 'excellent' to describe them and the candidate prints on his lithographed paper or campaign posters 'Endorsed by all Bar Associations'. What is the use of enlarging upon this point? It is a fact of common knowledge and leads to the main contention of this address, namely, that the duty of the bar in selection of judicial candidates is to exert its enlightened and collective influence *before* the political parties have actually nominated and the matter of selection becomes an accomplished fact.

* * *

"I tried a case once before a judge of political configuration against a corporation, the chief stockholder of which was a senator and the power behind the throne in the political organization that had put the judge on the bench. The judge and the senator had jointly and severally the nerve to permit the senator to sit by the judge's side on the bench while the trial was proceeding. I counted my client fortunate when I secured a mistrial. . . .

"Again, I went to another courtroom on a matter involving discretion and happened to see a certain political boss go into the judge's private room as I was on my way to the courtroom. The judge did not come in for half an hour beyond the appointed time. My application was denied. . . .

"We have all had unhappy experiences of this sort. We know that many judges are moved by 'human prejudice' and if there is anything more human than politics in these United States of America, I don't know what it is.

* * *

". . . the influence of the bar, collectively or semi-collectively, as at present exerted, does not amount to a hill of beans."

A federal judge, writing of the various aspects of an elective judiciary, provides a tragi-comic but seriously intended picture.[11]

[11] Jenkins, "The Troubles of an Elective Judiciary," 32 *American Law Review,* 237 (1898).

"1. The first trouble of an aspirant for judicial honors under an elective system begins long before his hopes can have fruition in a nomination for office. He must become known to and be popular with the masses; that is to say, he must cultivate the acquaintance of the ward bosses and of the great army of toilers who lead and control popular opinion—the saloon-keepers. He must learn to like, or must pretend to like, poor whisky, poor cigars and poor company. To accomplish this he must not too greatly woo that 'sweet restorer, balmy sleep,' but must be content to deny himself, to take up his cross, and spend the blissful hours of night in the discussion of grave affairs of state in a saloon, and in 'setting it up for the boys.' He may be ever so profound a lawyer, ever so great a jurist, but unless he can thus accommodate himself to the habits, the thoughts and the likings of the masses he will probably fail in the object of his ambition.

"2. He must secure a majority of delegates to the convention. Perhaps he has won the sympathy of the people, but it is the delegate who makes the decision.

"3. Having won the 'coveted nomination' he must electioneer, mainly at his own financial expense, and, if nominated by both parties, must contribute to the campaign of both. 'If he receives the nomination of both parties, it is not because of love for the man of an opposite faith, but because the party loves success more than it hates the man.

"4. His troubles are not yet over—he must make appointments to suit the political party, rather than to bring about the greatest efficiency. He is the prey of disappointed suitors. Refusal to submit to a political hierarchy means political ostracism, and refusal of nomination. He is subject to the venom of lawyers, and to the changeable whims of the public.

"5. Having succumbed to ambition, 'all too late he learns that the compensation is inadequate. He has lost his old clientele, so cannot return to the practice of his profession.'

"6. And when he comes before the Great Judge his only prayer will be that he may be appointed to some permanent position among the angels, and be not compelled to hold place by popular approval."

In writing of the extent to which judges are expected to contribute to campaign funds, Russel Whitman, a veteran lawyer of Chicago, who urged that the American Bar Association adopt a provision in its code of judicial ethics condemning certain party activities on the part of judges, speaks out of an unquestioned fund of realistic experience.[12]

"Another method of collecting campaign funds from judicial candidates is familiar. Where nominations are made by party conventions a sum is

[12] "Problems of Professional Ethics," 9 *Amer. Bar Assoc. Journ.*, 300, May, 1923.

frequently fixed as representing, in the judgment of the party bosses, the quota which the judicial nominees should severally be required to pay into the campaign fund. If there is a fair chance of election, this quota may be fixed at 5 per cent of the total salary to be received by the judge if elected; e.g., suppose the salary is $10,000 a year, and the term is five years. Then if a nominee has a reasonable chance of being elected, he might expect, as a prerequisite to his nomination, to be called upon to contribute 5 per cent of $50,000, that is $2,500, to the campaign fund of his party. Such contribution would not relieve him from demands or requests for further contributions during his five-year term of office; but he might expect that the amounts called for would not in any one instance be reckoned upon a basis of 5 per cent of his entire five years' salary. They would ordinarily be much less than this; and may in some degree depend upon how urgent the need for funds is in any given election."

* * *

"Conference with lawyers in attendance at Minneapolis tends to indicate unmistakably that political assessments levied upon judges or candidates for the bench constitute a deeply rooted and widespread evil. In Louisiana it is said that a candidate for judge has himself organized and is at present operating a political machine assembled and used for the purpose of collecting necessary funds and otherwise promoting the candidacy of the judicial aspirant who sits at the throttle. The bare mention of this seamy side of judicial elections brings from lawyers a shrug of the shoulders and the immediate questions 'What are you going to do about it?' 'How are they going to get elected or nominated if they do not "come across"?'"

In a speech before the Middlesex Bar in 1922 Alonzo R. Weed read a letter from a friend who had served for eighteen years as a member of a trial court in one of the great cities of the Middle West. The letter expresses the elective judge's envy of the conditions provided in such a state as Massachusetts.[18]

"My! what a wonderfully pleasing sensation one must experience to be lifted on to the bench without an effort. Think of it! No campaign; no politicians to see or truckle to. No campaign assessment to pay. No constituents for whom you don't care a hang to meet, address and harangue. No staying out late nights in stuffy smoke-laden halls and then above all no fears of ignominious defeat. Running for judge is in my judgment a low-down, degrading performance. I have made five campaigns, elected thrice and defeated twice. However, my campaign was more or less negligible, but the others who ran with me were on the job and went the

[18] The elective system of selecting judges as described by an elected judge. (Extract from a speech of Honr. A. R. Weed at the Middlesex Bar Dinner, Dec., 1922), *Mass. Law Quarterly*, No. 3, 25-26 (1923).

rounds, the result being that I was a poor vote-getter, still I was never defeated except when all the ticket I was on likewise went down in defeat. I always maintained, and results proved me right, that campaigning never elected a man judge, it was a condition which carried him in or left him out. I am glad that at my age no judicial campaigns can again confront me.

". . . he told me that by the established custom he paid a political assessment of $3,000 for each one of his five campaigns and he added $1,000 more in the last campaign because the contest became so critical. In other words, his five campaigns to be a judge cost him in all $16,000."

The records in two great political machines such as the Penrose Philadelphia machine and the Tammany system of New York show clearly that the appointment of judges even by a political boss is preferable to the scramble for office under the non-partisan system. Both the Penrose judges and the Tammany judges especially in the higher orders of judiciary have been fairly satisfactory at all times, and in some instances decidedly good. Under party control in New York City, without the intervention of the direct primary and the non-partisan judiciary ballot, the two parties have often entered into bi-partisan agreements which have contributed distinctly to the high quality of the bench, particularly the court of appeals. In 1927, for example, Judge Benjamin Cardozo was elevated to the head of the Court of Appeals by such an agreement with the result that the State of New York is able to command the service in high judicial office of one of the most distinguished jurists of his generation. This was possible not only because of the active intervention of lawyer politicians, but because of the very fortunate circumstance that judgeships are ordinarily not particularly valuable to the party in terms of appointments and spoils.[14]

IV. *The Politics of Non-Partisanship*

It is not, however, the political party itself which is the worst menace to an independent judiciary. It is rather the condition

[14] An interesting study remains to be made of the difference between appointments made by governors of various states to fill unexpired terms and those chosen through popular elections. A somewhat cursory examination in two or three states indicates that the governor's appointments, while often dictated by party expedients, are unquestionably better.

which is forced upon a judge by the necessity for keeping his name before the public. This condition is accentuated rather than lessened by removing the names of judges from party ballot while at the same time leaving them within the realm of popular election.

The effect of popular election upon the bench has unquestionably been accentuated rather than lessened by the advent of non-partisan elections. When judges are no longer subject to the protection and sponsorship of political parties, they are compelled to become their own political managers. They must at all times keep their politically apperceptive faculties alert. They must recognize that politics in a great city requires that religious and racial groups, labor and capitalistic organizations, and, above all, the public press, are gods whose good will the judge must retain.

In the years from 1900 to the outbreak of the Great War, a definite revolt developed in the various states against old forms of party government and in favor of non-partisan elections. Thinking that it would be possible to improve the bench, many states abolished party nominations and party elections of judges and substituted for them direct primaries and non-partisan judicial elections. Adequate evidence is lacking as to the complete effect of this change upon the bench, but such studies as have been made indicate striking results.

The experience of Ohio is typical. In 1911-12, the constitution and laws of Ohio were changed to provide for nomination of judges by direct primary or petition and for the placing of these names on the ballot without party designation. The purpose of this was not only to abolish the nomination of judges by party conventions, but to remove the names of judges from the party ballots and to place them on a separate ballot paper without party designation of any kind. In order to compare the old partisan method with this new non-partisan method of election, all elections or appointments to the bench from 1885 to 1920 were listed, and in each case the entire public and professional career was determined. A comparison of the group attaining the bench before the use of the non-partisan method with that following it indicates that the new system produced judges who were younger, who had less experience in private practice prior to election, and who had held some public offices as a preliminary to their judicial career.[15] When a judge is reduced to the necessity of providing his own campaign "thunder" under the non-partisan system, the laws which govern the attainment of publicity immediately operate upon him. He must of necessity bring his name before the voters often enough to provide more or less automatic response on their part when he runs for office. This requires that he do things which have news value, and, moreover, that he make contacts which will result in political assistance at election time. If he is relieved of the necessity of conciliating a political party, he does not thereby rise to complete independence. He finds that the world is not composed of individuals but of groups and of vote-gathering forces. He must, therefore, secure the support of labor organizations, capitalistic groups of various sorts, reform organizations, and religious groups, fraternal societies, racial aggregations, and, above all, he must achieve "news value" in the eyes of the newspapers. Some of the problems which he finds I have described elsewhere, in the following terms.[16]

"1. *The Traffic in Influence*—The atmosphere of the criminal court seems to favor the growth and prosperity of the petty politician. He serves as a kind of political broker. He preys upon both the public and the public official. The person caught in the toils of the law uses him because of his reputed influence with officials, the public official recognizes him because of his real or fancied power to deliver votes. In either case he profits, while the public interest is overlooked and the official is brought to a misuse of his official power.

"2. *The Appeal to Race and Religion*—The following passage from the *Survey* (263-264) deserves careful consideration by the advocate of a non-partisan judiciary. It describes a new influence upon the judiciary:

" 'In order properly to play the game,' observes one of the more sophisticated judges, 'it is necessary for a judge to attend weddings, funerals, christenings, banquets, barbecues, dances, clam-bakes, holiday celebrations, dedications of buildings, receptions, opening nights, first showings of films, prize-fights, bowling matches, lodge entertainments, church festivals, and every conceivable function given by any group, national, social, religious. A municipal judge is said to have refereed

[15] See graph illustrating this on page 256 of *Criminal Justice in Cleveland.*
[16] Moley, "Outline of the *Cleveland Crime Survey*," 17-19.

a prize-fight. Three judges of unquestioned character campaigned by visiting the saloons in the different foreign sections of the city, and were presented to long lines of foreign-speaking voters with the aid of an interpreter. No drinks were bought, not a cent was spent, only handshakes were exchanged, yet this was deemed essential campaigning.'

"One of the most disturbing features is the intensifying of racial and religious appeals. A man is elected or appointed because he is a Pole, a Jew, an Irishman, a Mason, a Protestant, and it is sometimes difficult for a committee to reject a candidate without being charged with discrimination. On the other hand, an even more vicious tendency has begun to appear—the formation of organizations with the avowed or unavowed purposes of 'knifing' every candidate who is not of a particular religion, nationality or color. It is estimated that one such organization last fall, through the expedient of issuing thousands of marked ballots at churches and other places, succeeded in swaying 50,000 votes among the regular nominees. The marked ballot carried nothing to indicate the sectarian nature of the organization, which bore a title similar to that of the Civic League, an impartial organization, and it is not to be supposed that many voters knew of the dominant motive behind the marked recommendations."

"3. *The Influence of Labor Organizations*—One of the respected leaders of labor says: 'The unions have lost faith in the courts; they believe the man who has the influence gets by.' This distrust is reflected in very serious efforts on the part of certain labor organizations to elect judges favorable to them and to defeat those suspected of hostility. Within recent years two very able judges have been retired because of the opposition of labor. One of these judges led the ticket in 1912 and was defeated in 1918. The *Survey* states, however, in connection with this activity on the part of labor, that little good can come from the simple partisan view that labor is largely to blame for the unsatisfactory manner in which judges are compelled to preserve their official lives. 'The folly of exposing a judiciary to every wind that blows and then blaming a particular wind is apparent'.

"4. *The Bench as 'News'*—Probably the most important influence with which a judge must reckon under a non-partisan system is the public press. While in the Cleveland newspapers editorial support of judges has in the main been wisely given, it is unfortunately true that editorial support is a minor factor in the influence of a newspaper upon elections. It is as 'news' that most people learn to know judges, and it is the 'news' or 'copy' value of a judge that largely determines his continuance on the bench. Some publicity is justly earned by a judge when he inaugurates a reform or hands down a decision on an important and unsual question—such publicity means public education. But, unfortunately, quantity of publicity seems to be more important than quality. The law of suggestion leads the public to vote for the most widely advertised name. For example, two candidates, hitherto comparatively unknown and of no marked fitness for the bench, have since 1912 been elected because they bore the same names as two retired judges who were widely known and respected. A blacksmith once running on the Socialist ticket for the Supreme Court carried Cuyahoga County because his name looked and sounded like that of the well-known probate judge. 'I don't care what you say about me, if you keep on publishing my name', remarked one ambitious official.

"In the making of publicity, the rules of newspaper enterprise govern. It is the unique and sensational thing that gets into the paper. It is not entirely inaccurate to say that the judge who acts like a judge is not good copy, but the judge who acts otherwise 'gets the front page'. For example, a presiding judge labors for long hours to clear up a badly clogged docket; he works nights and holidays, but few people hear of it. Another judge is prominently featured for having driven all the way to Canton with a sporting editor and other fight fans to attend a prize fight. Long study of a difficult case is not noted, but the newspaper carries the story that 'Municipal Judge —— ate candy as he listened to testimony Friday. "It keeps one from gettin' nervous," the judge says.'

"It has been aptly said that a relationship grows up between the reporter and the judge similar to that between the bumble-bee and the clover. The one exploits the other. The reporter needs the stories; the judge can give them. The judge needs the publicity which the reporter can provide.

"In the contest for publicity, service on the criminal bench is a distinct advantage. There are more 'stories' there; hence it has become customary for judges to seek service on the criminal bench in election year. The schedule is apparently conveniently arranged to provide judges seeking re-election with this needed means of publicity."

What lawyer, familiar with the conditions in the courts of great cities, has not seen newspaper men halt the progress of a judge, as he retires to his private chamber after adjourning court, with the request that he recount to them the "high spots" of the day, which they have been too busy to secure in a more regular manner? Even in our delightfully informal land of equality, some store is set upon the nice question of which person should call upon which. Many people with old-fashioned ideas of the dignity of the bench feel that the judge should be accorded the courtesy of receiving others. This custom still obtains in his relations with lawyers, who invariably must go to him to discuss matters affecting their cases. But we have seen the judge call, hat in hand, upon the newspaper proprietor. In one verified instance, he has on numerous occasions gone to the city editor, this practice almost assuming the form of a subordinate reporting at intervals to a superior.

Judges must get elected, and so conduct themselves as to attain reëlection. The term, in an overwhelming number of states, is six years or less, a period not long enough to permit even the newly elected judge to forget the necessity of building his following for the next election. A distinguished member of the bar, who had served a term on a state supreme court, said this in private conversation:

"I could not bring myself to run for reëlection. It meant constant breaking in upon the time which a judge sensitive to the quality of his written opinions should give to study. It meant traveling from town to town, climbing stairways to the offices of professionally unworthy but politically powerful lawyers. It meant accepting invitations to attend meetings of every sort, to speak on topics representing every kind of irrelevance. It meant accepting familiarities from the unworthy without flinching, rejecting improper requests without administering the rebuke which they deserved. It was a hard choice, for I wanted the office, but the price was more than I could pay."

If this is the verdict when the office is so far removed from political influences as is the state's highest court, what must be the humiliation which our political system visits upon the judges of county and municipal courts!

Interesting evidence concerning the wisdom of electing judges could be gathered in any judicial campaign by taking stenographic account of the speeches of all the judges who are candidates for office. Such a compilation has never been made but it would be a most powerful argument against an elective judiciary. What is a judge to discuss in a political campaign? It is true that he may promise faithful and incorruptible service. He may suggest that through his influence he will seek to bring about more expeditious judicial administration. He may not, however, suggest that in order to do so he will seek to influence his legislature, because that would perhaps be an improper activity for a judge. If he promises individual groups that he will give them special consideration, he is seriously violating the most primary of ethical principles. If he merely passes among all sorts and conditions of people, as is ordinarily done in a judicial campaign, he is wasting his own time and that of the people with whom he mingles. There is, moreover, very little public interest in judicial elections. The vote for judicial candidates usually runs markedly below that for other candidates.

V. *The Political Mind*

If such conditions exist as generally as these samples portray, the bent of mind of American judges must, in some degree, be influenced by the conditions through which they pass in achieving the high position which they occupy. If promotion and progress are dependent, as apparently they are, upon observance of certain political conditions which are inevitable in securing public office, the minds of the judges must be politically influenced. This is not to say that a political bent of mind is necessarily an unsatisfactory mind to use in trying cases, criminal or civil. It is, however, a faculty which will largely determine the conditions under which such judicial work is performed. It is not to be expected that men whose formative years have been given to public service in essentially political positions will be transformed when they reach the bench. They remain political. The political mind has been most admirably described in a great work on human psychology and behavior: [17]

"When a party politican is called upon to consider a new measure, his verdict is largely determined by certain constant systems of ideas and trends of thought, constituting what is generally known as 'party bias'. We should describe these systems in our newly acquired terminology as his 'political complex'. The complex causes him to take up an attitude toward the proposed measure which is quite independent of any absolute merits which the latter may possess. If we argue with our politician, we shall find that the complex will reinforce in his mind those arguments which support the view of his party, while it will infallibly prevent him from realizing the force of the arguments propounded by the opposite side. Now, it should be observed that the individual himself is probably quite unaware of this mechanism in his mind. He fondly imagines that his opinion is formed solely by the logical pros and cons of the measure before him. We see, in fact, that not only is his thinking determined by a complex of whose action he is unconscious, but that he believes his thoughts

[17] Hart, *Psychology of Insanity* (London, 1921), 65.

to be the result of other causes which are in reality insufficient and illusory. This latter process of self-deception, in which the individual conceals the real foundation of his thought by a series of adventitious props, is termed 'rationalization'.

"The two mechanisms which manifest themselves in our example of the politician, the unconscious origin of beliefs and actions, and the subsequent process of rationalization to which they are subjected, are of fundamental importance in psychology. They may be observed every day in every individual. That a man generally knows why he thinks in a certain way, and why he does certain things, is a widespread and cherished belief of the human race. It is, unfortunately, for the most part an erroneous one. We have an overwhelming need to believe that we are acting rationally, and are loth to admit that we think and do things without being ourselves aware of the motives producing those thoughts and actions. Now a very large number of our mental processes are the result of an emotional bias or complex of the type we have described. Such a causal chain is, however, incompatible with our ideal of rationality. Hence we tend to substitute for it a fictitious logical process, and persuade ourselves that the particular thought or action is its reasonable and natural result. This is the mechanism of rationalization seen in the example of the politician."

Specifically, it would seem that there are two marks of a political mind as shown in a judge's practical methodology. The first is determined either by his ambition for further office or for his continued and uninterrupted enjoyment of the one which he possesses. The other is a certain striving for that which is "practical"; that is, a consideration in the making of every decision of not only the merits in the specific problem before him, but the effect that his decision will have when viewed by the outside individuals who compose his public. That such a consideration is not entirely independent can be shown by certain examples of decisions which he must make where problems in which numbers of people are involved are to be decided and in which a decision must be made which will result in what is commonly called social justice, in spite of temporary injustice in an individual case.

It is quite common for classical exponents of jurisprudence, both ancient and modern, to declare that such a consideration should be foreign to the mind of a judge and that the law should be enforced without regard to its effect in individual cases. This, of course, is based upon a fallacious conception of the definiteness of law. We have indicated how indistinct the outlines of law really are. Another consideration in point, which the classical argument does not include, is the modern explanation of the process of rationalization. A consistent exponent of the ruling order will produce not only good arguments for a given course of action, but very often good law, in spite of his lack of appreciation that he is engaged in a process of justifying a prejudice.

But when these factors have been considered the stark fact remains that social problems are secondary to a wise determination of what to do in an individual case, and the skill necessary to make this determination is only partly implanted by education in politics. It may be necessary to do unpopular things and it certainly should be necessary to deny the claims of political influences, which are seldom based upon a clear, rational decision as to the needs of an individual defendant. Thus the political mind has, in the administration of criminal law, a tendency frequently to make temporary decisions which will seem to satisfy all concerned, when, in fact, such temporary decisions are merely a means of deferring an ultimate grapple with pretty fundamental considerations. It permits considerations of expediency to assume determining proportions when what is needed is courageous and final action. It unfortunately lends itself to types of leniency or types of severity which accord, not with an honest examination of facts, but with what an unenlightened public opinion demands. It is in these realms that the political mind fails as a factor in the effective enforcement of criminal law. A judge reaches the point where he must select a course of action in a world in which the plausible often poses as the truth, in which the strident and emphatic can easily be mistaken for the majority, in which the voice of propaganda may easily disguise itself as the voice of democracy, and in which the way of the majority may be the way of conservatism, devotion to the past, and, what is still more serious, devotion to prejudice.

There are exceedingly favorable sides of the political mind which give to the American judge qualities that often give him an advantage over some judges of a more independent mold. The practitioner of politics becomes highly sensitive to currents in opinion which frequently may be evidence of new and highly important developments in social attitudes. The political judge will become aware of the stirring of public opinion which is destined to determine the course of subsequent law, and through his intuition he will be able to anticipate legal changes and thus to accomplish something by way of bridging the gap which always separates public opinion and law. Through the very process of seeking methods by which he can bring about public approval for himself, the political judge will often become the constructive agent for important judicial innovations and reforms. He is able, particularly in criminal cases, to get the "feel" of the social situation out of which a criminal act has emerged and to administer wise counsel and prescribe effective treatment. In all matters affecting changes in economic life, which so often become seriously involved in an outworn legalism, the political judge is able to make skillful and often wise adjustments. It is quite probable that the political mind is less likely to identify its own ideas and beliefs as part of eternal truth. The give and take of political life has taught the politician the fallibility of human ideas and human purposes. These characteristics are likely to be lacking in a judiciary entirely independent of the currents of popular thought. "My duty as a judge," said Judge Cardozo, "may be to objectify in law, not my own aspirations and convictions and philosophies, but the aspirations and convictions and philosophies of my time. Hardly shall I do this well if my own sympathies are with the time that is past." [18]

VI. Meeting the Reality of Things

There seem to be in large, perhaps increasing numbers, judges who are the product of the conditions described in this chapter. They are in a sense "career men." Most of their adult life is spent in the public service, either in official positions or in active politics. Sometimes they progress from minor political positions, frequently prosecutorships of some sort, and proceed through a range of offices culminating in trial judgships. The most important reason for the frequency of this type of judge is the demand by political organization that judgships be granted to those who have served the party. This being true, the judgships fall to two types

[18] *The Nature of the Judicial Process* (New Haven, 1928), 173.

of lawyers. Some find difficult competition in strictly private practice and discover that following a political star is easier and more profitable. Others, who are men of spirit and of an idealistic turn, deliberately forsake the higher economic return of private practice and enter the vicissitudes of politics. To an increasing degree those lawyers who look forward to a strictly private practice, particularly of a specialized nature, are avoiding the digression of a flyer in politics. They realize that to hold public office, even to attain the temporary advertising value which it provides, is to defer and seriously to interfere with the slow process of building professional equipment and status. Moreover the "higher" ranges of corporation practice regard their office-holding brethren with some degree of dis-esteem. A very serious corporation lawyer was quite unaware of the quiet humor of his remark about another practitioner, "He is a good lawyer with a good record except that once when he was young he drifted into Congress."

The time seems to be passing when the lawyer grown to maturity in the active practice of the law, crowns his career with service on the bench. This is inevitable, because of conditions in the political world, and in the actual practice of law. The average practicing lawyer becomes highly specialized. If he is desirous of distinguished service at the bar he must renounce for the most part active interest in politics, not because it interferes with his impartial activity as a lawyer, but because he can not afford to give the time to it. A political machine is like every other human institution. It must, under pressure of self-preservation, provide some reward for long and, let us assume, honest and disinterested service in public office and party activities. This kind of reward for the lawyer-politician is elevation to the bench. It is, moreover, essential to the man who has spent his years between admission to the bar and the age of forty in political office that some provision be made for economic security other than the practice of the law because the lawyer at the age of forty faces an almost impossible problem if he then attempts to enter the active profession of the law. He must either join the ranks of what are commonly known as political lawyers who sell, not legal skill and knowledge, but political influence, or he must be content with scanty returns. Service on the bench provides a respectable and honorable alternative.

The most commonly urged corrective for the influence of politics in the judiciary is an increased interest and activity by the organized bar in judicial elections and appointments. These efforts proceed upon the principle that the organized bar under the influence of its leaders can guide the electorate or the appointing authority. The bar is presumably best able to define the qualifications of the judicial office, to determine the character of service which judges are giving and to discover among those who are available, the persons best suited for selection. Bar associations, national, state and local, have been active in attempts to improve the personnel of the bench, local organizations frequently polling their membership to arrive at a joint recommendation and endorsement. A very few, notably the Cleveland Bar Association, have actively campaigned for their preferences, seeking in this way to relieve the judicial candidates of the embarrassment of a direct appeal to the voters. These efforts have undoubtedly resulted in the defeat of some unfit judges and in the election of worthy ones.

Two ideas seem to be uppermost among those American lawyers who deplore the present elective system in the selection of judges, and who wish to make suggestions of a so-called constructive nature. One is to abolish the elective system and to provide for the appointment of judges by the governor or by some other official. The other idea takes for granted the permanence of the elective system and attempts to eliminate the influence of politics to some degree from the selection of judges by galvanizing into action the various bar associations for the purpose of lifting from the judges the burden of making their own campaigns. It would seem that, before much further effort is made upon these two assumptions, it would be desirable to gather some concrete and specific information which unfortunately we now lack. In the first place, what evidence have we that the selection of judges by governors would be appreciably better than the selection by public election? The fact seems to be assumed, although it is commonly known that most governors accept the recommendation of political leaders, and that these

preferences are not unlike those which the same political leaders
would act upon in nominating judges for a popular election. It
would seem for the most part that the superiority of the
appointive system rests largely upon the assumption that the
nomination of a judge by a political leader is better than the
self-advertising necessary under the non-partisan system. This
assumption is probably well founded, but there is too little evidence on the question to justify a general statement that appointment by the governor would be superior to elections after party
nomination. A very careful examination of the appointments
made to the New York Supreme Court in the first and second
departments shows clearly that with one or two exceptions the
persons appointed by the governors to fill unexpired terms were
about the same persons who would have been nominated for the
office by the political organization for popular election. The
slight superiority of the New York City magistrates over the
judges of the Chicago Municipal Court hardly justifies the
assumption that the appointive system is preferable. The superiority is probably due to the longer term and better salary. The
fact is that an organization mayor will usually accept the recommendations of an organization in which the magistracy is located.
If it is a vacancy in the Bronx, the mayor usually accepts upon
the recommendation of the Bronx Democratic organization, and
in like manner in each of the other four boroughs. A very careful
study should be made in a number of states to determine, if
possible, the relative qualifications of judges appointed by governors and those elected by the people. A study should take into
consideration some of the personal qualifications mentioned in
this chapter and should, moreover, make detailed investigation
to determine the exact extent to which recommendations by the
bar, the political organization and other agencies are weighed
in making appointments. Such a study would seem to be necessary before we really assume that the improvement of the
bench in this country is merely a question of appointment versus
election.

The other question concerns the extent to which bar associations may remove a judge from the necessity of participating
actively in politics. The theory upon which this program is based

is that the responsible members of the bar who will presumably control the activities of the professional associations will know more intimately the qualifications of judges and of those who are candidates for the bench, and that they will make certain that the public or the appointing power is informed concerning the relative merits of those who are candidates for office.

The permanent value of such intervention as well as that of the desirability of appointive judges, must wait upon further information. Very careful studies of the exact extent to which bar associations have attempted to operate in the field of judicial selection should be made, and consideration ought to be given in such studies to the effect which such activities have had upon the bar associations themselves. It is, as will be pointed out subsequently, quite probable that the nature of the controlling group in bar associations will change when such associations become powerful political factors. In other words, it is quite easy for the best minds of the bar to wield dominant influence in an association which does little but to commemorate yearly the deceased members and to provide a platitudinous annual program. It seems quite probable that to change the character of the objectives of an association will necessarily bring about a change in the association itself.

Those who call upon the bar to reform the administration of justice are thinking of the profession in terms of a neat and compact little guild. The bar in America has far outgrown such a conception. The vast market for legal knowledge, the interrelations of the bar and business, the ease with which legal education can be acquired in many of the less rigorous law schools, and the lax conditions of admission to the bar in many states have resulted in a vast bar membership which is very difficult to organize as an effective unit. The ever present conflict between the personal injury lawyers and their opponents is a basis of disunion altogether too difficult effectively to overcome, particularly where the selection of judges is concerned. Instances are to be found where the two groups of interest have come to form rival bar associations.

One of the reasons why a great many persons and organizations favor a judiciary more independent of popular control is the fact that under present circumstances the American courts particularly those of last resort in the states are called upon to decide purely political questions. The most important of these questions is the determination of the constitutionality of laws passed by legislative bodies. There are, also, other questions constantly coming before them which involve questions closely related to politics. The injection of economic problems, such as disputes involving the relative rights of labor and employer, means in substance that these two great influences will be used in the selection of judges, and for this reason labor will always be on the side of an elective bench. In fact, a great deal of the talk that we hear about an independent judiciary simply means that some people want the judiciary independent of the influence of their opponents. When, in a happier day for them, judges were selected from their own ranks and largely through their own influence, they were not so articulate on the question of independence.

All of this points to the necessity for an elimination from the mass of business which the courts are compelled to consider, questions which are, after all, not justiciable in accordance with the standards of traditional jurisprudence, but are really adjustments between conflicting economic groups within the state. The most effective way to reduce the problem of judicial administration to proportions which offer some hope of solution may be to remove from the business which courts are called upon to decide, questions which can be determined by politically selected boards and commissions equipped to weigh in the balance the seriously debatable questions of economic interest.

The apparent pessimism of the foregoing comments is intended to serve as a warning to those who feel that the problem of judicial personnel in America is a simple one of method. The problem is, in fact, rooted in a number of very important and, it may be, permanent characteristics of American public and professional life. There are certainly questions involved which need just as active consideration as the ones which we have mentioned. These are questions which in part must quite permanently remain unanswered, because they involve problems of relative values which must in the last analysis depend upon the attitude of the person who is attempting to weigh them.

In spite of everything, the political party remains the most powerful influence in the selection of the bench in American states. It is a factor which is to be permanently reckoned with. This being true the making of provision for education for the bench with reference to the administration of criminal justice is a possibility for those interested in reform. The judges of criminal courts will probably to an increasing extent acquire educational stimulation from certain community associations. It is common for juvenile judges to find their close professional associations with social welfare workers, educators and psychiatrists, rather than with lawyers. The same thing is likely to be increasingly true of criminal judges. The educational value of such contacts is important. Judges are also to a degree educated by their own probation departments which are constantly bringing into their reports significant new sociological and psychological facts.

Such casual educational contacts are not to be depended upon for the serious preparation of judges of criminal courts. He should be a bit of a physician and a psychologist, a good deal of a sociologist and of course, a lawyer. It may be that within discreet limits there should be some differentiation in the law schools between the education of a "public" and that of a "private" lawyer. This would probably best be met by some extension of a system of optional choice of courses in the law school itself and a liberal reconstruction of the traditional courses in criminal law and procedure. If circumstances decree that we shall have career men as judges our educational processes may well consider means for their preparation.

In any final consideration of the question of how far the democracy may be expected to acknowledge its inability to choose its own judges it must be kept in mind that relative values are concerned. Popular election, universal suffrage, local self government and other democratic institutions acquire unexpected friends when such innovations as an appointive judiciary are proposed. Irrelevant but significant weighing of values takes place and the less tangible but older and more sentimental side of the scale will probably continue to prevail.

Considering what the sovereign democracy compels its judges to suffer, it is served better than it deserves. American state trial judges are, in spite of unfortunate exceptions, a hopeful group of public servants. The observer, as he goes from state to state, comes to recognize that in character, and common sense, judges are the best of those who are in public life. They are in every way, as a class, superior to the ranges of other branches of government. The public is not unaware of this because as respect is given to the public service in America, the judges are highly held. This is a reason why more power may safely be placed in their hands. And it provides some reason for the presence of tempered optimism in the face of many grim realities.

APPENDIX A

RULES IN M'NAGHTEN'S CASE (1843)

10 C.L. AND F. 200 AT P. 209

(*Q*. I.) "What is the law respecting alleged crimes committed by persons afflicted with insane delusion in respect of one or more particular subjects or persons: as for instance, where, at the time of the commission of the alleged crime, the accused knew he was acting contrary to law, but did the act complained of with a view, under the influence of insane delusion, of redressing or revenging some supposed grievance or injury, or of producing some supposed public benefit?"

(*A*. I.) "Assuming that your lordships' inquiries are confined to those persons who labor under such partial delusions only, and are not in other respects insane, we are of opinion that notwithstanding the accused did the act complained of with a view, under the influence of insane delusion, of redressing or avenging some supposed grievance or injury, or of producing some public benefit, he is nevertheless punishable, according to the nature of the crime committed, if he knew at the time of committing such crime that he was acting contrary to law, by which expression we understand your lordships to mean the law of the land."

(*Q*. II.) "What are the proper questions to be submitted to the jury where a person alleged to be afflicted with insane delusion respecting one or more particular subjects or persons is charged with the commission of a crime (murder, for example), and insanity is set up as a defense?"

(*Q*. III.) "In what terms ought the question to be left to the jury as to the prisoner's state of mind, at the time when the act was committed?"

(*A*. II *and* III.) "As these two questions appear to us to be more conveniently answered together, we submit our opinion to be that the jury ought to be told in all cases that every man is to be presumed to be sane, and to possess a sufficient degree of reason to be responsible for his crimes, until the contrary be proved to their satisfaction; and that to establish a defense on the ground of insanity it must be clearly proved that, at the time of committing the act, the accused was laboring under such a defect of reason, from disease of the mind, as not to know the nature and quality of the act he was doing, or, if he did know it, that he did not know he was doing what was wrong. The mode of putting the latter part of the question to the jury on these occasions has generally been, whether the accused at the time of doing the act knew the difference between right and wrong; which mode, though rarely, if ever, leading to any mistake with the jury, is not, as we conceive, so accurate when put generally and in the abstract, as when put with reference to the party's knowledge of right and wrong, in respect to the very act with which he is charged. If the question were to be put as to the knowledge of the accused solely and exclusively with reference to the law of the land, it might tend to confound the jury, by inducing them to believe that an actual knowledge of the law of the land was essential in order to lead to a conviction: whereas, the law is administered upon the principle that everyone must be taken conclusively to know it, without proof that he does know it. If the accused was conscious that the act was one that he ought not to do, and if that act was at the same time contrary to the law of the land, he is punishable; and the usual course, therefore, has been to leave the question to the jury, whether the accused had a sufficient degree of reason to know that he was doing an act that was wrong; and this course we think is correct, accompanied with such observations and explanations as the circumstances of each particular case may require."

(*Q.* IV.) "If a person under an insane delusion as to existing facts commits an offense in consequence thereof, is he thereby excused?"

(*A.* IV.) "The answer must, of course, depend on the nature of the delusion; but making the same assumption as we did before, namely, that he labors under such partial delusion only, and

is not in other respects insane, we think he must be considered
in the same situation as to responsibility as if the facts with
respect to which the delusion exists were real. For example, if,
under the influence of his delusion he supposes another man to be
in the act of attempting to take away his life, and he kills that
man, as he supposes, in self-defense, he would be exempt from
punishment. If his delusion was that the deceased had inflicted
a serious injury to his character and fortune, and he killed him
in revenge for such supposed injury, he would be liable to punishment."

(*Q*. V.) "Can a medical man, conversant with the disease of
insanity, who never saw the prisoner previously to the trial, but
who was present during the whole trial, and the examination
of the witnesses, be asked his opinion as to the state of the prisoner's mind at the time of the commission of the alleged crime,
or his opinion whether the prisoner was conscious at the time of
doing the act that he was acting contrary to law, or whether he
was laboring under any, and what, delusion at the time?"

(*A*. V.) "We think the medical man, under the circumstances supposed cannot, in strictness be asked his opinion in the
terms above stated, because each of those questions involves the
determination of the truth of the facts deposed to, which it is for
the jury to decide, and the questions are not questions upon a
mere matter of science, in which case such evidence is admissible.
But where the facts are admitted, or not disputed, and the question becomes substantially one of science only, it may be convenient to allow the question to be put in that general form,
though the same cannot be insisted on as a matter of right."

APPENDIX B

THE "INSTRUCTION" OF ETCHEPARE
From Brieux's La Robe Rouge
Translation by Celeste Jedel

Mouzon (juge d'instruction). There's a way to prove your innocence, since you pretend you *are* innocent. Establish one way or another that you were not at Irissary on the night of the crime, and I'll let you go. Where were you?

Etchepare. Where was I?

Mouzon. Yes. Where were you? Were you home?

Etchepare. Yes.

Mouzon. You're certain?

Etchepare. Yes.

Mouzon (getting up a little theatrically, his finger pointing at Etchepare). All right! Etchepare, this settles you. *I know* that you went out. When you were arrested you said to your wife, "Don't *ever* let them know I was out last night." I'll tell you more, too. Somebody saw you. A servant. She told the police how she passed you at ten o'clock a short way from your house. Well?

Etchepare. It's true . . . I did go out.

Mouzon (triumphantly). Aha! . . . My God, it's hard to make you open your mouth. . . . But I can see it on your face when you're lying. It's obvious. I read it as though it were written in big letters like this—And the proof, my man, is that *not a soul* saw you go out! But I would have sworn it on a stack of Bibles— W-E-L-L! We've made some progress now. (To the clerk) Have you got that confession? Fine! (To Etchepare) Now that you've begun, come on! Finish it up! These policemen here want to go eat their soup. Do you confess? No? Then tell me, why did you insist that you had stayed at home?

Etchepare. Because I said it to the policemen and I didn't want to contradict myself.

Mouzon. And why did you say it to them?

Etchepare. Because I thought they were arresting me for smuggling.

Mouzon. Good. Then that night you didn't go to Irissary?

Etchepare. No.

Mouzon. Where did you go?

Etchepare. To the mountains to look for a horse that escaped the night from a bunch we were bringing from Spain.

Mouzon. Good! Fine! Not badly thought out! It can be defended. You went to look for a horse lost in the mountains. A horse escaped from a lot you were smuggling in. Perfect! If true! It depends on you now whether I'll let you go. You're just going to tell me now to whom you sold the horse. We'll send for the buyer and if he confirms your statement, I'll sign your release. To whom did you sell it?

Etchepare. I didn't sell it.

Mouzon. You gave it away?

Etchepare. No! I didn't find it.

Mouzon. A-ah! You didn't find it. Damme! That's not so good. . . . All right! But *of course* you didn't go all alone into those mountains.

Etchepare. Yes, I did.

Mouzon. Now isn't that too bad. Next time, you know, you'll really have to take a companion along. Did you stay out long?

Etchepare. All night. I came in at 5 A. M.

Mouzon. A long time.

Etchepare. We're not rich—a horse—it's worth a pretty penny.

Mouzon. Good. But you didn't stay out all night without meeting *someone*.

Etchepare. It was pouring.

Mouzon. Then you didn't meet anybody?

Etchepare. Nobody.

Mouzon. I didn't think so. Listen here, Etchepare. Do you think jurors are imbeciles? (Silence) I said a little while ago you were intelligent. I take it back. What kind of a rigamarole

are you handing me? A child of eight could have made up a
better one. It's ridiculous, I tell you. Ridiculous! The jurors will
shrug their shoulders when they hear it. Out all night, in the
pouring rain to look for a horse you don't find! And without
meeting a soul! Coming in at 5 A. M! It's daylight then! But
no! Nobody saw you. You didn't see a soul. Everybody became
suddenly blind! Is that it? There was a miracle and everybody
was stricken blind that night! You don't say that? No? Why?
It's just as probable as what you *do* say. Everybody wasn't blind?
You see what your defense is worth. My clerk and policemen are
roaring. Don't you admit it's ridiculous?

Etchepare (abashed, very low). I don't know— I—

Mouzon. If you don't know, *we* do. I have no advice to
give you. Just repeat that in court and see what happens. But
why not confess? Why not confess? I really don't understand
your stubbornness. I repeat it, I don't understand it.

Etchepare. My God! Even if it isn't me, must I say it is
anyhow?

Mouzon. Well then, you persist in your story? You persist?

Etchepare. How do I know? How do I know what I should
say? I'd do better not to say a word. Everything I say turns
against me.

Mouzon. It's because you invent stories that are utterly, entirely fantastic. Do you think I'm a fool to believe such nonsense?
I like your first story better. At least you've got two witnesses on
your side. Two pretty worthless ones. But two anyhow. . . .

Etchepare. Well? . . . (long silence)

Mouzon. Come on. Speak up!

Etchepare (hesitating). All right! I'm going to tell you, sir!
You're right. It's not true. I didn't go to the mountains. What I
said first was true. I didn't budge from the house. Before I was
all mixed up. First I denied everything, even what was true. I
was so afraid of you. Then, when you told me, I don't know
what any more—I don't know any more—But I know I'm innocent! Well, just before, I almost wanted to confess I was guilty
just to make you let me alone. What was I saying? I don't know
any more. Oh, yes! . . . When you told me—those things. I forgot—it seemed to me that it was better to say I went out. I lied!

(Sincerely) But I swear to you, I *do* swear that I'm not guilty.
I swear it! I swear it!

   Mouzon.   This time, now, you *were* at home then?
   Etchepare.   Yes, sir.
   Mouzon.   All right. Take him away. Keep him near though.
We're going to confront him. We're not done with him yet.

INDEX

INDEX

Aleyn, English magistrate, 14
American Institute of Criminal Law and Criminology, 94, 150
American Judicature Society, Journal of, 76, 84, 89
American Law Institute, Code of Criminal Procedure, 22; rejection of Continental system of inquiry, 41; model code of, 105
Arnold's case, 141
Augustus, John, 159

Baer, Judge George, quoted, 97
Bail, 43; in England, 44, 60; injustice of present administration of, 47; remedies suggested for evils of, 56
Bar associations, 252
Baumes Laws, 72
"Blue Ribbon" jury provision, 112
Bondsmen, 48
Brooklyn *Daily Eagle,* 54 f.
Brougham, Lord, quoted, 113
Bryce, Lord, quoted, 233
"Bushell's case," 115

California, Crime Commission, 27; publication of judicial statistics in, 61; Judicial Council, 76
Cardozo, Judge Benjamin, 241, 250
Centralization of courts, 78; proposal evaluated, 58
Chamberlain, Col. Henry Barrett, 213
Chicago *Daily News,* 205, 230
"Chicago," play, 66, 186, 189
Chicago Crime Commission, 57, 103, 212, 213
Chicago Juvenile Court, 157
Chicago Municipal Court, conditions in, 3; description of preliminary hearing in, 27; psychiatric services of, 32; description of prosecution in, 33; strong chief justice in, 78; description of branches, 80-81; education of judges in, 228
Chicago *Tribune,* 10, 205, 230
Chief justice, need of in circuit and state systems, 77; powers and duties of in Chicago, 78, 82

Claghorn, Kate H., 50
Clayton Act, provisions upheld by U. S. Supreme Court, 198
Clerical staffs, inferior quality of, 8, 31
Cleveland, status of prosecutor in, 33; Survey of Criminal Justice, 62, 231; Crime Commission, 216; Cleveland Foundation, 219; Bar Association, 252
Cleveland *Press,* 205
Clinics, 156
Cobb, Irvin, 189
Code of Criminal Procedure of Amer. Law Institute, 22, 105
Connecticut, public defender system, 70
Contempt power of courts, 198; in England, 199
Cooley, ——, *Constitutional Limitations,* quoted, 121
Court of General Sessions, New York, 162
Court organization: Need of reform in and suggestions for, 76
Crime Commissions, see under New York, Chicago, Illinois, Cleveland, Missouri.
"Criminal Code, The," 139
Criminal law, practice of, 62
Crowe, Robert, 216

Darrach, Dean William, quoted, 135
Daugherty case, 111, 112
Detroit, Recorder's Court of, 32, 77; experiment in specialization, 83; probation department, 162
Detroit Bureau of Governmental Research, report of, 85

Education, of judges, 229
Elmira Reformatory, N. Y., 164
Evidence, comment upon, 119
Expert testimony, 152

Fall-Doheny case, 109, 111
Felonies, small proportion of reaching jury in N. Y., 113
Fielding, Henry, quoted, 17-18
France, inquiry preceding trial, 37; press and laws governing it, 201
Frankfurter, Felix, 220

269

Criminal Justice in America

AN ARNO PRESS COLLECTION

Administration of Justice in the United States. 1910

Barnes, Harry Elmer. **A History of the Penal, Reformatory and Correctional Institutions of the State of New Jersey.** 1918

Capital Punishment: Nineteenth-Century Arguments. 1974

Chicago Community Trust. **Reports Comprising the Survey of the Cook County Jail.** [1923]

Connecticut General Assembly. **Minutes of the Testimony Taken Before John Q. Wilson, Joseph Eaton, and Morris Woodruff, Committee from the General Assembly, to Inquire Into the Condition of Connecticut State Prison.** 1834

Criminal Courts in New York State. 1909/1910

Finley, James B[radley]. **Memorials of Prison Life.** 1855

Georgia General Assembly. **Proceedings of the Joint Committee Appointed to Investigate the Condition of the Georgia Penitentiary.** 1870

Glueck, Sheldon, editor. **Probation and Criminal Justice.** 1933

Goldman, Mayer C[larence]. **The Public Defender.** 1917

Howe, S[amuel] G[ridley]. **An Essay on Separate and Congregate Systems of Prison Discipline.** 1846

Kohn, Aaron, editor. **The Kohn Report: Crime and Politics in Chicago.** 1953

Lawes, Lewis E. **Twenty Thousand Years in Sing Sing.** 1932

Los Angeles Police Department (Chief August Vollmer). **Law Enforcement in Los Angeles:** Los Angeles Police Department Annual Report, 1924. New Introduction by Joseph G. Woods. 1924

Maine Joint Special Committee. **Report of the Joint Special Committee on Investigation of the Affairs of the Maine State Prison.** 1874

Massachusetts, Commonwealth of. **Report of the Special Commission on Investigation of the Judicial System.** 1936

Moley, Raymond. **Our Criminal Courts.** 1930

Morse, Wayne L. and Ronald H. Beattie. **Survey of the Administration of Criminal Justice in Oregon.** 1932

National Conference on Bail and Criminal Justice. **Proceedings of May 27-29, 1964 and Interim Report, May 1964-April 1965.** 1965

New York. Kings County, Grand Jury. **A Presentment Concerning the Enforcement by the Police Department of the City of New York of the Laws Against Gambling by the Grand Jury for the Additional Extraordinary Special and Trial Term.** 1942

New York State. **Proceedings of the Governor's Conference on Crime, the Criminal and Society.** 1935

New York State. **Report of the Crime Commission, 1928.** 1928

New York State Committee on State Prisons. **Investigation of the New York State Prisons.** 1883

New York State Crime Commission. **Crime and the Community.** 1930

New York State Supreme Court, Apellate Division. **The Investigation of the Magistrates' Courts in the First Judicial Department.** 1932

O'Sullivan, John L. **Report in Favor of the Abolition of the Punishment of Death by Law, Made to the Legislature of the State of New York.** 1841

Pennsylvania Parole Commission. **The Report of the Pennsylvania State Parole Commission to the Legislature.** 1927. Two volumes in one.

Pennsylvania Special Grand Jury. **Investigation of Vice, Crime and Law Enforcement.** 1939

Reform of the Criminal Law and Procedure. 1911

Reporter of the Post. **Selections from the Court Reports Originally Published in the Boston Morning Post, From 1834-1837.** 1837

Shalloo, J. P., editor. **Crime in the United States.** 1941

Smith, Bruce. **Rural Crime Control.** 1933

Smith, Ralph Lee. **The Tarnished Badge.** 1965

Society for the Prevention of Pauperism. **Report on the Penitentiary System in the United States.** 1822

South Carolina General Assembly. **Report of Joint Committee Created Under Joint Resolution 662 of 1937 to Investigate Law Enforcement.** 1937

Sutherland, Edwin H. and Thorsten Sellin, editors. **Prisons of Tomorrow.** 1931

Texas Penitentiary Investigating Committee. **A Record of Evidence and Statements Before the Penitentiary Investigating Committee.** [1913]

Train, Arthur. **Courts and Criminals.** 1926

Train, Arthur. **The Prisoner at the Bar.** 1906

United States Department of Justice. **Attorney General's Survey of Release Procedures.** Volume II: Probation. 1939

United States Department of Justice. **Attorney General's Survey of Release Procedures.** Volume IV: Parole. 1939

United States. House of Representatives. Committee on the District of Columbia. **Investigation of the Metropolitan Police Department.** 1941

Waite, John Barker. **Criminal Law in Action.** 1934

Warner, Sam Bass. **Crime and Criminal Statistics in Boston.** 1934

Warner, Sam Bass and Henry B. Cabot. **Judges and Law Reform.** 1936

Wiretapping in New York City. 1916